Greening the Accounts

CURRENT ISSUES IN ECOLOGICAL ECONOMICS

General Editors: Sylvie Faucheux, *Professor of Economic Science* and Martin O'Connor, *Associate Professor of Economic Science, C3ED, Université de Versailles–Saint Quentin en Yvelines, France,* John Proops, *Professor of Ecological Economics, School of Politics, International Relations and the Environment, Keele University, UK* and Jan van der Straaten, *Retired Senior Lecturer, Department of Leisure Studies, Tilburg University, The Netherlands*

The field of ecological economics has emerged as a result of the need for all social sciences to be brought together in new ways, to respond to global environmental problems. This major new series aims to present and define the state-of-the-art in this young and yet fast-developing discipline.

This series cuts through the vast literature on the subject to present the key tenets and principal problems, techniques and solutions in ecological economics. It is the essential starting point for any practical or theoretical analysis of economy-environment interactions and will provide the basis for future developments within the discipline.

Greening the Accounts

edited by

Sandrine Simon and John Proops

School of Politics, International Relations and the Environment, Keele University

CURRENT ISSUES IN ECOLOGICAL ECONOMICS

Edward Elgar
Cheltenham, UK • Northampton, MA, USA

Published by
Edward Elgar Publishing Limited
Glensanda House
Montpellier Parade
Cheltenham
Glos GL50 1UA
UK

Edward Elgar Publishing, Inc.
136 West Street
Suite 202
Northampton
Massachusetts 01060
USA

HC
79
, I5
G72
2000

A catalogue record for this book
is available from the British Library

Library of Congress Cataloguing in Publication Data

Greening the accounts / edited by Sandrine Simon and John Proops.
    —(Current issues in ecological economics)
  Includes index.
    1. National income—Accounting—Case studies. 2. Sustainable
  development—Case studies. 3. Environmental economics—Case studies.
    I. Simon, Sandrine, 1970– II. Proops, John L.R., 1947– III. Series.

HC79.I5 G72 2000
339.3—dc21

00–055120

ISBN 1 84064 057 X

Printed in the United Kingdom at the University Press, Cambridge

Contents

Tables

Figures

Contributors

Christine Cooper, Department of Accounting and Finance, University of Strathclyde, Glasgow, Scotland.

Anthony M. Friend, School of Community and Regional Planning, University of British Columbia, Vancouver, Canada.

Kirk Hamilton, Environment Department, The World Bank., Washington DC, USA.

Rupert Howes, Forum for the Future, London, UK.

Steven J. Keuning, Central Bureau of Statistics Netherlands, Department of National Accounts, The Netherlands.

Glenn-Marie Lange, Institute for Economic Analysis, New York University, USA.

John Proops, School of Politics, International Relations and the Environment, Keele University, UK.

Fulai Sheng, Conservation Economics Unit, WWF Macroeconomics Program Office, Washington DC, USA.

Sandrine Simon, School of Politics, International Relations and the Environment, Keele University, UK.

Carsten Stahmer, Federal Statistical Office and Faculty of Economics, University of Heidelberg, Germany.

Ian Thomson, Department of Accounting and Finance, University of Strathclyde, Glasgow, Scotland.

Prashant Vaze, ECOTEC Research and Consulting Ltd., Birmingham, UK.

Preface

This volume is a contribution to the Current Issues in Ecological Economics series, which aims to provide comprehensive and authoritative overviews of a range of areas of interest to ecological economists.

Greening the Accounts is an early volume in the series for several reasons. First, it is an area of interest to John Proops, one of the Current Issues co-editors, and so seemed an obvious area to make an early start. Second, Sandrine Simon has made a special study of recent work in green national accounting, and is also a research fellow at Keele University, so her involvement was a further push in this area. Finally, and most importantly, green accounting is an area of great importance and current research effort, worldwide. Over the past five years, it seems that the dimensions of current research have stabilised somewhat, and a considerable amount of empirical work has become available, so a volume such as this is probably timely.

In trying to bring together this volume we have been fortunate to be able to draw upon a range of authors whose expertise is widely recognised. At the outset, we were purposely directive in our approach to the authors, laying down quite tight guidelines as to the content and structure of their contributions. We were delighted and grateful that such a range of eminent researchers was willing to be so directed. We hope that the outcome is therefore more coherent and less repetitive than one might find in an edited text, and that this volume will serve as a useful reference point for those working in, or interested in studying, this important and dynamic area.

Sandrine Simon and John Proops

School of Politics, International Relations and the Environment, Keele University, UK

1. Introduction

Sandrine Simon and John Proops

1.1 GREENING THE ACCOUNTS

Research in green accounting has been selected as one of the fundamental themes to be included in the Current Issues in Ecological Economics series. It is certainly an area of research that has been investigated by various researchers in numerous countries around the world, and in a range of institutional settings.

The familiar System of National Accounts (SNA) has been developed and used internationally, and has been referred to as a basis for international comparisons of economic progress. However, the shortcomings of the SNA, particularly concerning the proper accounting of nature, has led to much controversy, leading to a range of attempts to 'green' the accounts. It is now generally accepted that this reform of the SNA is of international importance.

Would the inclusion of research in green accounting in the Current Issues in Ecological Economics series also imply that it is, and has always been, carried out in the context of ecological economics? Nothing is less certain. However, what this book attempts to demonstrate is that, by exploring how research in green accounting has evolved, and by examining the state of the art at this stage in its development, it becomes clear that ecological economics is crucially helpful in green accounting. This is true not only because of its underlying principles, but also because of the technical insights and methodological approaches it puts forward.

Three main dimensions of research in green accounting are examined in this book and are presented in the respective parts.

Part One deals with the history of national accounting and its place in the debate concerning sustainability. Part Two describes issues related to the history of green accounts and the methodologies adopted. Finally, Part Three shows how green accounts are being constructed and used in various countries, and by national governments and corporate businesses. In the rest of this chapter we detail the contents of the three Parts in turn.

1.2 PART 1: THE HISTORY OF NATIONAL ACCOUNTS

This book implicitly assumes that research in green accounting can be compatible with ecological economics, and can also contribute to the representation and implementation of sustainability. To support this position, it is first crucial to understand why and how national accounting can be related to sustainability.

In Chapter 2, Christine Cooper and Ian Thomson address this issue by focusing on the epistemological dimension of national accounting. In particular, they stress the social and political roles of the SNA, showing how politicians use it as a policy tool and as a system of governance. They also assess some of the roles and myths associated with accounting.

Cooper and Thomson argue that national accounts cannot be assumed simply to represent the social, environmental and economic reality of a nation. Instead, they reflect and construct the methods of governance of the state, and the ways of maintaining national unity and of constraining potentially disruptive forces, whatever they are. The notion that accounting represents rational choice is also critically examined. Whilst accounting may have been designed originally as a rational information system, it is clear that it does not operate as such.

The authors also observe the 'language of accounting' and show to what extent it is a jargon, but also a type of discourse that cannot be separated from other historically derived social and cultural discourses. They explain how the accounting language has gained an important part of its power by appearing to be 'natural' and representative of the economic reality.

They also argue that the acquisition of accounting language is an important influence in the formulation of our subjectivity. Accounting at all levels (including national) is therefore offered as part of Lacan's 'symbolic order'. By this is meant the way in which societies are regulated by a series of signs, roles and rituals, which have meaning only in relation to each other, forming recognisable codes and being expressed in language. On acquiring accounting language, we accept a symbolic order which is already in place. Thus, national accounting cannot be seen as an objective, neutral, rational, comprehensive and scientific process. It reflects ideologies, and paradigms, and constructs realities that it presents following a certain rhetoric.

Cooper and Thomson therefore make it clear that the current SNA has been used as a justification for not changing our economic practices. It therefore must either be reformed or ignored in decisions related to sustainability. Chapter 2 therefore emphasises that the reform of the SNA is far from being a merely technical issue.

In Chapter 3, Anthony Friend examines the relationship between national accounts and 'nature' from an historical perspective. He suggests that the structure and use of accounts changed, even before a 'green reform' of the SNA was initiated. Friend concentrates on the roots of green accounting in the classical and neoclassical schools, and pays particular attention to themes such as the roots of self-organisation, conservation principles, and the share of wealth in green accounting. He also explains the distinction between the classical and neoclassical frames of reference in the greening of national accounts and discusses the fact that the research context for the development of national accounting has progressively shifted to being a very neoclassical one, dominated by the syntax of the mechanics of the neoclassical general equilibrium model. Friend concludes that the revision of the SNA, through its system of stock-flow balances, allows for a biological niche to enter the system. By extension, he shows that there is also a window of opportunity to pay more attention to the syntax and paradigm of ecological economics when pursuing research in green accounting.

In Chapter 4, Sandrine Simon notes that green accounting (as an analytical framework and a policy tool), sustainability (as a concept), and ecological economics (as a paradigm) were developed at different times, and were not originally linked. However, they can now be seen as fundamentally related and this chapter argues that we should gain from making them closer in practice.

First, the links between green accounting and sustainability are examined. Green accounting was an early element in the current research on 'indicators of sustainability', although green accounts are only just starting to be considered and constructed as such. The chapter argues that this new role is relevant and that green accounting can constitute a good indicator of sustainability, and hence help in representing and implementing the concept. This is true not only for structural reasons (related to some criteria that fulfill the requirements for the construction of indicators of sustainability and that the holistic accounting framework has) but also for political reasons (through the use of the accounting tool by policy makers).

Second, ecological economics is presented as the paradigm that has the potential to help in reforming the accounts if, in their 'green' form, they are to be related to the concept of sustainability.

1.3 PART 2: GREEN ACCOUNTING AS A POLICY INSTRUMENT

Part Two looks at more technical elements in the construction of green accounts.

The 'indicator' issue is first reviewed in Chapter 5 by Steven Keuning. He examines how green accounting can be interpreted as an indicator of

sustainable development and why we need such indicator. He then illustrates
this by explaining how the Dutch NAMEA (National Accounting Matrix
including Environmental Accounts) has been compiled as a 'framework of
indicators' and how it is used in the policy making process.

Next, Keuning comments on the need for an integrated accounting information system at an international level, that would encompass this notion of
'indicators' or 'indices' of sustainability. Eurostat, in particular, has expressed an interest in such developments and has advocated the construction
of a System of Environmental Indices matrices, partly inspired by the
NAMEA accounts, that would be consistent with the environmental themes
selected in the European Fifth Framework.

In Chapter 6, Kirk Hamilton focuses on the issue of modelling in relation
to the construction and use of green accounting. In particular, he discusses
the theoretical bases for various types of environmental accounts and makes
use of various models to explain these. He shows how these models are
interpreted and used in the context of policy making, such as the use of
natural resources and the issue of pollution. Finally, he relates them to the
notion of sustainability and how to put it into practice. He thus shows how
some sophisticated models permit the integration of resource and environmental information into macro-economic analysis.

Having examined both the notions of indicators and of modelling in
research on green accounting, this part then focuses on the 'revival' of input–
output (I–O) analysis in the context of research in green accounting.

In Chapter 7, Carsten Stahmer argues that the use of input–output analysis
could greatly contribute to improving our understanding of the complex
concept of sustainability in all its aspects, be they economic, ecological or
social. Various types of input–output tables are presented. They include I–O
in monetary units, in physical units and in time units. Stahmer explains that,
in order to carry out a comprehensive study of sustainability, and to use a
suitable database for such analysis, we need to construct and use these three
types of I–O tables, both separately and in combination.

After arguing the advantages of focusing on I–O analysis as a useful
complement to various types of green accounts, the author presents some
illustration of the types of I–O tables he wishes to promote, with the example
of German economic activities in the year 1990.

The main arguments put forward to defend the construction of such I–O
tables are concentrated on the shortcomings of national accounts and of the
neoclassical paradigm. Thus, the narrow concept of production used in the
conventional economic way, as well as the exclusive focus on monetary
transactions, are described as real obstacles to carrying out a comprehensive
activity analysis, and to attempting to study and operationalise the concept of
sustainability. I–O analysis also has the advantage of taking into considera-

tion temporal and indirect effects, that are rarely integrated in other existing representations of sustainability.

The combination of the various types of I–O tables, and their linkage with modelling of future scenarios, are both in need of being further developed, and would complement new advances in green accounting very well.

The construction of 'indicators of sustainability', the use of ex-ante modelling in relation to ex-post green accounting, and the reliance on I–O analysis, partly to observe and identify indirect effects of economic practices on the environment, all contribute greatly to the improvement of green accounting as a policy tool aimed at helping operationalise sustainability. These three elements, and the policy objective behind the construction of green accounts, have strongly influenced the way in which research in green accounting has been carried out, as well as its resulting outcomes.

Other factors have also influenced the way in which research in green accounting has evolved. In Chapter 8, Fulai Sheng and Sandrine Simon examine the motivations behind some of its main developments. They first show that the 'paradigm dilemma' (whether the reform of the SNA implies a reform of the economic paradigm) already underlay research in green ac-counting when it began, although it might not have been perceived as such at that time. The correction of the shortcomings of the SNA could either imply a reform in the construction of the accounts, and in the representation of the economic functioning and interdependencies with the natural environment, *or* encourage the introduction of environmental dimensions within the accounts left as they were, in order to calculate an adjusted GDP.

This is discussed in the debate on 'satellite accounts' versus 'aggregate indicator', and leads to the related issue of 'valuation' in green accounting. The development of different (sometimes incompatible) environmental valuation methods has resulted in the construction of a variety of types of green accounts, that have been typically grouped into 'physical accounts' and 'monetary accounts'. The issue of monetarisation has had great importance in research in green accounting, as it is perceived as an 'economic and policy language' issue. Recent advances have offered new monetary valuation methodologies that are less controversial and that take account of previous disagreements. Similarly, new research exercises have focused on the com-munication and use of outcomes provided by physical accounts. Also exam-ined is the representation of the complex and multidisciplinary concept of sustainability in an accounting framework of indicators.

Another issue addressed by the authors is the complementarity between various research efforts that are not exclusively focused on accounting *per se*, and the consequent shift of emphasis and opening of research 'in green accounting'. If one of the prime outcomes from this research is the operation-alisation of sustainability, we need to examine the policy-making process, who makes policy, and which policy tools are used and how. The issue of modelling and input–output analysis are presented as two main areas that complement research in green accounting.

1.4 PART 3: USES OF GREEN ACCOUNTING

Part Three leaves the more theoretical issues aside and concentrates on how green accounts are being dealt with in practice, and by whom.

First, in Chapter 9 Glenn-Marie Lange presents several case studies, showing how green accounts are being used in practice. She explains that environmental accounting provides essential technical information for monitoring and analysis, and also promotes effective policy dialogue. Because it is based on a systems approach, and on a proactive approach to policy making, green accounting also provides a new way of thinking about resource management.

Lange shows that the implementation of green accounting varies between countries, due to the economic needs and also to the institutional setting that does (or does not) link those who compile the accounts and those who use them.

When giving examples of the application of green accounting, the author concludes that a wide range of policy applications have been made through the construction of asset accounts for a better understanding of a country's wealth. She gives the example of Namibia (where physical asset accounts of the fish stock have been constructed) and of Botswana, a country highly dependent on mineral resources, which has used some asset accounts for manufactured and natural capital to monitor progress towards the diversification of the economy. The construction and use of activity green accounts is also presented. Activity accounts include three components (resources use, resource degradation and emission of pollutant, and expenditures for environmental protection) and their applications are consequently more extensive than in the case of assets accounts. Lange gives the examples of such accounts for a number of European countries and Canada. These countries have constructed some forms of eco-efficiency profiles, to compare industries in terms of their relative economic contribution and environmental burden. As opposed to these two types of environmental accounts, the summary monetary indicators, such as the environmentally adjusted national product, do not seem to be widely used.

Lange concludes that, although some creative uses of green accounting can be observed, the full potential of green accounting has not yet been tapped in many countries. She emphasises that, for green accounting to be useful and helpful, in practical terms, it must be driven by policy needs, since it is unlikely that policy applications will simply follow from the construction of the accounts.

This is an important message for future developments in research on green accounting. When a country is considering implementing environmental accounting, it needs to begin the process with an identification of the specific policy issues to be addressed, and how environmental accounting will address them before the accounts are constructed. This clearly implies that basing the reform of the SNA on correcting its shortcomings is not enough to make it useful in policy terms.

In Chapter 10, Prashant Vaze examines the construction and use of green accounts in the UK and, in particular, in the context of the Office for National Statistics (ONS), which deals with their construction. After explaining which different methodological approaches exist in research on green accounting, the author gives more detail concerning the green accounts that have been constructed by the ONS. He shows that various approaches have been initiated. First, some UK satellite (assets) accounts have been compiled for strategic resources, such as water, forest, and oil and gas. Some physical flow accounts were also developed in the UK. In common with other EU countries, the UK had to produce annual inventories of many gaseous pollutants as part of its commitment to the Montreal Protocol, the Framework Convention on Climate Change and the Convention on Long Range Transboundary Pollutants. Vaze explains how the ONS converted emissions from processes to the standard industrial classification, thus allowing the thorough study of emissions and their impact on the environment from a national and international perspective.

Environmental protection expenditure accounts have also been compiled in the UK, including 'end-of-pipe' investments and integrated processes, where pollution abatement is designed into the core structure of the equipment. Finally, Vaze mentions the importance of environmental taxation in the UK environmental policy debate.

In the general context of research in green accounting, Vaze shows that the development of satellite accounts in the UK has been recognised as a valuable and useful experience. The UK satellite accounting approach has even been recognised as exemplary at an international level since the SNA revision of 1993 explicitly mentions it; it was the only satellite account to be accorded this special treatment. He concludes that, from a policy perspective, the UK satellite accounts have some usefulness and that their construction and improvement deserves institutional and political support.

In Chapter 11 Rupert Howes deals with the application and construction of green accounts in the context of corporate businesses. This issue seems often to be treated separately from that of green national accounting, although it is recognised that the policy application of environmental accounting is worth investigating at different levels. This area of research is still relatively new, at least by comparison with research on green national accounting. However, it is an area which will certainly gain importance in the future, especially with the growth of environmental auditing.

Howes starts by explaining why corporate accounts need reforming, insisting on the role of natural capital and on the need to maintain it. Costs are being generated by companies, although they do not account for environmental degradation, or for environmental services provided by nature. Howes show that the key to resolving the conflict between profit and the environment lies in getting the prices right, and that one way to do this is through the process of ecological tax reform (ETR). However, as he points out, in the absence of a political will to implement such an ETR, companies committed to improving their environmental performance need to move beyond simple corporate reporting. They need to begin to account for both their internal environmental costs and their external impacts, in a more complete and transparent way.

He uses the example of a multinational manufacturer of carpet tiles, to show what is corporate green accounting and to explain how the accounts are compiled. Although such work is experimental, a detailed presentation of the firm's environmental consolidated accounts is provided.

Howes stresses that some companies are already beginning to respond to the challenge of corporate green accounting and have made significant progress in improving their environmental performance by using environmental accounting techniques. The UNEP's 1997 Benchmark Survey of 100 corporate Environmental Reports also suggests that the greening of corporate accounting will become an increasingly important issue.

Finally, Chapter 12 offers an overview of the concepts and issues developed in this volume, and suggests a number of directions for an ecological economics approach to greening the accounts.

The aim of this book is thus to explore the links between research in green accounting, ecological economics and sustainability from different angles, be they: social, political and epistemological; historical; conceptual and methodological; or theoretical and practical.

PART ONE

The History of National Accounts

2. The Social and Political Roles of National Accounting

Christine Cooper and Ian Thomson

2.1 INTRODUCTION

This chapter does not deal directly with the reforms of National Accounting practice; rather, it will challenge the assumptions of truth and objectivity associated with accounting information, by emphasising its social and political roles. To achieve these aims, we will:

- examine the relevance of national accounting to the sustainability debate,
- briefly describe how national accounts are used by policy makers,
- examine the construction of national accounts and how they reflect underlying political and economic paradigms, and
- critique some of the roles and myths associated with accounting.

To many, National Accounting and its statistical constructs Gross Domestic Product (GDP), Gross National Product (GNP), and Net National Product (NNP), stand for all that is unsustainable. They are symbols of modernity, industrialisation, rationality and masculinity, and are responsible for Western societies' current obsession with growth and its associated environmental and social destruction. They see reforming National Accounting as a futile exercise, analogous to re-arranging deckchairs on the Titanic. National Accounts can never reflect the full range of issues or the complexity of relationships associated with a more sustainable future. No single 'account' can adequately, truly or fairly represent the different realities experienced by different nations, different communities, different classes, different generations, and different genders throughout the planet.

This perspective has to be tempered by the recognition that to move towards a more sustainable planet will have to be a political process. We have to deal with the current systems of governance that are blocking progress and maintaining our current unsustainability. The way in which political decisions are made, the inputs into their decision processes, the methods of evaluating the success of political actions, the political rhetoric of success or failure and the methods of political accountability, therefore become relevant topics of investigation.

The reality is that National Accounts are used by politicians to make decisions. National Accounts are seen as objective, reliable, comprehensive financial measures, free from bias and politically neutral. National Accounts provide information about flows of money through the economy. However, GDP, GNP, NNP are incorrectly used as surrogates for value created by a nation and human happiness or welfare (Anderson, 1991).

National Accounts are not only regarded as measures of the effectiveness of politician's actions but also as an important statistical input into future policy determination, for example:

- Taxation policies are based on actual and projected National Income calculation.
- Public expenditure is determined by reference to National Accounting numbers.
- Certain expenditure items are calculated directly from GDP figures or estimates, e.g. Overseas Aid.
- Criticisms of healthcare and education are made by reference to other countries' public expenditure on these items as a percentage of their GDP.

The debate as to the accuracy of National Accounts, how well they reflect the reality of social, economic and environmental impact or performance, is perhaps irrelevant. The point is that people use them as if they are real and truthful. Important decisions are made using this information and their outcomes are measured by reference to the figures. Despite the technical and representational weaknesses of National Accounts, they will play a major part in the political processes required if the human race wishes to become more sustainable. It is unlikely that reforming National Accounts will make the world more sustainable, however it may play a part in a wider political movement in reducing our current unsustainability.

2.2 THE NATURE OF SUSTAINABILITY

Sustainability is conceived as possessing economic, social, psychological, cultural, moral and political dimensions. Sustainability, by its very nature, is complex, involving many conflicting factors and can be characterised as:

- multi-dimensional, multi-disciplinary and multi-sectoral,
- with non-monetary and monetary dimensions,

- extending across politico-geographical boundaries and time,
- involving conflicts between interests and ideologies,
- involving uncertainty and risk (Clayton and Radcliffe, 1996).

Knowledge is a critical part of the move towards a sustainable future. This knowledge base must consist of scientific, technical, political, economic ethical and philosophical elements. There is a need to evaluate the extent of our current knowledge, future knowledge requirements, and how to activate and communicate that knowledge. Knowledge is required about the key economic, social and environmental problems, how serious these problems are, and what are the associated risks and causes. It will be necessary to clarify degrees of uncertainty and to identify critical areas of ignorance. It is important to know about behaviour within natural and social systems. Information is needed about trends, how quickly situations are changing, whether this rate of change is accelerating or deteriorating, and to have threshold estimates of how and when these changes will significantly effect society. National Accounts form an important part of this knowledge gathering and communication process.

Sustainability is not a scientific problem and cannot be solved objectively. In practice, many of the decisions that will have to be taken will be based on estimates and guesswork. It is unlikely that there will be *clear-cut good and bad alternatives*; instead choices between alternatives that have different benefits and costs for different people at different times will need to be made. Such decisions involve value judgements as to the priorities and actions of society, rather than scientific or economic precision.

It is likely that sustainability will be driven more by political systems than by breakthroughs in knowledge about environmental systems. Herein lies a contradiction (Redclift, 1987), in that current acceptance of sustainable development must mean concessions from those currently holding political and economic power. If there truly is commitment to sustainable development, this must involve sacrifice from those in power, which many regard as optimistic at best and politically naive (e.g. Cooper et al., 1992).

Sustainable development is a political concept, utilised especially by the dominant Western bodies of power. It would be possible for one nation to maintain their local environment by exporting its toxic waste. However, this represents a short-term displacement rather than a solution. Sustainability can only be fully assessed at the global level, but such global concerns need also to be enacted at a local level. It will often be difficult to determine what the most effective action would be, because the links between our social and economic systems and the environment are so extensive and complex.

In order to move away from unsustainability fundamental reforms are necessary. These reforms will affect many different dimensions of human activities (see Table 2.1).

Table 2.1 Systems requiring reforms

Legislative and political systems	Production and supply systems	Physical resource systems
Financial systems	Physical infrastructure	Management systems
Market and systems of competition	Ethical value systems	Knowledge and learning systems
Communication systems	Systems of networking	Risk perception and management

These changes are unlikely to occur naturally within the present social-economic-political environment. They will require political action and intervention, locally, nationally, regionally and globally. The impact of these reforms as measured by National Accounts is a political reality that must be addressed.

Political actions that result in a reduction in the metric used to evaluate performance are less likely to be taken than political actions that improve reported performance. If the method of recording and reporting performance privileges a particular paradigm or political philosophy, then actions designed to change this paradigm are likely to be reported in a distorted fashion. National Accounts can be seen to be constructions of a particular political-economic paradigm and to exclude many factors and concerns embedded within a sustainability paradigm.

2.3 THE NATION AS THE SUSTAINABLE ACCOUNTING ENTITY

A pre-requisite for any accounts is an accounting entity. The selection of a sustainable accounting entity to evaluate progress towards sustainability will be a highly contested area. Sustainability manifests itself in a diversity of 'sustainability accounts' and 'sustainable accounting entities', with tensions surrounding different groups' acceptance of these accounts. Given that sustainability is an emergent dynamic process, arising from a complementarity of diverse and competing system dimensions, it is a reasonable conclusion that at present sustainability cannot be measured or adequately defined within existing National Accounting methodologies.

Sustainability is unlikely ever to be accounted for or directly measured using hard objective metrics with any degree of consensus. However, there are many 'real' proposals to 'solve' our current unsustainability. These include: The Rio Declaration, Kyoto Earth Summit, Agenda 21, third world debt reduction agreements, ISO14001, EMAS, Eco-labelling, Clean Technology, Industrial Ecology, Pollution Permits and trading, Environmental Regulations, Social and Environmental Reporting, Green and other redistributional tax schemes, anti-social exclusion legislation, consumer pressure groups, general market forces, national laws, community action and many others. A policy solution requires system closure, that is, an acceptance and understanding of the elements and their interactions within the system (or entity). As this is a human process, all solutions result from false and partial system closures. This observation does not mean that it is impossible to account for sustainability. It does mean that in accounting for sustainability we will need to take into account additional dimensions and perspectives.

Policy solutions require some form of evaluation as to their effectiveness in moving society away from unsustainability. This evaluation should account for the impact of each 'solution' in terms of its specific objectives and in its interrelationship with other solutions. This type of accountability requires a new approach to identifying the appropriate accounting entity. The assessment of a change factor's success or failure is heavily dependent on the construction of the accounting entity. If it is drawn too narrowly, it runs the risk of appearing to be effective, but actually it merely transfers the problem from one geographic region to another, or from the present to the future.

Many current 'problems' can be attributed to a failure of policies designed to 'solve' problems; e.g. pesticide resistant insects, uncontrollable forest fires, flooding, antibiotic resistant disease agents, and so on. The simple and partial accounting of these actions initially reported them to be successful, due to the use of inappropriate metrics, time-scales and accounting entities. These specific accounting exercises were inadequate, as they did not reflect the underlying complex reality of the situations of concern.

The partitioning of any world view into an entity and its environment (or non-entity) requires the imposition of some arbitrary separation. Any account must recognise that it not only defines the entity, it also constructs the considered environment. The solution, entity and considered environment are mutually reinforcing and interrelate in a reflexive manner. The use of National Accounts is seen as *one* of many important accounting entities in the sustainability debate. It is important in that it is associated with a particular nation and their policies, and as sustainability requires political solutions it is a relevant accounting construct to work with. Its concentration on the politically constructed state gives it validity when examining local (national) political decisions in relation to sustainability objectives. However, the use of National Accounts does not capture possible problems or risk transference outside the National Accounting entity. It is also the case that the concentration on the overall nation hides distributional issues within the state itself. It is possible for a state to reduce its total CO_2 emissions; however, this may be accomplished by concentrating on a centralised energy production facility that concentrates all of the CO_2 into a small part of the country, whereas previously this was evenly distributed around the country. National Accounts must recognise that they provide only a partial and simplified view of the problem and as such can provide only a partial evaluation and evidence of partial solutions. It is critical from a sustainability perspective to recognise that the state is only one of many possible accounting entities and other accounts and entities must also be considered is assessing sustainability.

2.4 SUSTAINABILITY THROUGH ACCOUNTING

Sustainability is often communicated and discussed using accounting analogies, e.g.

> Compare it to a large sum of money that pays interest. If you succeed in living on the interest, the capital will stay intact. It is possible to maintain such a situation indefinitely. On the other hand, if you use a small part of the capital as well as the interest, the end will come surprisingly fast. After all, because of the decrease in capital, the annual interest will also decrease. One will therefore eat faster and faster into one's capital (Buitenkamp, 1993).

What we include as the capital to maintain and how we measure the interest are problematic issues that need to be addressed. As will be shown, National Accounts contain an extremely narrow definition of National Capital. For example, National Accounts would normally exclude many valuable assets: the population, natural environment, the built environment, roads, towns, cities, the countryside, rivers, the sea, plant life, animals, birds and insects. If these items are excluded from the capital calculation, then National Accounting will not recognise their destruction or exploitation. National Accounts will be silent about the destruction of those things that meaningful life in a country ultimately depends upon.

It should not be assumed that the accounting profession has solved these problems, even in relation to company accounting. Accounting academics and practitioners are aware of the limitations of accounting techniques; however, these inadequacies are not always communicated or understood by users of accounts (see Chapter 11). Accounting information is enriched with values and properties that it does not possess, nor does it claim for itself. It is important that users of any accounting information are aware of these limitations and strip away the myths of objectivity, comprehensiveness, scientific precision and neutrality.

Bebbington et al. (1994) suggest that relationships between accountancy and sustainability arise on many levels including:

- Political economy theories in which the entity should provide a greater range and level of information to a greater range of stakeholders. Accounting legitimises activities; discharges responsibility for activities; and negotiates a social contract between the nation, its population and other nations.
- The potential for accounting to create selective pictures of reality (Gray et al. 1993; Hines, 1988; Hopwood, 1987). Current accounting representations recognise only those things that can be measured by economic pricing. As many aspects of sustainability are unrecognised by such measures, making decisions, identifying goals and concepts that affect sustainability will be incomplete.

There is a large body of literature which posits that environmental and social accounting can *at least* improve societal eco-efficiency through wider recognition of the associated costs and benefits (e.g. Gray, 1990; Gray et al., 1993; Macve and Carey, 1992; Owen, 1993). More recently, there have been suggestions for wider accounting for sustainability (e.g. Commission of the European Communities, 1992; Gray, 1992; Rubenstein, 1994). The UK government also supports wider economic costing, suggesting that better decisions about sustainability could be taken within government and in industry if the full economic costs of environmental considerations were taken into account (HMSO, 1994).

This approach is criticised, because it is grounded within the current system of capitalism (e.g. Maunders and Burritt, 1991; Puxty, 1986; Tinker et al., 1991), and the incompatibility of sustainability with the logic of the capitalist system (Wildavsky, 1994). There is felt to be a possibility that accounting for social and environmental issues could result in the capture of these issues within the existing unsustainable paradigm (Cooper et al., 1992).

Anderson (1991) provides evidence of capture in the context of National Accounts, in his evaluation of the inconsistencies of National Accounting measures and sustainability. These and other omissions are summarised in Table 2.2.

Western notions of trade and neoclassical economics heavily influence National Accounts. They only value actions that can be converted to commodities traded and captured in an accounting system. For example, National Accounts systematically under-report the contribution of women to the nation's well-being, particularly in relation to 'domestic' work and childcare. This can lead to strange decisions, whereby a mother looking after her own children is excluded from the calculation of GDP, but if others pay her to look after their children then this increases GDP. The 'logical' extrapolation is that the nation would be reported as 'better off', if we paid each other to look after others' children rather than looking after our own.

Table 2.2 National accounting and sustainability inconsistencies and exclusions

• Ignores unpaid domestic labour
• Excludes non-money transactions outside the household
• Ignores distributional issues
• Ignores differences in needs and circumstances of different nations
• Uses unstable exchange rates in international comparisons
• Ignores the value of peoples possessions and their associated 'depreciation'
• Ignores environmental wealth and its 'depreciation'
• Ignores human beings and their 'depreciation'
• Deals inadequately with positional goods
• Privileges work time over leisure time
• Ignores the quality of work
• Improperly accounts for reducing public provision of services
• Improperly accounts for ineffective private sector provision of services
• Value of output reflects the existing distribution of income
• Ignores biodiversity
• Ignores future generations
• Ignores future costs associated with current activities
• Ignores national externalities
• Diminishing marginal utility of money

The ability to measure in money is a major factor for inclusion in National Accounts. National Accounts ignore things that cannot easily be measured in money, or easily captured and reported. It can be seen from Table 2.2 that many reforms suggested by sustainability would affect items excluded from the National Accounts calculation; e.g. distribution of income, human beings and environmental resources. Degradation of the ecosystem is not currently a cost in the accounts. Social exclusion and relative poverty within a nation is not identifiable from the accounts. Policy initiatives that could reduce ecosystem destruction (e.g. energy conservation measures based on reducing energy use) will not show up in the national accounts. These actions, while resulting in real social and environmental improvements, will not be reported as such and therefore not 'valued' within the constrained rationality of National Accounts.

National Accounts introduce a series of biases and could support unsustainable actions. National Accounting is not an objective or neutral process. It is embedded within a western capitalist, masculine paradigm that only recognises transactions of 'value' within this partially constructed rationality. It is a system that ignores many crucial dimensions associated with sustainability. Policy actions that are required to move away from unsustainable practices may not be recognised as desirable in National Accounts, whereas socially and environmentally destructive policies may be mis-reported as beneficial to the nation.

2.5 SUSTAINABLE ACCOUNTING REFORMS

If National Accounts can support unsustainable actions, then it is possible that National Accounting reforms offer possibilities for change. New accounts would have the potential to offer new conceptions of the accounting entity. Power (1992) contends that changes in accounting can enact and reflect real processes of change as long as they allow the constitutive capacity of accounting to widen the discourse on the issues within the entity (state).

> . . . we can speculate that new languages of 'waste' and 'sustainability' albeit translated into existing organisational codes via the rubric of efficiency, can effect a new moral environment within the organisation. It is not so much a question of inventing new incentive structures for individual and collective behaviour but, more profoundly and problematical, changing the common sense phenomenology of the organisation; a new universe of facts for old behaviour, rather than existing behaviour in the existing universe of facts (Power, 1992, p. 3).

Stated simply, including currently excluded items in the National Accounts, or changing methods of valuation, could result in better (from a sustainability perspective) decision making. However, this change would occur only if it changed the nature and content of the discourse surrounding policy decisions.

2.6 ACCOUNTING AS A CONSTRUCTOR OF REALITY

Reality is created by, amongst other things, accounting representations (Miller and O'Leary, 1987; Hines, 1988; Burchell et al., 1980; Burchell et al., 1985; Hopwood, 1987). Understanding 'social reality' is informed by, and dependent upon, our experiences interpreted through symbols. Accounts, social and technical, are one such set of symbols. Technical quantified accounts are currently seen as a more powerful symbol than more qualitative and empowering accounts (Ezzamel et al., 1990). Accounts simultaneously create and interpret 'reality'. Accounting represents the entity and produces visibility on two levels (Miller and O'Leary, 1987, Hopwood, 1987):

- Accounting 'makes visible' actions and events that cannot be physically observed.
- Accounting 'makes visible' concepts and values that become enshrined in accounting systems providing a basis for their observation and control.

In the case of National Accounts, governments become accountable for their actions, their (in)efficiencies are shown via national accounting numbers and trends. Concepts, such as GDP, become real through national accounting. Accounting renders these things visible by transforming actions, people, concepts and values into numbers or 'facts'.

Accounting can be seen to have technical and social dimensions. The technological side of accounting is associated with measurement concepts, systems of evaluation and quantification metrics. The social side of accounting is as a discourse, language or communicative system which creates a link between the tangible activities of an entity and the less tangible interpretative schemes, values and beliefs of the entity (Laughlin, 1991; Power, 1992). Accounting categories and expressions provide the basis for discourse within an entity and accounting selectively makes visible and legitimises behaviour within the entity (Hines, 1988; Hopwood, 1987; Miller and O'Leary, 1987). In this constitutive capacity, accounting is seen as able to shift the terms of the discourse via changes in accounting techniques potentially contributing to change (Laughlin, 1991; Power, 1992; Gray et al., 1995).

National Accounting could also be said to have a role in managing the boundary between the nation and the environment and in preserving national unity. Llewellyn (1994) suggests that accounts, which define the entity in physical, legal and financial terms, are used to manage the boundary between the entity and its environment. The greater the society/entity interaction, the greater the demands on accounts to legitimise the entity. Accounts act as binding structures, which produce and reproduce the internal unity of the entity. By this process accounts direct attention to the 'right' areas of action (Macintosh and Scapens, 1990), regulate information coding and monitor performance which bind the entity by minimising uncertainties. Accounting functions are forms of calculation, which help govern and frame life within entities.

National Accounts cannot be assumed simply to represent the social,

environmental and economic reality of a nation, but as reflecting and constructing the method of governance of the state and ways of maintaining
national unity and constraining potentially disruptive forces. In some respects
they can be seen as political instruments for maintaining the status quo.

2.7 NATIONAL ACCOUNTING AND RATIONAL CHOICE

National Accounts can be seen to fulfil a number of alternative roles, apart
from the commonly held notion of providing useful information for political
decision makers. Accounting is often cited in decision making processes, as it
represents the rational choice. Accounting is a way to rid decision making of
subjectivity, emotional or political bias. Boland and Pondy (1983) consider
two different models, the rational and the natural. Rational models assume
managers[1] are confronted with an objectively knowable, empirically verifi-
able reality that presents demands for action. Managers analyse the apparent
cause-and-effect relations, calculate costs and benefits, and take action in
response to the requirements of the external environment and the technology
of production.

Natural models see managers as responsible agents who interact symboli-
cally and, in doing so, create their social reality and give meaning to their
ongoing stream of experience. Problems are not simply presented to managers, problems are constructed by them. Whereas quantitative, literal analysis
guides rational models, qualitative, symbolic interpretation guides natural
models.

The use of accounting can be seen to be both a natural and a rational
process. Accounting is seen as a set of formal symbols (for interpreting
experience) and as a language reflecting both rational and natural aspects of
entities. Accounting makes sense of the entity (rational) and is used to make
sense of the frames of reference used in the entity (natural). Accounting is a
rational mechanism filtering *objective measurable* reality through accounting
categories. Accounting is a natural mechanism in that the categories give
coherence to chaotic processes[2] within the entity. Each aspect is seen to serve
as a context for understanding the other aspect. The rational and natural
aspects are not necessarily exclusive but can be used to support each other,
with one being dominant and the other 'bracketed' or off-stage. Which aspect
will assume the dominant role will change over time and is likely to be
contingent on the circumstances of each individual decision context.

Whilst accounting may have originally been designed as a rational information system, it is clear that it does not operate as such. Any claims to the
rational integrity of its internal processes are irrelevant, as it is not used in a

rational world and is used by irrational humans. National Accounts did not evolve as a measure of value or happiness for a nation. They actually measure and report on a limited set of monetary flows in a defined nation for a clearly defined time period. However, National Accounts are used 'incorrectly' by people who do not understand the meaning of the words and numbers they invoke to prove their case or maintain their ideological perspective.

2.8 IS ACCOUNTING LANGUAGE IDEOLOGICAL?

Ideology is seen as working through accounting, to give certain signifiers an authoritative position in terms of their role of helping us to understand the world and, at the same time, silently to exclude other ways of understanding the world. For example, it sounds rather bizarre to stand up and say that you support a reduction in GDP or argue that inefficiency is a good thing. Yet, rather than being made aware of the closures brought about by accounting discourse, we are taught to believe that we are able to choose our values and understandings of the world (Belsey, 1985; Barrett, 1985). Many of the central postulates underlying accounting are conceived as being *natural and transhistorical* rather than ideological and historically contested. National Accounting has gone through major historical changes and has been used for different purposes over time; e.g. a philosophical exercise into notions of values and welfare, wartime planning, national efficiency programmes, and determining fiscal strategies. The changing construction of National Accounts reflects changes in dominant ideologies over time or external threats to the nation.

There are, of course, many different definitions of ideology. For example, ideology can be viewed as a discursive or semiotic phenomenon rather than a range of free-floating ideas, bringing a more materialist conception of ideology that 'grants the materiality of the word, and the discursive contexts in which it is caught up' (Eagleton, 1991, p.195). Hall's (1983) concept of ideology includes 'the languages, the concepts, categories, imagery of thought, and the systems of representation – which different social classes and groups deploy in order to make sense of, define, figure out and render intelligible the way society works'. Eagleton (1991) sees the term as denoting any significant juncture between discourse and political interests and also as a reference to the ways in which signs, meanings and values help to reproduce a dominant social power. We use this definition of ideology. Thus we are concerned with the *language of accounting*.

Accounting language could be described as 'jargon', in the sense that accounting uses words in very specific and, at times, confusing ways. For example, the word 'capital' in business accounting denotes the money put into a business by the owner rather than the more common sense meaning of the resources of the business: buildings, machinery, workforce, expertise, brand names and so on. The notion of capital in National Accounts is very different from the business notion of capital. To many members of the public it would come as a great surprise to learn that the National Accounts do not measure the nation's capital; they do not value our assets or measure our liabilities. National Accounting uses words differently from commercial accounting practice, adding yet another level of confusion.

Accounting is a particular discourse, but a discourse that cannot be separated from other historically derived social and cultural discourses. For example, to view accounting as an independent discourse may result in the failure to see the linkages between accounting and the development of our socially and environmentally destructive world order.

Ideology is best seen as a particular set of effects within the accounting discourse. It is in this sense that ideology brings about certain closures. This is consistent with Derrida's notion that all categories of thought are divided into binary opposites, the first term being valued at the expense of the second. Shearer and Arrington (1993) and Cooper (1992) note that many of the forms of signification which are silenced or considered to be 'worth less' are those which are considered to be 'feminine'. To Hall et al. (1977) it would be 'ideologically ungrammatical' to suggest that a loss is better than a profit. However, to many people losses may be preferred to profits: for example, if loss making means that the organisation has taken on board environmental concerns, or decided to pay good wages in a third-world country. Ideology makes certain signifiers dominant. In western culture dominant signifiers include profit, economy, efficiency, effectiveness, maintenance of capital, growth in GDP, asset, solvency, value for money and so on. Accounting language seems 'natural'.

2.9 THE NATURALISATION OF ACCOUNTING LANGUAGE

Classical descriptions of ideology see ideology's role as 'naturalising' and constructing social reality. Semiotic contributions to the study of language have again been enlightening regarding the links between ideology and discourse. The early, more structuralist, work of Roland Barthes (1972), by taking a 'two-stage' approach to the understanding of the sign, explained a linkage between ideology and language. Barthes saw 'scientific language' as being composed of three terms:

- the signifier, which is the empty acoustic image;
- the signified, the concept;
- the sign that is the associative total of the first two terms (the relation between concept and image).

The three terms together form a semiological chain. To Barthes, myths are forms of ideological language. Myths also contain signifiers, signifieds and signs, but are built upon pre-existing semiological chains, in which the sign in the first system becomes a signifier in the second. Barthes called this second order semiological system a metalanguage (see Figure 2.1).

Figure 2.1 Barthes' metalanguage

	1.Signifier	2. Signified	
Language	3. Sign		
MYTH	I SIGNIFIER		II SIGNIFIED
	III SIGN		

Source: Barthes (1972, p. 115, Figure 1).

Barthes' work throws light on accounting's mythical (or ideological) meanings. Take, for example, GDP as a measure of the standard of living or the measure of overall success and progress of a nation. This National Accounting measure (GDP) becomes mythical when it is 'robbed' of its technical book-keeping history. Instead, it becomes *mythical*, a sign of what is important about a nation, its efficiency, its position in national league tables and its strong government.

So accounting language gains at least part of its power by appearing to be natural and coterminous with reality but detached from the underlying building blocks of accounting. National income figures naturally insist that there is such a metaphysical thing as income. Thus this 'naturalisation' process adds an important dimension to our understanding of the way in which ideology works. We see the real multiple worlds in terms of unitary but mythical and ideological monetary information. Moreover we somehow forget how languages are formed out of a contested history.

Hall's (1982) concepts of historical traces and politics of signification help to understand language's history. To Hall, the outcome of struggles over definitions (including accounting definitions) depends upon the politics of signification. There is never the possibility of people accepting new ideas that are not in some ways grounded upon our pre-existing understandings. The pre-existing understanding that accounting discourse seems to resonate best with is neoclassical economics. Accounting discourse and much mainstream accounting theory draws strongly from the discourse of neoclassical economics (Tinker, 1980; Hunt and Hogler, 1990; Cooper and Zeff, 1992; Kinney, 1992; Williams, 1992). This allows accounting discourse to be considered 'ideologically grammatical' with capitalism's more socially and environmentally destructive tendencies. Ideology is 'working' through the alignment of accounting to such things as efficiency, neutrality, freedom, and 'optimum' allocation of resources. This has the effect of making it extremely difficult to question the discourse of accounting, because to do so would also mean questioning our historical traces or our pre-existing sedimented under-standings. Our 'common sense' tells us that accounting information *must be 'right'*. When accountants try to think about new problems, such as account-ing for the environment, they go back to the historically derived signifiers in order to develop practices to 'deal with' the problems. The associations between accountancy and other powerful discourses are difficult to break because their ideological terrain has been very powerfully structured.

In fact, when attempting to discuss, for example, a national income statistic, one will be confronted by two significant problems. If one questions the ontology of the number, one's argument will be marginalised and seen as somehow 'off the wall'. But if one argues that slightly different things (perhaps housework) should be included in the calculation of national in-come, one legitimises the ontology. But arguably, the biggest 'ideological mistake' that we make is to assume that we are the authors of our 'own' words and the rational decision makers regarding our 'own' actions. This mistake means that we believe that we choose which values we wish to adopt.

2.10 THE CONSTITUTION OF SUBJECTIVITY THROUGH LANGUAGE AND ACCOUNTING

One of the most significant contributions to understanding the basic ideologi-cal mistake that we can *readily choose* our values and understandings was made by Saussure (1965). He wrote that it is through language that people are constituted as subjects. Belsey (1985) notes that it is only by adopting the position of the subject within language that the individual is able to produce meaning. Many writers now believe that the only way in which we can understand the world is through language. Therefore, there is no unmediated access to the self, or to anything else. We are thus constituted by language. Once a child gains access to language it is 'already worldly' or as Volosinov (1986, p. 12) puts it:

. . . consciousness itself can arise and become a viable fact only in the material embodiment of signs' (p.11) . . . The individual consciousness not only cannot be used to explain anything, but, on the contrary, is itself in need of explanation from the vantage point of the social, ideological medium.

These insights indicate that the acquisition of accounting language is an important influence on the construction of our subjectivity. The role of language in the construction of subjectivity is one way of comprehending the invisible process of social control in which we 'willingly' adopt the subject positions and actions necessary to the continuance of the social formation; how we 'allow' closures and the dominance of certain signifiers. This clearly makes any discussion about how to change society extremely problematic. We are working with ideologically biased language. How can we escape from this?

2.11 RATIONALITY, SUBJECTIVITY AND ACCOUNTABILITY

The previous section, on the ideological mistake made in our understanding of subjectivity, gestures towards how accounting affects us personally. This insight is at present rather undeveloped (see for example, Miller and O'Leary, (1987), Cooper et al. (1992)). It is clear from the foregoing, though, that accounting somehow creates security; people seem to trust accounting numbers. Moreover, there is an overwhelming assumption in traditional accounting thought that we are *rational decision makers*. In this section our aim is to try to present an alternative view of the subject. Drawing upon French feminist insights, especially those of Helene Cixous (Cixous and Clement, 1986), and in particular her re-interpretation of Freud and Lacan (1979), it is suggested that we are insecure, anxious, contradictory, socially constructed subjects, whose prime desire is for security through recognition. One important feature of Lacan's (1979) work is his concept of the Symbolic Order. Lacan's Symbolic Order is the way in which societies are regulated by a series of signs, roles, and rituals which have meaning only in relation to each other, forming recognisable codes and expressed in language. The Symbolic Order is already in place in society and must be accepted and internalised by a child in order to function adequately as a social subject. At the same time as the child unconsciously internalises these sets of rules of language and behaviours, s/he is produced by them at the level of the uncon-scious. The symbolic order is not arbitrary, cannot be chosen at will, and is not accidental. Accounting at all levels, including National Accounting, is part of the symbolic order. The acquisition of accounting knowledge helps to structure our unconscious. Its acquisition presents us with an altered subjectivity. Accounting's signs, roles and rituals 'make sense' in terms of the broader symbolic order. Accounting is not *different* or threatening; on the contrary it reaffirms our self-perceptions, perceptions regarding others and our perceptions of the world.

Within a dominant, masculine-constructed subjectivity there is familiarity with, and adherence, to simple single monolithic accounts. Multiple accountings are considered strange, overly complex and are likely to be rejected. Qualitative accounts, narrative accounts, alternative representations, multiple and non-financial performance measures, are rejected by the masculine as representing the threatening feminine These alternative *feminine* accounts are subjected to criticisms of being weak, unscientific, subjective, irrational, useless and confusing to the decision making. The non-linearity and complexity associated with sustainability can be seen as a significant threat to the linear simplicity associated with masculine subjectivity. There is a masculine fear of losing control of the situation[3] and this will result in a rejection of the more feminine ontology associated with sustainability. This makes the problem of deriving a way of accounting for the environment particularly difficult. Sustainable accounts will have to become more feminine, using softer valuation concepts, multiple accounting entities, stressing interrelationship rather than dominance, stressing non-financial measures, using narrative, making less claim to objective scientific truth and giving voice to those silenced by current hegemonies.

Accounting can be seen to be part of a masculine exercise of power over people and nature, it is part of an existing symbolic order. It is not an independent objective scientific language or truthful representation of reality. Accounting does not form part of a rational decision process, as we are not independent rational subjects, but are rather 'already worldly', in the sense that, on acquiring (accounting) language, we accept a Symbolic Order which is already in place.

2.12 CONCLUDING COMMENTS

This chapter has briefly touched upon a wide range of issues connected with the economic, social and political role of accounting. It has drawn upon a wide range of critical studies of the practice of accounting and related them to National Accounting. The broad thrust of these studies is that accounting (in any of its manifestations) cannot be seen as an objective, neutral, rational comprehensive and scientific process. National Accounts reflect underlying ideologies and paradigms. National Accounts construct realities, they do not simply represent them. National Accounts can be used to define the nation within a particular ideology and to bind its constituent parts. National Accounts are part of a political process and form the basis of different political rhetorics. National Accounts silence those without power and distort the message of those who challenge existing hegemonies. National Accounts are simplistic and only offer a partial view of the nation they profess to represent.

National Accounting is also seen as part of the political problem of unsustainability and its reform must become part of the solution process. As it plays a part in policy decision making, it is important that those who use the information are aware of its inadequacies and omissions. We should identify and reduce the negative social environmental impact of conventional national accounting. We should reform the techniques for costing and valuing social and environmental activities. We should devise new forms of financial and non-financial accounting systems, information and control systems to support more sustainable policy decisions, develop new forms of perform-ance measures, new forms of accountability and reconcile the conflict be-tween conventional criteria and sustainable criteria.

National Accounting occupies a key space between social, environmental and economic systems. Conventional National Accounting has been used to defend current practices and used as a justification for the status quo. Na-tional Accounts provide a very selective but powerful representation of the national identity, through the detailed language of accounting. National Accounting provides the categories through which policy makers perceive their territory. Making the social and environmental impacts of political decisions more transparent through the national accounting system is critical for good political decision making. It is important for today's decision makers to be aware of the current, future and potential social and environ-mental costs and benefits of any decision they take. National Accounts do not currently do this and therefore must either be reformed or ignored for deci-sions relating to sustainability. Many policy options relating to sustainability are systematically penalised or handicapped by the distortions of National Accounting methods. National Accounting can never create a single set of figures that will wholly represent the sustainability problematique and must be interpreted in conjunction with other accounting entities. However, Na-tional Accounts must, as far as possible, reflect sustainability issues, and users of these accounts must also be educated as to their partiality and often naïve simplicity, if they are to play an effective part in the wider political process towards sustainability.

REFERENCES

Anderson, V. (1991), *Alternative Economic Indicators*, London: Routledge.
Barrett, M. (1985), 'Ideology and the cultural production of gender', in J. Newton and D. Rosenfelt (eds), *Feminist Criticism and Social Change*, London: Methuen.

Barthes, R. (1972), *Mythologies*, London: Paladin.

Bebbington, J., I. Thomson, R. Gray and D. Walters (1994), 'Accountants' attitudes and environmentally-sensitive accounting', *Accounting and Business Research*, **94**, 109–20.

Belsey, C. (1985), 'Constructing the subject: deconstructing the text', in J. Newton and D. Rosenfelt (eds), *Feminist Criticism and Social Change*, London: Methuen.

Boland, R.J. Jr, and L.R. Pondy (1983), 'Accounting in organizations: a union of natural and rational perspectives', *Accounting, Organizations and Society*, **18** (4), 223–34.

Buitenkamp, N. (1993), *Sustainable Netherlands – Environmental Space*, Amsterdam: Friends of the Earth Netherlands.

Burchell, S., C. Clubb, A.G. Hopwood., J. Hughes and J. Nahapiet (1980), 'The roles of accounting in organizations and society', *Accounting Organizations and Society*, **5** (1), 5–27.

Burchell, S., C. Clubb and A.G. Hopwood (1985), 'Accounting in its social context: towards a history of value added in the United Kingdom', *Accounting, Organizations and Society*, **10** (4), 381–413.

Chua, W.F. (1986), 'Radical developments in accounting thought', *The Accounting Review*, October, 601–32.

Cixous, H. and C. Clement (1986), *The Newly Born Women*, trans. B. Wing, Minnesota: University of Minnesota Press.

Clayton, A. and N. Radcliffe (1996), *Sustainability: A Systems Perspective*, London: Earthscan.

Commission of the European Communities (1992), *European Better Environment Awards for Industry*, Brussels: Commission of the European Communities.

Cooper, C. (1992), 'The non and nom of accounting for (m)other nature', *Accounting, Auditing and Accountability Journal*, **5** (3), 16–39.

Cooper, W.W. and S. Zeff (1992), 'Kinney's design for accounting research', *Critical Perspectives on Accounting*, **3** (2), 87–92.

Cooper, C., D. Pheby, K. Pheby and A.G. Puxty (1992), 'Accounting, truth and beauty', paper presented to European Accounting Association, Madrid.

Eagleton, T. (1991), *Ideology: An Introduction*, New York: Verso.

Ezzamel, M., K. Hoskin and R. Macve (1990), 'Managing it all by numbers: a review of Johnson and Kaplan's Relevance Lost', *Accounting and Business Research*, **20** (78), 153–66.

Gray, R. (1990), *The Greening of Accountancy: The Profession After Pearce*, Certified Research Report 17, ACCA, London: Certified Accountants Publications Ltd.

Gray, R. (1992), 'Accounting and environmentalism: an exploration of the challenge of gently accounting for accountability, transparency and sustainability', *Accounting, Organizations and Society*, **17** (5), 399–425.

Gray, R., J. Bebbington and D. Walters (1993), *Accounting for the Environment*, London: Paul Chapman.

Gray, R., D. Walters, J. Bebbington and I. Thomson (1995), 'The greening of enterprise: an exploration of the (non) role of environmental accounting and environmental accountants in organizational change', *Critical Perspectives on Accounting*, **6** (3), 211–39.

Hall, S., (1982), 'The rediscovery of Ideology: return of the repressed in media studies', in M. Gurevitch, T. Bennett, J. Curran and J. Woollacott (eds), *Culture, Society and the Media*, London: Methuen.

Hall, S. (1983), 'The problem of ideology: Marxism without guarantees', in B. Matthews (ed.), *Marx: A Hundred Years On*, London: Lawrence and Wishart.

Hall, S., I. Connell and L. Curtis (1977), 'The unity of cultural affairs television', *Cultural Studies*, **9** (1), 3–19.

Hines, R.D. (1988), 'Financial accounting: in communicating reality, we construct reality', *Accounting, Organisations and Society*, **13** (3), 251–61.

HMSO (1994), *Sustainable Development: The UK Strategy*, London: HMSO.

Hopwood, A. (1987), 'The archaeology of accounting', *Accounting Organisations and Society*, **12** (3), 207–34.

Hunt, H.G. and R.L. Hogler (1990), 'Agency theory as ideology: a comparative analysis based on critical theory and radical accounting', *Accounting Organisations and Society*, **15** (5), 437–54.

Kelly, M. and M.J. Pratt (1992), 'Purposes and paradigms of management accounting: beyond economic reductionism', *Accounting Education*, **1** (3), 225–46.

Kinney, W.R. (1992), 'Issues in accounting research design education', *Critical Perspectives on Accounting*, **3** (2), 93–7.

Lacan, J. (1979), *The Four Fundamental Concepts of Psychoanalysis*, trans. A Sheridan, Harmondsworth: Penguin.

Laughlin, R. (1991), 'Environmental disturbances and organizational transitions and transformations: some alternative models', *Organizational Studies*, **12** (2), 209–32.

Llewellyn, S. (1994), 'Managing the boundary: how accounting is implicated in maintaining the organisation', *Accountancy, Auditing and Accountability Journal*, **7** (4), 4–23.

Macintosh, N.B. and R.W. Scapens (1990), 'Structuration theory and management accounting', *Accounting, Organizations and Society*, **15** (5), 455–77.

Macve, R. and A. Carey (1992), *Business, Accountancy and the Environment: A Policy and Research Agenda*, London: ICAEW.

Maunders, K.T. and R.L. Burritt (1991), 'Accounting and ecological crisis', *Accounting, Auditing and Accountability Journal*, **4** (3), 11–26.

Miller, P.C. and T. O'Leary (1987), 'Accounting and the construction of the governable person', *Accounting, Organisations and Society*, **12** (3), 235–65.

Owen, D. (1993), 'The emerging green agenda: a role for accounting?', in D. Smith (ed.), *Business and the Environment: Implications of the New Environmentalism*, London: Paul Chapman.

Power, M. (1992), 'Corporate responsibility and environmental visibility: the role of accounting and audit', presented at Ecological responsibilities of enterprises, Florence.

Puxty, A.G. (1986), 'Social accounting as immanent legitimation: a critique of a technist ideology', *Advances in Public Interest Accounting*, **1** (1), 95–112.

Redclift, M. (1987), *Sustainable Development: Exploring the Contradictions*, London: Methuen.

Rubenstein, D. (1994), *Environmental Accounting for the Sustainable Corporation: Strategies and Techniques*, New York: UNEP/CICA.

Saussure, F. (1965), *Course in General Linguistics*, New York: McGraw-Hill.

Shearer, T. and C.E. Arrington (1993), 'Accounting in other wor(l)ds: a feminist without reserve', *Accounting, Organisations and Society*, **18** (2/3), 253–72.

Tinker, A.M. (1980), 'Towards a political economy of accounting: an empirical illustration of the Cambridge controversies', *Accounting, Organisations and Society*, **5** (1), 147–60.

Tinker, A.M., C. Lehman and M. Neimark (1991), 'Falling down the hole in the middle of the road: political quietism in corporate social reporting', *Accounting, Auditing and Accountability Journal*, **4** (2), 28–54.

Volosinov, V.N. (1986), *Marxism and the Philosophy of Language*, trans. L. Matejka and I.R. Titunik, Cambridge, Mass.: Harvard University Press.

Wildavsky, A. (1994), 'Accounting for the environment', *Accounting, Organisations and Society*, **19** (4/5), 461–81.

Williams, P. (1992), 'Prediction and control in accounting "science"', *Critical Perspectives on Accounting*, **3** (2), 99–107.

NOTES

1   In this chapter the notion of manager is used in a wide sense to include politicians and policy makers charged with the responsibility of managing the nation.
2   Included in the natural aspect are symbolic, political, ritualistic and ceremonial functions of accounting. This expanded by Chua (1986) and in Kelly and Pratt (1992).
3   This is often associated with a psychological fear of castration (Lacan, 1979).

3.   Roots of Green Accounting in the Classical and Neoclassical Schools

Anthony M. Friend

3.1 INTRODUCTION

Our inquiry may justifiably start with the great intellectual enterprise of eighteenth-century 'enlightenment', with a notion that individual well-being is inseparable from the prosperity of the kingdom as a whole; a vision of a shared 'Common-Wealth'.[1] Thus, in liberal economic texts of the classical economists can be found a concept of a national fund or stock of capital to create the wealth of nations:

> The annual labour of every nation is the fund which originally supplies it with all the necessaries and conveniences of life which it annually consumes, and which consists always either in immediate produce of that labour, or what is purchased with that produce from other nations (Smith, 1994, p. lix).

This introductory statement to *An Inquiry into the Nature and Causes of the Wealth of Nations* clearly places labour (i.e. work) and capital (i.e. the fund) as the central fact in the creation of national wealth. Natural capital, composed of the stock of the Earth's biological, geological and cycling resources, in the classical economics scheme of things, is the provisioner of humankind's materials and energy, and 'work' (the creation of order) is the driving force behind the concept of a volume measure of the national 'fund'. This conception is coherent with Green Accounting, insofar as the existing stock of natural, economic, and cultural capital is a true measure of the National Dividend. The coincidence of the classical and ecological economics conceptual framework is traceable to the notion that 'the general stock of any country or society is the same with that of all its inhabitants or members, and therefore naturally divides itself' into three kinds of stocks; those 'reserved for immediate consumption', those reserved for 'fixed capital', and those reserved for 'circulating capital' (Smith, 1994, p. 304). If we replace the word 'reserved' with the contemporary concept of 'conserved value' we have the essence of Greening the Accounts, *qua* conservation accounting. Moreover, by linking the volume of the stock of fixed capital (i.e. a capacity measure of future output) with actual flow of circulating capital (i.e. the goods and services produced) and subtracting capital consumption from gross revenue to obtain 'neat' revenue, the classical theory of production is in all particulars compatible with the modern concept of a sustainable economy.[2] In this way a connection is made between the maintenance of a stock of commodities available for consumption and the source of supply drawn from natural capital. In the words of Adam Smith:

> To maintain and augment the stock which may be reserved for immediate consumption, is the sole end and purpose both of the fixed and circulating capital. It is this stock which feeds, clothes and lodges the people. Their riches or poverty depends upon the abundant or sparing supplies which those two capitals can afford to the stock reserved for immediate consumption. So great a part of the circulating capital being continually withdrawn from it, in order to be placed in the other two branches of the general stock of society; it must in its turn require continual supplies without which it would soon cease to exist. These supplies are principally drawn from three sources, the produce of the land, of mines, and of fisheries. These afford continual supplies of provisions and materials, of which part is afterwards wrought into finished work, and by which are replaced the provisions, materials and finished work continually withdrawn from circulating capital (Smith, 1994, p.307–8).

The accounting identities of saving and investment is also noted:

> Every saving, therefore, in the expense of maintaining fixed capital, which does not diminish the productive powers of labour, must increase the fund which puts industry into motion, and consequently the annual produce of land and labour, the real revenue of every society (Smith, 1994, p. 317).

3.2 THE ROOTS OF A SELF-ORGANISING STRUCTURE IN GREEN ACCOUNTING

Smith assumes a cultural-institutional structure for a self-regulating market of a liberal economy which satisfies the human 'disposition to truck, barter and exchange'. A model of an economy whereby the sum total of all individual (productive) actions, motivated by nothing less than self-interest to better themselves improves the (economic) well-being for all. While prima facie a model for chaos, order appears in this laissez-faire system in the form of a mysterious force of an invisible hand. A metaphor, according to Mirowski (1989), taken from the Newtonian Laws of motion and applied to commodities-in-exchange.[3] In effect, the law of conserved force of two colliding (mass) bodies transmuted into a two-body transaction account between the producers and consumers of economic commodities. Conserved is the symmetry of 'value' found in a closed 'accounting loop' of the National Accounts. This is typically illustrated to the unwary first-year student of economics as an enclosed hydraulic system describing a two-way flow production services and consumer purchases (Samuelson and Scott, 1966, p. 195).

Students of ecological economics would likely recognise this 'mysterious force' in the Prigoginean concept of an emergent property of a dissipative structure (Prigogine and Stengers, 1984). The 'invisible hand' represents at one and the same time the 'conserved value principle,' or 'natural price' of the classical theory, and the 'self-organising principle' generated by the actions of a large number of producers and consumers in a competitive economy. Note that market prices act both as stabilising and destabilising force in an economy. The latter is a result of speculation and expectations (i.e. positive feedback loop) and the former a result of the market clearance mechanism (i.e. a negative feedback loop).

The classical economists clearly did not intend to advocate 'chaos' in establishing the principles of a competitive society. They therefore gave much thought to the political framework designed not only to provide the conditions of a liberal economy but, more importantly, to regulate and control the natural instinct of a political-commercial elite to exact monopoly and privilege from the State. The classical texts took great pains to describe social-political means to attain economic ends, in contrast to neoclassicism which took the politics out of the formalism of the economic model.

The concept of a competitive society could escape entirely neither from its negative connotation of the 'survival of the fittest', nor from its Marxist interpretation of capitalism being the exploiter of a powerless multitude (working class) by a privileged few (owners of capital). This was further exacerbated by the multiplier-effect of population growth and capital accumulation hitting the 'wall', so to speak, of the 'fixity' of nature's resources. The conclusion drawn from the growth model is that the ultimate destination of the capitalist system is a 'stationary state' and its implied zero-sum outcome in the distribution of income. This outcome is caused by the law of diminishing returns and would result in:

- Exhaustion of natural resources inducing an ever-increasing rise-in-rent for land.
- Population explosion reducing labour to a subsistence level of existence (i.e. an 'iron law of wages').
- Exponential accumulation of capital reducing the rate of profit to zero.

While progress toward increasing wealth and affluence of the people was seen as a (temporary) reward for liberating trade, the permanent state of prosperity seemed forever haunted by the Malthusian spectre. While Malthus described the mechanics of population growth, Smith intuitively perceived the problem in the Darwinian 'struggle for survival'.

> Every species of animals naturally multiplies in proportion to the means of their subsistence, and no species can ever multiply beyond it. But in civilized society it is only among the inferior ranks of the people that the scantiness of subsistence can set limits to the further multiplication of the human species; and it can do so in no other way than destroying a great part of the children which their fruitful marriages produce (Smith, 1994, p. 91).

The System of National Accounts (SNA) is an abstract (linear) database of a national production system, deeply embedded is a syntax of a self-regulatory market system. It is described by a transaction matrix between buyers and sellers, and within the (system) boundaries of a prescribed institutional framework of economic agencies (or units). The pre-analytic vision embedded in the SNA is the classical view of an economy as a 'self-organizing' adaptive system for the provision of goods and services. Adam Smith's great insight is that an individual who 'intends only his own gain, . . . is led by an invisible hand to promote an end which is no part of his intention', and in so doing promotes 'the public interest' (Smith, 1984, p. 485). Described is a commodity space model of productive activity motivated by 'self-love'.[4]

Here we may note, as does Mirowski (1989), that the economists, perhaps intuitively, have borrowed from classical physics the formalism of the principle of 'least action' (or seeking the most efficient energy path in the motion between two points) as an algorithm for a laissez-faire economy.[5] Translated into economics, this assumes that an inherent property of the dynamics of a competitive society is the allocation of a (scarce) resource to its most productive use; a constructed syntax of a random collision of particles (chaos) drawn towards an equilibrium state by the law of the conservation of energy, (order). This is made concrete in the (Walrasian) general equilibrium model of many sellers and buyers, none of whom can control, or influence in any way, the allocative mechanism of a long-term equilibrium price. In this model, value is conserved by marginal cost (producers) and benefit (consumers) of all individual transactions which add-up for the whole system to the familiar accounting identity of:

Production (supply) = *Consumption (demand)*

For this model to work requires at least three axioms; the existence of a rational decision maker; a perfectly competitive market; and a perfect flow of information among economic transactors. Classical economics greatly simplified the dynamics of efficient allocation by positing a 'natural price' embodied in an exchangeable commodity. Underpinning this notion is a conserved substance theory of value, identified as embodied labour, in which a price for a commodity in exchange gravitates towards 'centre of repose', also identified as the production cost.[6] The neoclassicists rejected the substance value theory and replaced it with an ephemeral psychology of a 'willingness-to-pay' as the determinant of an equilibrium price. The 'Hand' thus became still further obscured in an optimum utility field which changes its form with every marginal quirk in taste, fashion and lifestyle.

3.3 THE ROOTS OF THE CONSERVATION PRINCIPLE IN GREEN ACCOUNTING

The Greening of the National Accounts (and its constituent database) in effect transforms the invisible hand of market transactions to an equally invisible hand to conserve natural capital. The formalism of a neoclassical production-consumption equilibrium state is described by an abstract idealised (economic) behaviour that is neither isomorphic with, nor anchored to, the observed (real-time) accounting variables of resource depletion and ecosystem degradation. The equilibrium supply–demand condition is characterised by differential equations, which possess infinite (marginal) adjustment mechanisms with respect to change in price, change in available stock of human-made and natural commodities, and incentives to invest in new capital stock. Since this takes place over time, the expected return is discounted for risk and foregone consumption by an inverted interest rate, to obtain the present value of any given investment schedule. *Ipso facto*, future supply is equilibrated to future demand by the sum total of all individual investment decisions discounted to present value.

Thus, the neoclassical framework has introduced a conservation principle in terms of a servomechanism of 'expectation', internalised in the model itself and not, as in the classical framework, an (external) function such as population growth, technology and fixed land. In the latter case the total value, by definition, is conserved in exchange but the limit function of fixed resources effectively (re)distributes the conserved share of wealth. The neoclassical framework does not directly integrate nature's limit function in its model of wealth creation, but nonetheless incorporates the conservation principle indirectly through social choices, prices, and technology. Identified servomechanisms applied to conserving natural capital include, *inter alia*:

- Trade-off value (i.e. willingness-to-pay to conserve or restore an ecosystem function).
- Supply price reducing demand and thus conserving a natural resource.
- Substitution of economic for natural capital.

- Expectation of new technologies applied to reducing consumption of materials and energy (i.e. dematerialisation of an economy).

The classical concept of an absolute limit to (economic) growth and its substance theory of value, in a sense is reified in conservation accounting. Conserved value, anchored to physical exchange, is analytically more robust in dealing with environment-economy transactions than the indeterminacy of a psychological value anchored in a consumer preference function. Ricardo (1973) suggested corn units rather than money units be used as the numéraire for relative valuation among commodities. This idea was reintroduced in modern literature by Sraffa (1960) in his model of price determination and distribution of an economy, described in terms of a dynamic input-output accounting of circulating capital (i.e. Production of Commodities by Means of Commodities). Conserved value has nonetheless taken a more complex hue in ecological economics than that afforded by the simpler classical theory of embedded labour. While work, described as kinetic energy, is the baseline numéraire of conserved value in exchange of an (open) thermodynamic system, this is modified by a detailed analysis of a complex, and generally unique, property of an ecosystem function. This is further modified, where feasible, by an explicit recognition of an ethical principle and/or cultural value entailed by any given stock of natural capital (Friend, 1996).

A primitive form of environment-economy transaction accounting is found in the eighteenth century *Tableau économique* of the Physiocrats, also known as the Economists. The underlying assumption is that all wealth originates from the bosom of the earth, and an economy merely circulates value among labour, landlords, and manufacturers. Secondary production, or manufacturing, does not in itself create new value.[7] Here, the concept of nature's surplus is applied in much the same sense as the solar energy inflow driving the biosphere's primary productive system in thermodynamic analysis. While this conception of a source of wealth is a child of a predominantly agricultural society, it also presupposes that humankind is sustained by nature's bounty in the form of minerals of the earth, the wood from the forest and the fish in the ocean. It is also viewed, and is clearly expressed in Ricardo, as a limit function of economic (and population) growth. It should be noted that while nature is ultimately treated as a fixed, and thus scarce, commodity, surplus capital and labour are necessary ingredients to improve not only the productive quality of land and livestock, but accessibility to distant stocks. Colonialism is therefore a means to expand the effective supply of inputs into domestic production and, of course, convenient land available for a surplus population.

National Accounts recognise land (i.e. natural resources) as a factor of production, but curiously disconnect it from the classical concept of the interdependency of Man and Nature and its *sui generis* spatial-qualitative properties (i.e. heterogeneity of natural capital). Explicit in the 'Inquiry' is that, along with human labour, Nature adds value directly to a commodity. This efficacious property of 'land' is a double dividend obtained by the marriage of labour and capital.

> No equal capital puts into motion a greater quantity of productive labour than that of the farmer. Not only his labouring servants, but his labouring cattle, are productive labourers. In agriculture, too, Nature labours along with man; and though her labour costs no expense, its produce has its value, as well as that of the most expensive workman (Smith, 1994, p. 393).

GDP is only weakly connected to the flow of environmental goods and services generated by the nation's stock of natural capital. This is implicit in the transaction accounts recording the cost involved in the protection, conservation and restoration of an ecosystem function, and explicit in the natural assets identified, and included, in the capital asset accounts. SNA (1993) recommends that the economic value of a privately owned natural resource stock be estimated to its present discounted value.[8]

This provides an economic value for natural capital in the nation's fixed physical stock account (i.e. balance sheets). Changes in the (economic) value of natural capital, if data are available, may be estimated from physical data on depletion and accretion of biological resources, degradation and restoration of cycling assets, rates of depletion of exhaustible resources (e.g., mineral and fossil fuel reserves) and write-off in catastrophic losses. The value of new natural capital stock again, if the data are available, may be added to the previously identified stocks in the balance sheets by discoveries (e.g. oil reserves), privatisation of previously public domain assets (e.g. water authorities) and direct investment in natural capital (e.g. forest plantations).

The SNA (1993) revision has emphasised the importance of stock accounting, and to the extent that natural assets are included in the 'Volume of Asset Accounts', a thin wedge is available for prying open the economy to an environmental limit function. Nonetheless, recommendations so far are partial, conservative with respect to valuation methods, and selective with respect to which resources to include or exclude. Moreover, values are market equivalents, disconnected from ecosystem functions, and are arbitrary with respect to their boundary conditions (e.g. classified to timber stocks as opposed to ecosystem forest types).

3.4 THE ROOTS OF SHARE OF WEALTH IN GREEN ACCOUNTS

The classical division of the National Dividend share among workers, capitalists and landowners, has survived in the modern National Accounts, as factor payments to labour (wages and salaries), factor payments for the use of capital (interest, dividends, and capital consumption allowance), and factor payments for the use of land and the rights for resource exploitation (rent, royalties, concession fees, etc.). However, the associated social-class categories are now subsumed in a more neutral division among (economic) functional transaction categories, namely households, business, government and foreigners.

While in the classical world the national income pie devolves into a distinct social class structure, these are not necessarily watertight with respect to economic functions. The self-employed artisan who owned his own tools, the yeoman farmer who improved his own land and the small-scale trader who owned his shop, are at one and the same time a labourer, capitalist and rentier. Nonetheless, there has been much discussion on whether the share of wealth is in the natural order of things, controlled perhaps by an 'invisible hand' of economic laws, or is a socially determined power relationship stemming from some sort of 'initial conditions' entailed by the economic system. In effect, this would be an historical resolution of conflicting values of a land owning aristocracy (e.g. *noblesse oblige*), a merchant-capitalist (e.g. willingness-to-pay) and the mass of the labouring class, (e.g. a fair wage for a fair day's work). Karl Marx (1906), who thought long and hard about this problem, concluded that all wealth originated in theft, and share is the power to appropriate newly created wealth (i.e. the surplus product of labour). Since this viewpoint is historical, the share of the National Dividend is thus an entailment property of the (social-economic) system (i.e. the struggle for 'surplus value').

The liberal economists recognised that actual share, despite the apparent equanimity of an invisible hand, is not a 'just' reward for work, but the resolution of complex dynamics of competition for (scarce) resources. Distribution is thus resolved by effective demand, in the form of an equilibrium price, among those who own, and have command over, the use of the productive resources of labour, capital, both physical and financial, and the property rights for the use of natural capital. Thus, an explanation is needed in (embodied) labour theory of value to explain how a 'non-productive class' can appropriate the product of a 'productive class'. The dynamics of distribution, particularly as expounded in Ricardo, analyse the problem in Malthusian terms of an exponential growth of population, a steady accumulation of (physical) capital, and an (ultimately) fixed quantity of land. Under these conditions, the only conclusion to draw is that:

- *Wages* tend towards subsistence by the growth in surplus labour.[9]
- *Profits* tend towards zero by the law of diminishing returns on fixed capital and, its corollary, diminishing opportunities for circulating capital (i.e. falling interest rates).
- *Rents* tend toward the maximum for the use of a non-expanding (fixed) resource.

Services, including the cost necessary to transport and/or distribute goods, in the classical sense of economic product, are unproductive.[10] These are part of the circulating capital which, when consumed, 'perish the very instance of its production', or is withdrawn from circulation through taxation imposed on productive labour, capital or land. In effect, this is an accounting rule which treats services as 'transfer payments' from the productive to the non-productive sector, i.e. GDP remains unchanged. Furthermore, services according to Adam Smith, while at times necessary and at time frivolous, could only be a drain on the real wealth of a nation; a diversion of resources from productive to non-productive uses. Parsimony, or abstinence of consumption, is a necessary condition for saving required to augment the fund of circulating capital. While part of this sum remains in circulation for the purchase of goods for resale, thus adding nothing to the national product, part is withdrawn and added to a fund for investment in labour and capital, to produce an additional supply of goods for future consumption. Saving, in a roundabout way, adds to the productive wealth of the nation, whereas profligacy, in a similarly roundabout way, subtracts from the wealth of the nation, in particular as expenditure on wars.

> The labour of some of the most respectable orders in society is, like that of the menial servants, unproductive of any value, and does not fix or realize itself in any permanent subject, or vendible commodity, which endures after labour is past, and for which an equal quantity of labour can be procured. The sovereign, for example, with all the officers both of justice and war who serve under him, the whole army and navy, are unproductive labourers . . . In the same class must be ranked, some both of the gravest and most important, and some of the most frivolous professions; churchmen, lawyers, physicians, men of letters of all kinds; players, buffoons, musicians, opera-singers, opera-dancers, etc. . . . . Like the declamation of the actor, the harangue of the orator, or the tune of the musician, the work of all of them perish the very instance of its production (Smith, 1994, p. 361).

This classical conception of production is later echoed by Kuznets' concern about the treatment of certain kinds of public expenditure in national income. In his view, the national production takes place within a given social framework of administration, laws, security and defence. While these constitute a necessary condition, they are not part of the net output of an economy. This view of accounting clearly reflects the objective function of an economy as an 'index of economic welfare', in which growth of output is not an end but a means. In Kuznets words:

> . . . national income is a measure of net output . . . within a given social frame-
> work, . . . the flow of services to individuals from the economy is a flow of eco-
> nomic goods produced and secured under conditions of internal peace, external
> safety, and legal protection of specific rights, and cannot include those very
> conditions as services . . . There is little sense in talking of protection of life and
> limb as an economic service to individuals – it is a precondition of such services,
> not a service in itself (Kuznets, 1952, pp. 193–4).

Rent on land and resources is similarly viewed as 'unproductive' insofar that the property owner contribute nothing to production, such as land improvement, but merely obtains a right, so to speak, to appropriate nature's production.

> As soon as the land of any country has all become private property, the landlords,
> like all other men, love to reap where they never sowed, and demand a rent even
> for its natural produce. The wood of the forest, the grass of the field, and all the
> natural fruits of the earth , which, when the land was in common, cost the labourer
> only the trouble of gathering them, . . . have an additional price fixed upon them.
> He must pay for a the licence to gather them, and must give up to the landlord a
> portion of his labour either collects or produces (Smith, 1994, p. 56).

Ricardo described rent as ' . . . that portion of the produce of the earth which is paid to the landlord for the use of the original and indestructible powers of the soil' (Ricardo, 1973, p. 33). This is qualified in that part of rent, like improved land, is apportioned to payment for the use of investment capital. The actual level of rent is shown as a price of diminishing return of new and less productive land bought into production. At the margin the rent is zero. Rent can be viewed, in particular for biological resources, as a right of property, and thus a permit to appropriate nature's surplus product. While Adam Smith considered rent as a payment for the use of a productive resource, Ricardo formalised rent as a dynamic exponential function of growth in demand and a fixed supply. The difference in conception of rent is important, in that in one case rent is justifiably passed on as a value-added to a commodity, whereas in Ricardo it is ultimately a monopoly price, and thus a value-subtracted from a commodity.[11]

The question of the appropriate concept of 'rent' for the use of natural resources in the National Accounts is still with us today. The choice of treatment is critical for non-market valuations (i.e. shadow prices) in Green

Accounts. Rent, as a market transaction, is a factor payment to those who own the right of access to a natural resource.[12] No distinction is made, therefore, between a user-cost payment for the consumption of natural capital and a market-value user right. However, one may assume that rent implies a normalised cost for resource management and, in the case of an exhaustible resource, a time-discounted capitalisation cost. In Green Accounting, user cost is equal to the supply price of Nature (i.e. replacement cost for the used-up stock) and, where feasible, adjusted by social-cultural values. In the case of a biological resource, user cost is a complex (heterogeneous) variable calibrated to an associated ecosystem production cost function. The user cost of an exhaustible resource is more straightforward, being a discounted present value of a 'reserve' stock, or inventory, for which the revenue is (re)invested in a alternative capital flow of (sustainable) income (El Serafy, 1992).

Actual rent is usually based on a 'bidding price' for the use of a natural resource and not, except coincidentally, a calculated 'user cost', or the 'conservation price' for the sustainable utilisation of natural capital. While the theory of economic valuation of 'rent' assumes an (economic) opportunity cost, this may not, and usually does not, assume a full user cost for conserving the health and integrity of a ecosystem (steady-state) production function. Nor is there any allowance made for intrinsic cultural and environmental values independent from a willingness-to-pay or social benefit-cost analysis. Economic valuation, of course, implies a conservation value in policies for establishing national parks, heritage sites, and protection of rare and endangered species. It should be noted that conservation value, while a social-political choice, requires an ecological accounting metric such as ecological prices, properly to value an environment-economy (exchange) transaction.[13] The classical school already recognised the inherent ambiguity of rent in an economy, insofar that they identified the locus of value not with those who 'love to reap where they never sowed', but in the 'indestructible powers of the soil'.

3.5 THE ROOTS OF NEOCLASSICAL THOUGHT IN GREEN ACCOUNTING

The neoclassical school shifted the discourse of economics from the 'cause' to the 'mechanics' of wealth creation. Abandoned is the search for the origin of value and the (moral) justification of share of the National Dividend, in favour of a purely formal and completely general theory of functional interdependence (Roll, 1956). Abandoned also is the 'dismal science' conclusion of an ultimate state of subsistence living for the mass of the population, in favour of optimism of 'progress' and economic growth. The economy is thus conceived of as an expanding utility field, a metaphor according to Mirowski (1989), borrowed from theoretical physics law of motion/inertia and the conservation principle of thermodynamics. While the latter formalises the principle of conserved value-in-exchange, the former formalises the actions leading to an efficient allocation and distribution of scarce resources, assumed in a self-regulatory (competitive) market for goods and services. Thus is a general equilibrium model reified in the income-expenditure identity of the National Accounts.

Nonetheless this formal, and elegant, equilibrium price system has proven to be the Achilles heel for an explanation of the existence of non-equilibrium states of the economic system, externalities of production and the unpredictable evolutionary dynamics of the creative/destructive economic process (Schumpeter, 1934). Ellul (1994), among others, has observed that a technological society is less directed by rational choices circumscribed by cultural values, traditional norms and standards assumed in a self-regulatory market, than driven by the logic of technology itself along often unchosen, and clearly unpredictable, paths. The poverty of the mechanical analogy was noted by Alfred Marshall in his introduction to the Principles of Economics.

> The Mecca of the economist lies in economic biology rather than economic dynamics. But biological conceptions are more complex than those of mechanics; a volume on Foundations must therefore give a relatively large place to mechanical analogies; and the frequent use of the term 'equilibrium,' which suggests something of a statical analogy (Marshall, 1920, p. xiv).

The accounting of a 'national dividend' shifts from a stock (classical) to a flow (neoclassical) conceptual framework. Marginal analysis and the 'mechanics' of wealth creation underpins the logic of employing national income as opposed to national wealth as a the proper measure of a nation's well being. Marshall, in his 'Principles', provides a rationalization of the money approach to measure a people's prosperity:

> The money income, or inflow, of wealth gives a measure of a nation's prosperity, which, untrustworthy as it is, is yet in some respects better than that afforded by the money value of its stock of wealth. For income consists chiefly of commodities in a form to give pleasure directly; while the greater part of national wealth consists of the means of production, which are of service to the nation only in so far as they contribute to producing commodities ready for consumption (Marshall, 1920, p. 80).

While money value is a now well-established numéraire of GDP, it is clearly an 'untrustworthy measure' of a nation's sustainable prosperity. Here, the classical concept of income being services flowing from a physical stock of capital is of greater relevance. Marshall would likely approve of the conservation of the 'means of production,' when a hundred years later, the depletion of natural capital jeopardises a future generation's welfare function. Indeed, Marshall considered the Malthusian prediction of a declining per capita utility as substantially correct, but that it is *deferred* in a growing economy:

> . . . it was not Malthus' fault that he could not foresee the great development of steam transport by land and by sea, which have enabled Englishmen of the present generation to obtain the products of the richest lands of the earth at a comparatively small cost (Marshall, 1920, p. 180).

Marshall assumed, like Adam Smith, that while the productivity of nature is a 'free gift', a clear distinction needs to be made between free-for-all exploitation and the necessity to maintain the productivity of nature's bounty by careful husbanding, nurturing and stewardship. In his chapter on the 'The Fertility of Land' is found an environmental perspective of 'land' broadly defined, not only as an input of natural resource to an economy but as an holistic landscape of ' . . . seas and rivers, in sunshine and rain, in winds and waterfalls'. Secondly, land is viewed in much the same manner as the classical school in terms of a critical, and indispensable, source of wealth, subject to diminishing returns. Thirdly, recognised is the efficacy of human input to enhance the productivity of natural capital, by the same token, a neglect to do so leading to environmental degradation. However, the bottom line is that man has 'little control' and thus must respect nature for itself, nor can its services be effectively replaced by man-made substitution.

> Those free gifts of nature which Ricardo classed as the 'inherent' and 'indestructible' properties of the soil, have been largely modified; partly impoverished partly enriched by the work of many generations of men . . . Every acre has given to it by nature an annual income of heat and light, of air and moisture; and over these man has but little control. He may indeed alter the climate a little by extensive drainage works or by planting forests, or cutting them down. But, on the whole, the action of the sun and the wind and the rain are an annual annuity fixed by nature for each plot of land. Ownership of the land gives possession of this annuity: and it also gives the space required for the life and action of vegetables and animals; the value of this space being much affected by its geographical position (Marshall, 1920, p. 147).

While land is a source of material goods, its spatial fixedness drew the attention of its *sui generis* properties.

> The area of the earth is fixed: the geometric relations in which any particular part of it stands to other parts is fixed. Man has no control over them: they are wholly unaffected by demand; they have no cost of production, there is no supply price at

which they can be produced . . . .We shall find that it is this property of 'land' which, though as of yet insufficient prominence has been given to it, is the ultimate cause of the distinction which all writers of economics are compelled to make between land and other things. It is the foundation of much that is most interesting and most difficult in economic science (Marshall, 1920, p. 145).

Marshall, was familiar with land improvement and selective breeding but knew little of ecosystem dynamics. Nonetheless he noted the distinction between the resilience of natural selection and the vulnerability of the economically desirable but artificial hybrids and cultivars which ' . . . has given him plants that have but little resemblance to their wild ancestors'. He then goes on to say:

For while nature left to herself would select those which are best able to take care of themselves and their offspring, man selects those which will provide him the most quickly with the largest supplies of the things he most wants; and many of the choicest products could not hold their own at all without his care (Marshall, 1920, p. 148).

The 'Principles' clearly recognised the existence of natural production as an 'annuity fixed by nature' and the existence of an economic product that has no associated 'cost of production' nor 'supply price'. It is clearly a small step to identify nature's product as an integral part of the National Dividend valued at ecological prices (i.e. nature's supply cost). One further step is required to arrive at the Green Accounting concept of optimisation of the neoclassical utility field constrained by a 'limit function' of environmental carrying capacity. That is the notion of fixed geometry of productive properties of land which Marshall noted ' . . . (is) the foundation of much that is most interesting and most difficult in economic science'. This, when translated into policy arrives at:

- Internalisation of environmental costs in the economic production function (i.e. polluter pays principle).
- Conservation of natural capital in order to maintain a steady-state flow of ecological goods and services.

The law of diminishing returns underpins the Marshallian environment-economy analysis. A distinction, however, is made between the Ricardian sense of a capacity limit of a fixed quantity of land and that of reproducible capital. The latter, as Marshall noted, is expandable, and thus it is always profitable to add one more unit up to the point where the marginal cost equals the marginal benefit. This indeed is generalised for ' . . . all affairs of life'.

> Excessive application of any means to the attainment of any end are indeed sure
> to yield diminishing returns in every branch of business; and, one may say, in all
> affairs of life (Marshall, 1920, p. 407).

The problem of a 'fixed' supply and growing 'demand' requires a solution for a sustainable economy, let alone a growing economy. Paradoxically, diminishing returns (i.e. increasing marginal cost of production) resolves itself through the price mechanism, by reducing demand and by substitution of a scarce with a more abundant resource and, if all other means fail, waiting in the wings is the *deus ex machina* of technology. In the celebrated fable of the 'Tragedy of the Commons', Hardin (1968) claims that there exists no technical solution to the continuous human expropriation of natural capital. An optimum population of the Planet, for instance, could not satisfy, at the same time, the Benthamite goal of the greatest good for the greatest number. The logical implication of substitution of human-made for natural capital is the zero-sum outcome expressed as an equal value gain for an economy and an equal value loss for an ecology. Nature's contribution to GDP thus shrinks while that of the economy grows in equal measure.

That the diminishing marginal returns in economic output have not set in, might suggest that there is a technical solution. Even more telling, per capita income, as measured by the SNA, might further suggest that even where environmental limits have set in, these have been more than offset by substitution of human-made for natural capital. Marshall, however, did insist that while the law of diminishing returns can be 'deferred,' it cannot be postponed forever. Even deferral has its negative consequence.

> Against this must be set the growing difficulty of getting fresh air and light, and in
> some cases fresh water, in densely peopled places. The natural beauties of a place
> of fashionable resort have a direct money value which cannot be overlooked; but
> it requires some effort to realize the true value to men, women and children of
> being able to stroll amid beautiful and varied scenery (Marshall, 1920, p. 166).

3.6 DISTINCTIONS IN THE CLASSICAL AND NEOCLASSICAL FRAME OF REFERENCE IN THE GREENING OF THE NATIONAL ACCOUNTS

The antecedents of concepts and definitions of National Accounts stem from the various threads of classical and neoclassical thought on what exactly constitutes income, wealth, production, consumption, and capital. The classical thread is woven into the whole cloth of society in the form of an embedded labour theory of value in physical product, available for immediate consumption of goods and/or intermediate consumption of capital. The distribution of wealth is similarly woven into a whole fabric of society and divided among the labouring, capitalist and rentier classes. The neoclassical economics focused on abstract behaviour of economic actors in reference to the dynamic forces of a general supply–demand equilibrium. In effect, there is a paradigm shift in the theory of production from one of substance of material product to one of immaterial choices of psychic satisfaction. Eric Roll, in *A History of Economic Thought*, put it this way:

> . . . (the) new theory . . . is based upon . . . the transition from an objective to a subjective approach [and] brought about a major change in the relationship between economic analysis and its sociological antecedents. In nearly all classical literature, economic analysis was allied with an historical view of the structure of society which underlay the whole economic process. In its place was put a view of society as an agglomeration of individuals. The subjective theory of value is only compatible with an individualistic view of society . . . (Roll, 1956, p. 371).

The new theory transforms the Common-Wealth from a circulating flow of a physical stock of material goods to a income flow of money-valued transactions for the exchange of goods and services. This constitutes a utility field optimised in a system of competitive markets. Moreover, since the individual utility function is additive, it is but a small step to objectify this (hypothetical) field function to an imperative of economic growth.

The neoclassical concept of share, on the other hand, is more convoluted than the straightforward classical school's historically-determined rule for the division of the National Dividend. Required is an hypothesis of an 'invisible hand' for equalizing, in an exchange economy, the marginal utility of the consumer with the marginal productivity of the producer. Inferred is that no one economic agent can improve his/her position without jeopardising the optimum state of the sum-total economic pie. The corollary is that the economy is at a sub-optimum position if any factor of production, labour, capital and land (natural resources), is not fully employed at the marginal productivity level. While critics have pointed to the underlying tautology of the Marginalist approach, it nonetheless assumes a compelling (neutral) social justification for the existing inequalities in the distribution of wealth.

At the macro-level of national accounting it is assumed that while people may not actually make, in all cases, rational *Homo œconomicus* calculations, its ontological validity is claimed in the statistics of large numbers given an opportunity to make a consumer choice among an array of alternative products and a given budget constraint. As many scholars have noted, there is a wide, and some believe unbridgeable, gap between the micro-level hypothetical models and macro-level observation of historical facts (i.e. statistical data). In its extreme form, the utility function is an expression of a national aggregate of psychic satisfaction.[14] Clearly, this is not a satisfactory concept for defining an objective function for the measure of a National Dividend. The confusion on whether per capita income is a satisfactory surrogate of human well-being, or merely a volume measure of an individual's throughput of material and energy, stems, in part, from the neoclassical rationalisation of the utility field function for a nation writ large. This is a confusion arising from the metaphysics of a 'pre-analytic' vision for an economy formalised in the differential equations of statistical mechanics but which, unlike the natural sciences, depends on a deductive, as opposed to inductive, form of inquiry to confirm ' facts'. For Jevons (1905) the principles of an economy can be deduced from an analytic system of laws embedded in 'the mechanics of utility and self-interest', but Roll noted that:

> Jevons, himself a statistician, did not deny that empirical studies were an essential part of the total economic studies; but urged that the ultimate laws of economics were of so general a character that they could rightly be compared with the laws of the physical sciences, which have their basis more or less obviously in the general principles of mechanics (Roll, 1956, p. 378).

3.7 CONCLUSION

The National Accounts, as currently conceived, are firmly grounded on the syntax of the mechanics of the neoclassical general equilibrium model. The revised SNA (1993), through its system of stock-flow balances, allows for a biological niche, however tentatively, to enter the System. This is found in the Accumulation Accounts entitled 'Natural growth of non-cultivated biological resources' and duly entered as account number K5. Here is clearly a window of opportunity for not only Greening the Accounts but introducing the ecological economics syntax of 'emergent' properties of dissipative structures, based more or less obviously in the general principles of thermodynamics.

As we have noted in this chapter the contribution, and criticality, of Nature's production function to the National Dividend is well established in classical economic theory. The shift in the value theory from 'work' to 'willingness-to-pay' somewhat obscured, but did not completely obviate, Nature as a limit function to economic growth. The Law of Diminishing Returns, a manifestation of the Entropy Law (Georgescu-Roegen, 1971), points to the exponential growth in energy and social costs to maintain a steady-state thermodynamic equilibrium of a technologically advanced, complex, large-scale, and hierarchical, system of production. While it is not difficult to argue that the thermodynamic (non-linear) framework for Greening the Accounts is theoretically compelling, the necessity to do so may be resisted by those for whom the (mechanical) utility approach has served well in pursuance of expanding market economies as an end in itself. Therefore, essential prerequisites are empirical studies, and the requisite data collection, that truly reveal the sustainable state of an economy and the health and integrity of its interdependent ecosystem production functions, and thus compel, at the level of public discourse, the introduction of thermodynamic principles into the SNA.

REFERENCES

Boulding, K.E. (1949), 'Income or wealth', *Review of Economic Studies*, **17**, 77–86.

Edgeworth, F.Y. (1881), *Mathematical Psychics*, London: Kegan Paul.

Ellul, J. (1994), *The Technological Society*, New York: Vintage Books.

El Serafy, S. (1992), 'Sustainability, income measurement, and growth', in R. Goodland, H.E. Daly, S. El Serafy (eds), *Population, Technology, and Lifestyle*, Washington DC: Island Press.

Friend, A.M. (1996) 'Sustainable development indicators: exploring the objective function', *Chemosphere*, **33** (9), 1865–87.

Friend, A.M. (1999), 'Unearthing ecological pricing buried in conservation accounts' (unpublished manuscript).

Georgescu-Roegen, N. (1971), *The Entropy Law and the Economic Process*. Cambridge Mass.: Harvard University Press.

Hardin, G. (1968), 'Tragedy of the commons', *Science*, **162** (3859), 1243–8.

Jevons, W.S. (1905), *Principles of Economics*, London: Macmillan.

Kuznets, S. (1952), 'Government product and national income', in *Income and Wealth*, Series I, Cambridge: Bowes and Bowes.

Marshall, A. (1920), *Principles of Economics*, 8th edn, London: Macmillan.

Marx, K. (1906), *Capital: A Critique of Political Economy*, New York: The Modern Library.

Mill, J.S. (1985), *Principles of Political Economy*, Books IV and V, Harmondsworth: Penguin.

Mirowski, P. (1989), *More Heat than Light: Economics as Social Physics, Physics as Nature's Economics*, Cambridge: Cambridge University Press.

Penguin Books (1983), *Dictionary of Physics*, Harmondsworth: Penguin Books.

Prigogine, I. and I. Stengers (1984), *Order Out of Chaos: Man's New Dialogue with Nature*, New York: Bantam Books.

Ricardo, D. (1973), *The Principles of Political Economy and Taxation*, London: Everyman Library.

Roll, E. (1956), *A History of Economic Thought*, Englewood Cliffs: Prentice-Hall.

Samuelson, P.A. and A. Scott (1966), *Economics: An Introductory Analysis*, (Canadian Edition), Toronto: McGraw-Hill.

Schumpeter, J.A. (1934), *The Theory of Economic Development*, Cambridge Mass.: Harvard University Press.

Smith, A. (1994), *An Inquiry into the Nature and Causes of the Wealth on Nations*, New York: The Modern Library.

SNA (1993), *System of National Accounts, 1993 Revisions*, New York: United Nations Press.

Sraffa, P. (1960), *Production of Commodities by Means of Commodities*, Cambridge: Cambridge University Press.

NOTES

1   The concept 'share,' while prima facie a static analysis of given quantity of a stock of wealth, draws its essence from the dynamics of growth in GNP. Economic growth as an end in itself is rationalised by the notion of the 'trickle down effect' whereby the rich become richer, and the poor, less poor. Absolute growth assumes that the whole society is better off, even if temporarily some people are worse off, the so-called Kuznets curve showing a widening gap between equity and early stage industrial development. The classical tradition, especially as expounded by the Ricardo model, saw absolute growth leading to a maldistribution of income because of the dynamics of population growth and a fixed quantity of productive land. Mill went so far as to advocate a 'stationary state' for a Nation that has already reached a satisfactory level of prosperity on the grounds that:

> If the earth must lose that great portion of pleasantness which it owes to things that the unlimited increase of wealth and population would extirpate from it, for the mere purpose of enabling it to support a larger, but not a better or a happier population, I sincerely hope, for the sake of posterity, that they will be content to be stationary, long before necessity compels them to it (Mill, 1985, p. 116).

2   While the concept of 'fixed capital' is the familiar human-made capital of the national accounts, circulating capital is more akin to the concept of national product. Adam Smith makes the distinction between money as the means to circulate the 'wheel of production' and the commodities produced but not yet distributed to its 'proper consumers'. This is made up of work-in-progress, inventories held by producers and merchants, and finished products not yet sold. What is important in this context is that sustainability requires a 'withdrawal' of human consumption of environmental goods and services (i.e., circulating capital) in order to conserve the stock of natural capital. It is the revenue, *qua* surplus, left over after maintaining stock (i.e. neat revenue) that is the definition of sustainable wealth of a nation, both in the classical and Green Accounting sense.

> The gross revenue of all the inhabitants of a great country, comprehends the whole annual produce of their land and labour; the neat revenue, that remains free to them after deducting the expence of maintaining; first, their fixed; and secondly, their circulating capital; or what, without encroaching on their capital, they can place in their stock reserved for immediate consumption, or spend upon their subsistence, convenience, and amusements. Their real wealth too is in proportion, not to their gross, but to their neat revenue (Smith, 1994, p. 311).

3   Newton's Third Law states that when a body applies a force upon a second body, the second body applies an equal and opposite force upon the first.

4   The following is the oft quoted passage in the Wealth of Nations on the nature of self-interest:

> It is not from the benevolence of the butcher, the brewer, or the baker, that we expect our dinner, but from their regard to their own interest. We address ourselves not to their humanity, but to their self-love, and never talk to them of our own necessities but of their advantages (Smith, 1994, p. 15).

5   The least action principle is defined as a state variable in a conservative dynamic system where the motion between two points has a stationary value for the actual path as compared with the various paths between the same points for which the total energy has the same con-

stant value. (Penguin Books, 1983). Note that the Hamiltonian equations of neoclassical fame are based on this principle.

6   It is interesting to note that 'gravity' employed in the Inquiry as a metaphor for natural price is inconsistent with Newton's 'action from a distance' and proportional to an object's mass, but, nevertheless, is consistent with the older Aristotelean concept of 'natural place' of 're-pose'. The stone rolled downhill because its natural place is the bottom of the valley (Smith, 1994, p. 65).

7   Smith disagreed with the claim of the Physiocrats that the sole source of 'productive wealth,' *qua* value, is from agriculture. In his view all 'productive labour' is 'value added'. However, what constituted production was severely restricted to material transformation, and excluded what we today call services. Mirowski thought that Smith essentially misunderstood the Physiocrats schema of an integrated analysis of the distribution of 'national product'.

    If one chooses, as did the Physiocrates, to locate the augmentation of value in a single sector, then it follows that trade between sectors can readily be defined as trade of equivalents: this is the real meaning of the *Tableau économique*. In this schema, production is well defined as the locus of increase of the value substance; trade or circulation as where value substance is conserved, and finally, consumption as the locus of final destruction (Mirowski, 1989, p 159).

8   Arguably the proper discount rate for natural capital is zero, or even negative if strong conservation measures are required for stock survival. This, in fact, is the case when a moratorium is announced on fisheries. The negative discount rate is a value of the compound recruitment rate of the fish stock in each reproductive cycle, a kind of compound interest rate. In other words, the present value of the stock is its future volume when the fish stock is assumed to be of sufficient volume for harvesting to resume.

9   It was frequently noted among the classical economists that wages were higher in North America than England. It was, they reasoned, due to a wage rate just equal to an alternative cost of clearing virtually free land at the frontier of settlements. Naturally, the native people who already occupied the land, referred to as 'savages,' were displaced by the mere fact that they could not produce the same volume of output per unit of land in competition to the 'civilized races'. *Eh bien*, once again the working of the invisible hand!

10   Today this position appear quaint insofar as the bulk of GDP in a modern economy is generated by the immaterial output of the service sector. However, the Greening of the Accounts has once again raised interest in the material stock-flow accounting. Reduced to its purest form, all income is a stream of services flowing from stocks of fixed and circulating economic and natural capital. The only truly immaterial stock is 'know-how and knowledge' lodged in the minds and talents of people. This is sometimes referred to as cultural capital. For a discussion on income as a flow from stock see Kenneth Boulding's (1949) well-reasoned article on 'Income or Wealth'.

11   The current debate about 'product stewardship' is similarly concerned with the question of 'value added' and 'value-subtracted' with respect to the use of environmental goods and services. Stewardship assumes a value net of environmental costs.

12   The notion is that of 'property rights' and includes not only private, but also communal and public lands. The concept of the 'commons' is that of free access to air, water, and land resources.

13   I have proposed elsewhere that the 'invisible hand' of conservation is an ecological price, (or metric) to maintain and/or restore a steady-state output stream of an ecosystem production function. This is proposed as a direct 'user-cost' method of valuation for natural capital (Friend, 1999).

14   A British economist, Edgeworth (1881), wrote an economic text entitled 'Mathematical Psychics' which developed the theme of indifference analysis for preference ordering in making choices between two goods. This approach to economics is still found in introductory economic text under the chapter on 'welfare economics'.

4. Sustainability, Ecological Economics and Green Accounting

Sandrine Simon

4.1 INTRODUCTION

In this chapter, I shall address three important areas of research: green accounting, sustainability, and ecological economics.

Research in Green Accounting started a little more than 25 years ago, when it focused on the shortcomings of the System of National Accounts (SNA), the problems these shortcoming generated, and the ways to correct them. This research was initiated in the context of an 'indicator crisis' (Henderson, 1993), which questioned the validity of the signals on which policy makers rely (in particular, signals such as the aggregate economic indicators generated from the SNA). These criticisms were based on the fact that important considerations, such as environmental degradation, were not correctly taken into account, since they were seen as increasing the value of our 'economic performance' but not denounced for threatening our future life support base. Since then, research in green accounting has come a long way; different methods have been developed, and research is still evolving.

Turning to sustainability, the context for the development of this concept was already set when research in green accounting was initiated. However, it was only in 1980 that the concept was first promoted and widely publicised with the launching of the World Conservation Strategy. It was popularised, in 1987, by the final report of the Commission for Environment and Development, entitled 'Our Common Future' (WCED, 1987). It has been defined by Costanza et al. (1991, pp. 8–9) as:

> . . . a relationship between human economic systems and larger dynamic, but normally slower changing ecological systems, in which (1) human life can continue indefinitely, (2) human individuals can flourish, and (3) human cultures can develop; but in which effects of human activities remain within bounds, so as not to destroy the diversity, complexity, and function of the ecological life-support system.

Finally, ecological economics is a young 'discipline', the need for which was recognised only recently. As explained by Faber et al. (1998), different authors in the field, with different intellectual backgrounds (ecology, physics, chemistry, engineering, mathematics, economics, political science, etc.) have different emphases on the new interdisciplinary area of ecological economics. However, a brief definition of ecological economics is that it studies how ecosystems and economic activity interrelate. Ecological economics therefore relates to scientific aims and problems, but also to political and ethical issues, and this subject matter embraces some of the most serious problems faced today, such as deforestation and species loss, and the use of fossil fuels and carbon dioxide emissions.

These three popular themes of research (green accounting, sustainability, ecological economics) are different in that:

• Green Accounting is an analytical framework, a policy tool.
• Sustainability is a concept.
• Ecological Economics can be described as a paradigm.

They were developed at different times, and not originally linked.

However, it is becoming clear that these three areas are closely related and are fundamentally linked. In the case of ecological economics and sustainability, the link is very clear, in that sustainability is a key concept in ecological economics.

The links between green accounting and sustainability, and between green accounting and ecological economics are, however, more controversial, although the tendency seems to be more in favour of consolidating these links rather than not.

First, let us examine the link between sustainability and green accounting. Current debates on indicators of sustainability mention green accounting as a potential 'indicator of sustainability'. Although, ideally, this could be the case, at present traditional systems of green accounts should not be interpreted as indicators of sustainability. However, researchers generally agree that the national accounting framework has some advantages in the representation of sustainable processes. Also, green national accounting could be a very useful representation of sustainable processes and consequently become an indicator of sustainability.

The link between green accounting and ecological economics is important with regards to previous, but also and most important, future research in green accounting. So far, many systems of green accounts have been constructed by using some methods (in particular valuation techniques) that are characteristics of neoclassical economics, rather than ecological economics. This has been criticised (Aaheim and Nyborg, 1993; Common, 1990), since there seems to be a paradox in wanting radically to reform the SNA by using the methodologies that have originally created the shortcoming of the SNA. Further, ecological economics needs to be more involved in policy making; it has been criticised for not being sufficiently practically oriented (cf. Viederman, 1994). Using the contribution of this paradigm to develop green accounts would therefore be useful in the effort to operationalise sustainability.

In this chapter, I shall examine these linkages and argue that they need to be expressed in a clearer way if future research in green accounting is to contribute to the operationalisation of sustainability. As green accounting is the main subject of this book, it constitutes the point of departure of my discussion.

In the Section 4.2, I examine the compatibility between research in green accounting and the research paradigm of ecological economics. The direct link between green accounting and ecological economics is through the concept of sustainability. Thus, this section ends with a discussion of the necessity of taking account of the concept of sustainability in research in green accounting if this type of research is to be carried out within the ecological economics paradigm.

Section 4.3 focuses on how green accounts can help to represent and operationalise sustainability. I highlight the fact that research in green accounting represents a fundamental opportunity to operationalise sustainability. Both methodologically and politically, the accounting framework fulfils some interesting criteria that are useable when constructing an indicator of sustainability. The institutional dimension constitutes one important area of research which will need developing in the context of research in green accounting if green accounts are to help the policy making process find ways to put sustainability into practice.

In Section 4.4 I offer some conclusions.

4.2 GREEN ACCOUNTING AND ECOLOGICAL ECONOMICS

The current SNA describes the whole set of economic activities which take place in a country in one year (Malinvaud, 1964, p. 7). The way in which the SNA describes these economic activities, and the way in which it is used, has changed with time and needs. The creation of national accounts, as they exist now, originated in the inter-war period. In the 1930s, all industrialised countries accelerated research on economic statistics and systems of accounts, under the influence of the developing macroeconomics, in particular the Keynesian approach. With the inter-war economic crisis, and the perceived need to regulate the economy, governmental intervention in economic matters became more and more frequent. Consideration was therefore given to the construction of such indices as national product and income and other indicators derived from the national accounts. In general, it is important to notice that the development of economic information and of national accounting is linked with the development of intervention of the state in economic life (Archambault, 1988).

4.2.1 Definition and Aims of Green Accounting

This type of intervention is not negligible in the context of environmental policies, and we need to examine the way in which this has led to the 'greening' of the national accounts.

As noted above, research in green accounting started a little more than 25 years ago, when debates on sustainability still focused on the *definition* of the concept rather than on its operationalisation. The perceived shortcomings of the SNA can be summarised as follows:

- The traditional SNA focuses on flows only and ignores stocks, be they environmental or cultural. People interested in environmental issues have realised that stocks have a great importance, as in the way in which certain ecosystems stocks respond to external shocks. In turn, these stocks influence the interactions between natural ecosystems and human societies.
- Negative externalities, such as environmental pollution or crime, are not taken into account in the assessment of economic performance and progress.
- Distribution and inequality issues are not taken into account in the current SNA. For example, the SNA uses average income per head in any analysis of the performance of the economy.
- The SNA focuses on production processes that generate monetary exchanges solely. Hence, the use of services that do not involve monetary exchange (e.g. use of 'free' air or 'free' housework) are not considered as contributing to economic welfare.

For all of these reasons, the current SNA gives the wrong signals and needs reforming. The rationale for Green Accounting is therefore to correct these shortcomings, because the current SNA generates and encourages unsustainable economic development. Two general approaches have been developed.

The first advocates the addition or subtraction of elements related to the environment from the existing SNA (i.e. environmental heritage, 'patrimonies' and environmental depreciation)

The second advocates changes in the structure of the accounts to completely change the faulty 'policy signal'.

For some time, completely changing the structure of the account has been seen as unfeasible but, slowly, this opinion is being reviewed.

The aim that is common to the two attitudes towards green accounting is to reform the SNA policy tool, to make sure that it takes account of important environmental issues and that it helps policy makers steer economic development towards a more sustainable state.

4.2.2 How to Green the Accounts?

Although the development of green accounting did not use an ecological economics paradigm *per se*, the principles underlying both the development of the paradigm of ecological economics and the reform of the policy tool (the national accounting framework) are very close. This section indicates what are these principles. It also suggests why, in future research in green accounting, the greening of the accounts would be appropriately carried out in the context of ecological economics.

The first element to mention is the 'indicator crisis' (Henderson, 1993), first observed at the end of the 1960s. A series of criticisms was addressed to the SNA in particular, and to other elements related to our economic practices in general. These criticisms progressively evolved into a serious questioning not only of the way in which we manage our economies, but also the way in which we perceive our human societies in relation to the surrounding natural environment, and how all of these elements are illustrated through indicators. Paradoxes were highlighted. While apparent progress was being made, according to traditional economic indicators, environmental pollution was also clearly worsening.

The 'indicator crisis' resulted in a 'value crisis'. The gap existing between what economic indicators announced and what was observed in reality not only highlighted problems of measurement. It also stressed that some important elements were being ignored, which also deserved consideration when measuring 'progress' or 'welfare'. It was thus stressed that such dimensions should be included in indicators of progress, individually and also as related to each other. This would allow us to understand the economic functioning in a new way, as one aspect of a whole ecological and social fabric; a living system composed of human beings in continual interaction with one another and with their natural resources, functioning with certain kinds of scarcity and values. As a result of both the indicator and value crisis (Henderson, 1993), the debate on economics became progressively more concerned with what to measure, rather than how to measure it. This is very much related to a debate concerning the confusion of means and ends in economic analysis, a debate already initiated by Boulding (1963), and further developed by some ecological economists who focused on the reform of the economic paradigm and economic policy tools.

This leads us to the third important point. Both the indicator crisis and the value crisis allowed us to understand the problems underlying the paradigm of economics. The fusion of the 'indicators crisis' (Henderson, 1993) and the 'value crisis' resulted in a 'paradigm crisis'. The neoclassical economic way of thinking and acting was seen as too focused on 'chrematistics'[1] dimensions. Those in favour of a questioning and reform of this paradigm argued that economic analysis would benefit from revisiting the notion of 'oikonomia', which is basic to economic practice (Daly and Cobb, 1989). It is in this context that the paradigm of ecological economics started being developed. As Viederman (1994, p. 468) noted:

> The principles of ecological economics suggest that addressing the real world issues at the intersection of economics and ecology – the human household and nature's household – are our reason for existence. . . . Ecological economics is characterised by a problem focus, pragmatism, and concern for sustainability. It takes a comprehensive global view, over the long term and in context. Ecological economics is also concerned with the process of institutional change, expressing a tolerance for uncertainty and a willingness to explore questions for which we do not at present know the answers. While efficiency is the policy objective of conventional economics, ecological economics is concerned with resiliency, safety, and common sense.

Ecological economics therefore provides a new way of understanding how our human societies and economic systems function, through their interactions with the natural environment.

Research in green accounting and the progressive formulation of ecological economics are, therefore, not only compatible, but they have some common objectives. Indeed, it could be argued that green accounting is the crystallisation of ecological economics, in that it is the illustration, in practical and policy terms, of how ecological economics can contribute to practical changes.

However, research in green accounting has shown that the process of correcting the shortcomings of the current SNA can deviate from the principles of ecological economics. When solely focused on the addition or subtraction of environmental elements to or from the aggregate indicators generated by national accounts, research in green accounting has proved to rely on very chrematistically-based evaluation methods, i.e. monetary evaluation reflecting neoclassical principles. Here, there is a paradox between the methodology followed and the ultimate aim pursued. If green accounts are constructed using the traditional economic paradigm, there is a risk that they will not bring anything new, nor be compatible with the new type of economic analysis and practices intended to promote environmentally and socially centred values.

This leads us to conclude the following. The 'indicators crisis' stimulated a 'value crisis', which itself encouraged a questioning of the economics paradigm. The next step is to make sure that the policy indicators are being reformed using the paradigm which the indicator originally stimulated.

For green accounting to really bring something new in terms of indicators of performance and policy tool, its construction has to follow the principles of ecological economics.

4.2.3 Should Green Accounts be Related to Sustainability?

At this point, we need to introduce the notion of 'sustainability' in green accounting. The concept of sustainability was introduced through the concept of 'sustainable development', which term was first promoted and widely publicised with the launching of the World Conservation Strategy in 1980. It was popularised by the final report of the World Commission for Environment and Development (WCED, 1987), entitled 'Our Common Future'. The two most widely used definitions of 'sustainable development' are those from this text and from 'Caring for the Earth' (IUCN, 1991). The former states that it is 'development that meets the needs of the present without compromising the ability of future generations to meet their own needs' (WCED, 1987, p. 43). The latter document describes sustainable development as 'improving the quality of human life while living within the carrying capacity of supporting ecosystems and sustainability as a characteristic of a process or state that can be maintained indefinitely' (IUCN, 1991, p. 211). The notion of sustainability is much more politically ambiguous, even considered as 'politically treacherous' (O'Riordan, 1988), since it challenges the status quo. Viederman (1995, p. 37) has been describing sustainability as:

> . . . a vision of the future that provides us with a road map and helps to focus our attention on a set of values and ethical and moral principles by which to guide our actions, as individuals, and in relation to the institutional structures with which we have contact – governmental and non governmental.

Sustainability is a key term in ecological economics, since it is what this new paradigm ultimately seeks to achieve, in practical terms. It must therefore also be of prime importance in policy tools developed in the context of ecological economics.

In relating sustainability to research in green accounting, it is important to stress that the original criticisms of the SNA were fundamentally directed towards the notion of 'performance'. Calculating the Gross National Product (GNP), as with standard accounting techniques, does not allow us to envisage the structure of our societies in a more sustainable way. Neither does an adjusted GNP, for which the adjustments (inclusion of environmental elements measured in monetary units) have been based on a neoclassical evaluation methodology. The economic performance we are interested in, in ecological economics, should concentrate not solely on monetary exchanges and values. Those who question the SNA are interested in the 'performance' that is related to sustainability itself.

A green system of national accounts should therefore not only help policy makers orientate economic developments towards sustainable development, but also help to illustrate the way in which a sustainable economy would function. In green accounting, we are really trying to construct an integrated indicator of sustainability. There is, therefore, a fundamental shift in the way in which economic performance can be envisaged. Only the paradigm of ecological economics is in agreement with the way in which such an understanding of economic performance has evolved.

4.3 CAN GREEN ACCOUNTING REPRESENT AND HELP OPERATIONALISE SUSTAINABILITY?

From what has been said in the earlier sections, we can conclude that, for green accounting fundamentally to change the outcome of economic policies, it has to become an indicator of sustainability, constructed in the context of ecological economics.

One could, however, wonder: why focus on green accounting? Perhaps another type of 'indicator of sustainability' could be constructed, in a new way, using new ecological economics principles. Although one could feel that there are advantages in so doing, the disadvantages are as follows:

Important, if not revolutionary, attitudes of questioning have been generated by criticising the SNA. This policy tool cannot be left untouched after such debates. Also, this policy tool is currently politically powerful and the version of 'economic performance' it gives prevails. The development of a new, parallel, policy tool would be unlikely to replace the unreformed SNA.

Institutionally, the construction of the current SNA is powerful. The structure of this policy tool and its use results from a whole methodological construction, involving institutions which also need reforming, or at least need to be more aware of points stressed by advocates of green accounting.

Looking at these political and institutional dimensions, we need also to look at the methodological dimension. In the same way as ecological economics encourages us to question the prevailing economic paradigm, dominated by chrematistics, in order to re-understand the oikonomia foundations of economic analysis, green accounting invites us to look back at the original characteristics of national accounting. By doing so, we can see that the

structure of national accounts could help in representing sustainable processes, and therefore ultimately constitute an 'indicator of sustainability'.
National accounting actually fulfils certain criteria for indicators of sustainability.

4.3.1 Methodologically

The structure of the national accounts is such that they illustrate what happens in an economy during a year. The flows of goods and services exchanged between economic sectors (that generate monetary exchanges) are
registered in monetary units, in what can be described as inter-sectoral
matrices. These accounts are ultimately used to calculate some economic
macro and aggregated indicators, such as GNP, and it is these that are used
by policy makers as indicators of the performance of economic activities.
These indicators help policy makers choose between various alternatives for
future economic developments.

In the earlier sections, it was argued that the indicators crisis of the 1970s
(Henderson, 1993) was, to a large extent, generated by problems related to
indicators such as GNP. Here, we are looking more specifically at the tables
that form the national accounts and which are used to calculate the aggregate
economic indicators. The structure of these tables, which constitute the
national accounting framework, is representative of neoclassical economics'
understanding of the way in which the economy functions. The choice of
some economic sectors, the neglect of some others (informal sectors, unpaid
domestic work, etc.), the grouping of sectors, are representative of the current
type of economic analysis.

The way in which these accounting tables have been constructed has
presented some problems, in particular with regard to the lack of accountability for environmental considerations. However, some characteristics of the
structure of the national accounts are interesting from the point of view of a
potential representation of sustainable processes.

There follow some criteria of national accounts that present some interesting characteristics for a potential indicator of sustainability, apart from the
fact that it is an internationally recognised policy tool.

In national accounting, data are collected and aggregates are calculated
for each year. Although this might not be an adequate time interval to detect
significant trends from a sustainability point of view, it is still possible to use
the information provided by national accounts in the context of a general
plan, which covers more than one year. The fact that national accounting is
based on the frequent collection of up-to-date information, constitutes a
useful characteristic, to be used and maintained.

An indicator that has a predictive or anticipatory ability offers a tremendous advantage to managers and decision makers. The information generated in national accounts can be used in simulation models to help the policy making process. The complementary development and use of green accounts and ecological economic models is not impossible, and would constitute a very positive contribution to policy making towards sustainability.

Trends are meaningful when analysed in the context of reference values. Some research projects in green accounting have focused on this particular aspect, comparing the current state of the environment and state of the interactions between economic developments and ecological functioning, and some threshold values characteristic of a sustainable functioning of ecosystems (see Ekins and Simon (1998) for details).

Most importantly, the holistic representation of the 'economic functioning' is a useful characteristic of the national accounts, from the sustainability point of view. The interdependencies existing between economic sectors are illustrated in one snapshot, interpreted as a whole. Many people working on sustainability and sustainable processes agree that the concept of sustainability encapsulates various dimensions (social, ecological and economic) that all need to be taken into account. Sustainable processes similarly involve not only various sectors but, for instance, certain ecological processes from a certain ecosystem, and social intervention by a local community. What makes the process sustainable is that it actually creates the links between these various dimensions, and that it does it in a special way. When representing the sustainable processes, we therefore need to take account of interdependencies between various elements, new elements to be taken into account in the 'equation', and also a new 'system dynamic' (Clayton and Radcliffe, 1996), unique to sustainable processes.

The use of inter-sectoral matrices is therefore promising and helpful when attempting to represent sustainable processes.

In the debate on indicators of sustainability, it is important to note that there is a general tendency to develop frameworks of indicators, rather than lists of individual indicators. Thus, the European Commission (Ohman, 1999) is in the process of developing matrices of pressure and state environmental indicators, aimed at providing holistic information useful to policy making, and to gain insights on the practical effects of unsustainable processes. In parallel, directly related to research in green accounting, the Dutch NAMEA approach (National Accounting Matrices including Environmental Accounts) have been constructed using a variety of environmental themes and indicators related to each others in an accounting framework (see Chapter 5). The interest in the NAMEA is because it does not result in calculating an aggregated indicator such as an adjusted GNP: the matrix, in itself, provides enough relevant and policy oriented information to be useful as a whole (Keuning and de Haan, 1998). In line with this, many debates on indicators of sustainability are highlighting the need to disaggregate information and not to rely on aggregated information, especially if expressed in monetary units (O'Connor, 1998).

The relatively recent policy interest in sustainability and sustainable processes, is progressively shifting research efforts from the refinement of the definition of sustainability as a concept, to the explanation of how sustainable processes function, and how the successful performance of such systems and processes can be represented. I feel that green national accounting could help in this endeavour.

4.3.2 Politically

As mentioned earlier in this chapter, green accounting is a powerful policy tool, which generates indicators that are influential and heavily used. Governments, economists and the media, all use these indicators, all over the world, as a way to measure the various countries' economic performance and to compare them. The United Nations is working on reforms of the SNA which, in turn, are applied everywhere in the world. If the traditional system of SNA is criticised, it therefore has to be done in a general manner, and the changes should benefit every user of national accounts. The progressive reform of the SNA would certainly have a bigger impact than the development of individual ways of constructing indicators of sustainability usable in policy making.

At this point, it is important to remind ourselves that we are discussing 'ideal' systems of green national accounts, that could constitute indicators of sustainability and help to operationalise sustainability. These could be the subject of future research on green accounting.

Such systems of green accounts have not yet been developed. Current systems of green accounting are still very experimental, and cannot be considered *per se* as indicators of sustainability. In fact, the systems of green accounting that are used in environmental policy (which are very few), often focus on so-called 'strategic resources' (e.g. forests, oil and gas resources), individually, rather than working at an integrated policy approach of resource management that is closer to sustainable management.

There are two types of problems related to the policy implications of currently existing systems of green accounts.

The first relates to the popularity of, and current debates around, 'indicators of sustainability'. In this context, green accounts are often presented as 'indicators of sustainability'. This is premature, considering the state of research in green accounting.

The second problem is that, when observing the policy implications of green accounting or, more precisely, the way in which green accounting contributes to environmental policy making, it is clear that green accounts, as currently formulated, do not particularly help operationalise sustainability as such. When talking about green accounting as an indicator of sustainability, it is therefore fundamental to stress that it is what research in green accounting should tend towards, but has not yet achieved. If this is not made clear, there is a risk that both green accounting and the concept of sustainability will lose some credibility.

Research in green accounting therefore needs to be kept dynamically responsive to new insights concerning the understanding of the concept of sustainability. It also must be policy oriented if it is to be helpful, at some stage, in the operationalisation of sustainability. The way in which research is evolving should be oriented towards putting sustainability into practice.

The debates concerning the links between indicators of sustainability and green accounting have the potential for regenerating interest in research on green accounting and the direction it ought to take in the near future, if green accounts are really to become indicators of sustainability *per se*.

The exercise of greening the accounts had the important effect of boosting the debate on environmental values and the questioning of the meaning of economic performance. This should progressively have a policy effect in itself, rather than solely indirectly. Thus, if we aim at creating a new type of policy tool in a type of framework that is familiar to policy makers (accounting inter-sectoral framework), we therefore imply that the type of policies derived from using these tools will also be different from the one currently used. This, in turn, would imply that the policy making process, from an institutional point of view, should also be different. This institutional dimension is the subject of discussion of the next section.

4.3.3 Institutionally

As Boulding (1963, p. 54) stressed, any study of policy should concern itself with three things. What we want (the ends), how we get it (the means), and who are we, that is, what is the nature of the organisation or group concerned. With the rise of the 'citizen', and the growth of democratic institutions, the concept of the 'Power State' has been challenged by that of the general 'welfare state'; i.e. a state that exists to promote the general welfare of its inhabitants. Governmental institutions have an important role to play in the construction of policy tools such as green accounts. This is because it is governmental institutions that will use the indicators generated by the green accounts. However, they should not be the only ones and, if the SNA is modified, partly through modifying the type of policies made, the formulation of environmental policies towards sustainability generated by the new type of accounts should involve more participation from a broader range of stakeholders. This participation should manifest itself in the implementation of policies towards sustainability, and also in the construction of the accounts. This participation could help redefine important economic principles.

These issues have been examined by people interested in 'cultural capital' (Berkes and Folke, 1994) and also in the context of what Michael Jacobs calls 'institutional environmental economics' (Jacobs, 1994, p. 84).

Berkes and Folke stress the importance of natural capital and the relationship between natural capital and human capital in ecological economics thinking. They use the term 'cultural capital' to refer to factors that provide human societies with the means to deal with the natural environment. They stress:

> Aspects of cultural capital, such as institutions, involved in the governance of resource use and the environmental view, are crucial for the potential of a society to develop sustainable relations with its natural environment' (Berkes and Folke, 1994, p. 128).

It is clear that research in green accounting has so far concentrated mainly on 'natural capital' (Harrison, 1990), to the exclusion of cultural or social capital. However, the social dimension of the concept of sustainability is given more and more importance and this also needs to be reflected in research on green accounting.

Institutional environmental economics (Jacobs, 1994) could contribute greatly to the introduction of social dimensions into research in green accounting. It is very close to the underlying principles of ecological economics, since it rejects the methodological individualism that underpins the neoclassical analysis. Institutional environmental economists argue that economic behaviour is culturally determined, and that institutions in society (such as governments, regulations and property rights) are not 'market imperfections', but are the very structures which allow markets to operate. The research carried out in institutional environmental economics asks, for example, what is going on when people value the environment. They conduct empirical research to look at how people think and behave towards different aspects of the environment. These types of research initiatives can also attempt to develop social institutions that are able to reflect how people think and behave towards the environment, so that public decisions are more able to represent a democratic choice.

Institutionalists examine how, in practice and in principle, political institutions do, and should, work to make decisions on the environment. For this reason, they could help to identify how a system of green accounts could describe the relationships between natural and cultural capital, how environmental values could be expressed and represented in these accounts, and how decisions should be formulated if sustainability is to be put into practice.

Thus far, the institutional and social dimensions of sustainability have generated the least effort in research on green accounting. However, if these reformed accounts are to be related to sustainability, they need to include these dimensions. Ecological economics and institutional environmental economics could be the appropriate paradigms on which to base this type of research.

4.4 CONCLUSIONS

In this chapter, research in green accounting has been presented as a potential and promising way to operationalise sustainability, provided that this research is carried out in the context of the ecological economics paradigm. Reciprocally, ecological economics has been presented as the way of thinking and analysing economic dynamic functioning, which will help our better understanding and operationalising of sustainability. This is provided that the important principles it is based on are concretised through a policy tool, actually recognised and used, such as green accounting.

The complementarity, and quasi-symbiosis, between the concept of sustainability, the paradigm of ecological economics, and the national accounting policy tool, leads us to a number of conclusions.

First, it is clear that, in the context of the operationalisation of sustainability, green accounting, sustainability, and ecological economics are all very relevant issues. As shown in this chapter, these three 'themes' have been developed separately, although they are related to each other.

Second, in our attempt to construct 'indicators of sustainability' which would be useful in policy making, we have tended to interpret green accounts as such indicators. However, as stressed in this chapter, this constitutes a confusion between 'old' and 'future' research in green accounting, which deserves careful examination.

We conclude that, ideally, further research in green accounting would greatly benefit from being carried out in ecological economics. However, we also acknowledge that earlier research in green accounting (carried out in a predominantly neoclassical environmental economics context) has led to the construction of accounts that cannot and must not be interpreted as indicators of sustainability.

The general conclusion has important implications for future research in green accounting. If we seek to develop green accounts whose prime aim is to help operationalise sustainability, we need to recognise that such research has to be carried out consistently, within the ecological economics paradigm. We also need to differentiate clearly between newly developed green accounts and those that have been constructed long ago and that risk compromising the understanding of sustainability if badly interpreted and applied.

REFERENCES

Aaheim, A. and K. Nyborg (1993), 'Green National Product: good intentions, poor device?', Statistics Norway, Discussion paper No. 113.

Archambault, E. (1988), *Comptabilité Nationale* (National Accounting) (4th ed.), Paris: Economica.

Berkes, F. and C. Folke (1994), 'Investing in cultural capital for sustainable use of natural capital', in A. Jansson, M. Hammer, C. Folke and R. Costanza (eds), *Investing in Natural Capital*, Washington DC: Island Press.

Boulding, K. (1963), *Principles of Economic Policies*, London: Staples Press.

Clayton, A. and N. Radcliffe (1996), *Sustainability: A System Approach*, London: Earthscan.

Costanza, R., H.E. Daly and J.A. Bartholomew (1991), 'Goals, agenda, and policy recommendations for ecological economics', in R. Costanza (ed.), *Ecological Economics: The Science and Management of Uncertainty*, New York: University of Columbia Press.

Daly, H. and J. Cobb (1989), *For the Common Good: Redirecting the Economy Towards Community, the Environment and a Sustainable Future*, London: Green Print.

Ekins, P. and S. Simon (1998), 'Determining the sustainability gap', in P. Vaze (ed.) *UK Environmental Accounts*, London: Stationery Office.

Faber, M., R. Manstetten and J. Proops. (1995), 'On the conceptual foundations of ecological economics: a teleological approach', *Ecological Economics*, **12**, 41–54.

Faber, M., R. Manstetten and J. Proops (1998), *Ecological Economics: Concepts and Methods*, Cheltenham: Edward Elgar.

Faucheux, S. and M. O'Connor (1998), *Valuation for Sustainable Development. Methods and Policy Indicators*, Cheltenham: Edward Elgar.

Harrison, A. (1990), 'Introducing natural capital into the SNA', in Y.J. Ahmad, S. El Serafy and E. Lutz (eds), *Environmental Accounting for Sustainable Development*, Washington DC: World Bank.

Henderson, H. (1993), *Paradigms in Progress. Life Beyond Economics*, Indianapolis: Knowledge Systems Inc.

IUCN (1991), *Caring for the Earth: A Strategy for Sustainable Living*, Switzerland: IUCN, UNEP and WWF.

Jacobs, M. (1994), 'The limits to neoclassicism: towards an institutional environmental economics', in M. Redclift and T. Benton (eds), *Social Theory and the Global Environment*, London: Routledge.

Keuning, S. and M. De Haan (1998), 'Netherlands: what is a NAMEA? Recent results', in K. Uno and P. Bartelmus (eds), *Environmental Accounting in Theory and Practice*, Dordrecht: Kluwer.

Malinvaud, E. (1964), *Introduction à la Comptabilité Nationale* (Introduction to National Accounts), Paris: Imprimérie Nationale.

O'Connor, M. (1998), 'Ecological-economic sustainability', in S. Faucheux and M. O'Connor (eds), *Valuation for Sustainable Development. Methods and Policy Indicators*, Cheltenham: Edward Elgar.

Ohman, I. (1999), *Towards a European System of Environmental Pressure Indicators and Indices*, New York: United Nations.

O'Riordan, T. (1988), 'The politics of sustainability', in K. Turner (ed.), *Sustainable Environmental Management: Principles and Practices*, Boulder: Westview Press.

Viederman, S. (1994), 'Public policy: challenge to ecological economics', in A. Jansson, M. Hammer, C. Folke and R. Costanza (eds), *Investing in Natural Capital*, Washington DC: Island Press.

Viederman, S. (1995), 'Knowledge for sustainable development: what do we need to know?', in T. Tryzna (ed.), *A Sustainable World: Defining and Measuring Sustainable Development*, Sacramento: IUCN.

World Commission on Environment and Development [WCED] (1987), *Our Common Future*, Oxford: Oxford University Press.

NOTES

1 Daly and Cobb (1989, p. 138) explain the important distinction made by Aristotle between 'oikonomia' and 'chrematistics'. The former is the root from which the word economics derives. Chrematistics can be defined as the branch of political economy relating to the manipulation of property and wealth so as to maximise short-term monetary exchange value to the owner. Oikonoima, by contrast, is the management of the household so as to increase its use value to all members of the household over the long run. If we expand the scope of household to include the larger community of the land, of shared values, resources, biomes, institutions, language, and history, then we have a good definition of 'economics for community'. It appears that in modern usage the academic discipline of economics is much closer to 'chrematistics' than 'oikonomia'.

PART TWO

Green Accounting as a Policy Instrument

5. Indicators and Accounts of Sustainable Development: the NAMEA Approach

Steven J. Keuning

5.1 INTRODUCTION

It is often argued that society is steering with the wrong compass, namely Gross Domestic Product (GDP) growth, and for that reason the definition of GDP should be changed to make it the true indicator of sustainable development. This chapter argues that GDP was never meant to be a complete welfare indicator, and that it never will be so, irrespective of how its definition is altered. The best approximation to changes in social welfare, or sustainable development, is to compile not one but a (limited) set of aggregate indicators. In fact, this is nothing new, as the most important target variables of present-day policy making include unemployment, inflation, government deficit, GDP volume growth, and so on. The real challenge is to extend this list of core policy indicators with one, or a few, environmental indicators.

Adjusting GDP by monetarising an unsustainable use of the environment cannot be done by means of simple accounting deduction, but requires an explicit and quite complex model. As elaborated below, this is because assigning hypothetical prices to pollution requires the incorporation of all kinds of very sizable second-order effects, which substantially mitigate the original downward adjustment of GDP. In turn, this means that a single, undisputed estimate for green GDP cannot be computed. An additional complication is that, because a correctly estimated green GDP requires an extensive model, this indicator is not suitable for use in modelling or forecasting analyses. Such analyses require indicators which are straightforward and not the result of 'a model within the model'.

The most suitable indicators are those that can directly and simply be derived from an accounting framework, preferably extended national accounts. Environmentally adjusted national accounts enable model simulation experiments, in which the trade-offs between one or more environmental objectives, and most other objectives of macroeconomic policy, become explicit. Environmental indicators can then play an important role, not only in the design of environmental policies, but in all major fiscal, monetary and other economic policy analyses.

An extended national accounts framework which has attracted considerable attention, particularly in Europe and Japan, is the National Accounting Matrix including Environmental Accounts (NAMEA). This is a statistical information system that provides a synthesis between the conventional national accounts and data on all kinds of environmental problems. It yields a few summary environmental indicators that are easily understood, ready for insertion in all kinds of treaties and other political contracts (cf. the CO_2 emission target), and appropriately incorporated in the core economic policy models. Aggregation of various kinds of emissions that contribute to a single problem (e.g. the greenhouse effect or water pollution) is done on the basis of the relative contribution of each pollutant to the problem at hand. Of course, scientific insights in the relative harm of various pollutants may change over time. That would then require a revision of the NAMEA series, similar to the regular implementation of new insights of economic theory in a revision of the standard national accounts.

This chapter sketches the NAMEA-approach, its impact to date, and its suitability as an international standard accounting system for sustainability. The next section, however, first reviews indicators of sustainable development (see also Chapter 4).

5.2 INDICATORS OF SUSTAINABLE DEVELOPMENT

The relationship between national income, or Gross Domestic Product (GDP), and social welfare is quite similar to the relationship between personal income and personal welfare; undoubtedly income is an important determinant of welfare, but welfare is also influenced by other attributes, such as health, wealth, educational attainment, leisure and the state of the environment. Of these attributes, usually only income and wealth are precisely quantified, if only for tax purposes.

In the case of a person, a precise quantification of all welfare attributes is not necessary. For instance, health problems are rarely quantified, but people generally know whether or not they are ill. Of course, for a society as a whole quantification of non-monetary welfare attributes is even more complicated, in view of severe difficulties of comparability and aggregation of these attributes. At the same time, it is not feasible to know, much less judge, the changes in living conditions of all individual inhabitants of a country. For that reason, aggregate statistical indicators are quite useful, provided that their limitations are realised. For example, GDP summarises billions, perhaps trillions, of transactions in a single number. It is unrealistic to assume that such a number is equally exact as an estimate of the distance between Amsterdam and London, say. *A fortiori*, this applies to GDP volume change, the common measure of economic growth. In that case, there is the additional difficulty of breaking down value changes in all transactions into price changes, on the one hand, and quantity plus quality changes on the other. In particular, a quality improvement is not easily distinguished from an 'ordinary' price rise.[1]

Yet, the opposite option, compiling no aggregate indicators at all, is even more unsatisfactory. The alternative to indicators is an unmanageable information overload, probably consisting of a combination of innumerable incoherent qualitative impressions and many databases full of micro-data. That would certainly lead to less informed policy making. In addition, transaction costs would explode, since every administration, business interest and pressure group would create an aggregate reality which best suits its own interests. If, on the other hand, all parties involved agree about a manageable summary of the present state of affairs, as reflected in a limited number of aggregate indicators for a set of welfare attributes, a much more fruitful debate can be held about the relative weight of each of these attributes, and about the most suitable measures to improve the situation. Defining and computing a set of fairly undisputed aggregate welfare indicators is, in fact, a principal role of official statistics.

Once a reasonable degree of consensus exists that the best approximation of changes in social welfare, or sustainable development, is to compile a limited set of aggregate indicators, attention can shift to the attributes that must be quantified and to the construction of the aggregate indicators. The selection of attributes is a political matter. Although social scientists or statistical offices can propose a list of attributes that might be quantified, the inherently subjective nature of that list has to be emphasised and the more public debate there is about this selection, the better. Anyhow, attributes that are seemingly difficult to operationalise, let alone quantify (such as some aspects of sustainable development), should not a priori be omitted from that list. In most cases, a far from perfect quantitative expression of a serious societal concern is preferable to a complete lack of summary information on that issue.

5.2.1 Constructing Aggregate Indicators

The next step concerns the methodology of constructing aggregate indicators. To start with, several criteria for good indicators can be listed, such as:

... scientifically sound, understandable, sensitive to the change they are intended to measure, measurable and capable of being updated regularly' (Custance and Hillier, 1998, p. 4).

Moreover, there will always be political pressure to construct a single indicator, if only because of the obvious advantages of steering society on a single compass. Yet, the disadvantages of such a composite indicator exceed the advantages, as can be illustrated with the example of the familiar Green National Income.

In a Green National Income (also labelled Eco-Domestic Product or Sustainable National Income), the depletion and degradation of the environment is valued and confronted with the conventionally defined National Income. However, a correct Green National Income can only be the result of an explicit and quite complex modelling exercise.[2] The main reason is that, if prices had been introduced for an (unsustainable) use of the environment, virtually all prices and volumes in the economy would have changed radically. Therefore, the composition and size of National Income *itself* would have been totally different if the environment had been priced. Just subtracting (hypothetical) environmental costs from actual National Income (or national saving) yields an incoherent and essentially meaningless figure.

This can be illustrated as follows. Every commodity is produced in an unsustainable way or uses inputs (e.g. paper products in services production) that were produced in an unsustainable way. Incorporating environmental costs thus means that, in the reference year, almost all commodities would have become more expensive. Clearly, not all prices would have been affected to the same degree, and in fact the actual price changes would have depended on many factors (e.g. whether or not the rest of the world had introduced these 'true scarcity' prices as well). In turn, these diverging price changes would have set in motion all kinds of substitution processes, so that 'in the end' the economy would have looked completely different from the one we actually lived in. Probably, the original effect on National Income would have been mitigated. Moreover, somebody would have *received* all this money charged on behalf of the environment, and even if it had all been saved and only used for the acquisition of financial assets, this might have lowered interest rates with a concomitant positive influence on investment (in environment-extensive industries). This again would have had a sizeable upward effect on Green National Income.

Some still hold the view that the use of the environment, resulting in its depletion or degradation, should be treated just like the consumption of fixed capital ('depreciation') in the economic accounts. This proposal, however, overlooks the fundamental differences that exist between the consumption of fixed capital and the depreciation of natural assets. Consumption of fixed capital reflects an actual monetary outlay for investment in the past, that is spread out over the number of years the asset is in use (on average). However, nobody ever paid anything for the right to use environmental assets.

In addition, the consumption of fixed capital is a cost that has actually been internalised at the micro-level. All companies make provision for the depreciation of fixed assets, and this is subtracted from their receipts before taxes are paid, dividends are decided upon, new investment is planned, etc. However, introducing a provision for the depreciation of natural assets as a cost item at the company level would have created a completely new situation. The appearance of such a new cost item would probably have led to higher output prices, but even if this had not been the case (so that only the remuneration of the factor inputs in the industry concerned was lowered), the eventual effect of the lower net value-added on national consumption, saving, investment, NDP, etc., hinges on the incidence of this new cost item among value-added categories and institutional (sub)sectors (which earned less?). Also, if factor markets work reasonably well, the effects of introducing such a new cost item would spill over to all other industries and sectors of the economy; as a consequence, the macroeconomic effects can only be simulated with the help of an economy-wide, price-endogenous model.

Summarising, depletion and degradation are very real in physical terms, but they have not been taken into account in anybody's income or saving. A correct estimation of Green National Income thus requires a recalculation of National Income, simulating what would have been its size if the economy had been sustainable. Such a model requires realistic assumptions on the (major) economic impacts of introducing shadow prices for (over)exploiting the environment. Note that a Green National Income assumes that in the reference year all emissions and extraction of resources had been instantaneously reduced to a (politically defined) sustainable level. In reality, this would have implied a complete upheaval of the economic system. For that reason, rather than constructing a model to simulate a highly unlikely situation in the past, it may be more efficient to build a model for simulating the prospects for achieving sustainability in ten or twenty years time, say.[3] Besides, such a more gradual change is relatively easier to model than the radical Green National Income scenario.

In Germany, the federal government has officially declared that '... the original goal of developing a single highly aggregated indicator to represent economic and ecological development cannot be achieved' (Bundesministerium für Umwelt, Naturschutz und Reaktorsicherheit, 1996, p. 16). In the Netherlands, the Ministers of Economic Affairs and of the Environment have written to Parliament:

> In reality, the Green National Income does not exist, and therefore it can only be determined by model calculations . . . Since the results of such calculations are highly sensitive to assumptions, model specifications and the environmental standards applied, many alternative Green National Incomes can be calculated. It is unlikely that such calculations would ever produce one incontestable figure. It is not clear in advance whether a recalculated income figure concerning a past year is useful enough to warrant the extensive research needed. In our opinion, it would be more interesting and practical to take a more future- and policy-oriented approach to meet the demand for a Green National Income. This can be realised by assessing the possible medium- and long-term size of national income, in the event of a future decrease in the environmental pressure arising from politically determined environmental standards (Tweede Kamer, 1996, p. 1).

A similar conclusion is drawn in a EU-commissioned study on this subject (Brouwer and O'Connor, 1996), written by a broad international research group; refer also to Brouwer et al. (1996).

In fact, it is much more cumbersome to construct a methodologically correct composite indicator from phenomena that, in the real world, are expressed in different measurement units (e.g. sales in dollars and emissions in kilograms) than from data expressed in the same measurement units. In the latter case, the meaning of the indicator is also more easily communicated. In turn, transparency in constructing the indicator will enhance its public acceptance. An additional consideration is that, ideally, indicators are used in modelling analyses, simulations and forecasts which provide an indication of the causes and consequences of the present situation, on the expectations for the future, and of the likely effects of intended policy measures. Such models are typically rather complex, so that the computation of the indicators that result from such a model should be straightforward and preferably not the result of 'a model within the model'. On the other hand, it is much less of a problem for a simulation model to yield estimates for more than one aggregate indicator (e.g. GDP, unemployment, inflation and greenhouse gas emissions).

Since the most useful aggregate indicators are those that can also be incorporated in all kinds of (modelling) analyses, these indicators should be directly derived from an accounting framework, such as extended national accounts. Such a statistical information system also enables the modelling of feedbacks from non-monetary to monetary variables. If one aimed at maximising an environmental objective, operationalised by an indicator that is not derived from an accounting framework, it would be impossible to assess the repercussions of another value of this indicator on other macro-economic objectives. This shortcoming is remedied if an indicator is based on an integrated statistical system which also yields indicators such as (un)employment, inflation, GDP and government deficit, that is, the national accounts. In fact, environmentally extended national accounts enable model simulation experiments, in which the trade-offs between one or more environmental objectives and most other objectives of macroeconomic policy are made explicit. As a consequence, it becomes feasible to show the impact on environmental indicators as an integral part of, not only environmental policy analyses, but *all* fiscal, monetary and other economic policy analyses. This, then, is conducive to embedding sustainable development as a core objective of government policy, on a par with reducing unemployment or the government deficit, say.

An accounting framework, or a statistical information system, in which detailed data all have a specific relationship with each other, has the advantage of its analytical usefulness. It also improves the reliability of the data, including the aggregate indicators, because many individual statistics are then confronted and corrected with the help of a consistent set of definitional equations (supply equals demand, input equals output, value equals price times quantity, changes in emissions result from changes in production and changes in the emission coefficients). Furthermore, aggregate indicators which are embedded in an accounting framework can be defined more precisely, namely by explicit reference to other parts of the system. As a consequence, they are usually better comparable across nations and periods than 'footloose' indicators. In addition, their definition may be less liable to change if the outcomes are politically unwelcome, as such an adjustment requires an overhaul of the complete information system. In turn, such a stability of definitions will probably enhance public acceptance of the indicators.

5.2.2 Sustainable Development

How can all of this be applied to the issue of sustainable development? First of all, it must be clarified that sustainability itself is not a neutral concept. Sometimes, this is operationalised as a choice between strong and weak sustainability (e.g. Serageldin and Steer, 1994). However, the subjectivity of the concept exceeds such a simple dichotomy, as it depends crucially on the society's attitudes toward risks, which cannot be assessed in a 'technocratic' way, but only as the outcome of a political process. A typical example of an important environmental issue which (intermittently) features high on the political agenda, with quite different outcomes over time and between countries, is the (un)desirability of nuclear energy generation. Everybody realises that there are risks involved, and that these are a legitimate environmental concern; however, for the time being, views on the sustainability of these risks differ widely, so that setting a norm for, e.g., nuclear waste generation cannot be left to statisticians. In conclusion, nuclear waste generation is certainly an environmental 'theme' that is worth monitoring, but without an undisputed norm it cannot be weighed against greenhouse gas emissions in a single sustainability indicator, let alone be combined with GDP in a Green GDP model.

Secondly, it should be realised that various aspects of sustainable development are already incorporated in the standard national accounts. In particular, this concerns environmental problems for which proper ownership rights have been defined and allocated. A familiar example concerns the depletion of natural oil and gas reserves. In most instances, governments have established ownership over these reserves and have subsequently sold or rented the right to deplete these resources to private corporations. Particularly in the case of eternal concessions, it is obvious that the corporations concerned will long anticipate the eventual depletion of the resource (which would otherwise put them out of business), and will start developing alternatives. Moreover, if that is not done to a sufficient extent, or not successfully enough, financial markets will soon detect this, so that the (forward) market price of the resource in question will rise to the extent that the use of the resource will decrease, and (originally too costly) alternatives will be developed and implemented. Summarising, as soon as ownership rights over resources are sufficiently defined, their depletion becomes a purely economic problem, which does not need additional consideration and separate statistical indicators in a sustainable development strategy. Clearly, the situation is very different, at the moment, for many facets of the degradation of the environment (air, water pollution, etc.), since in these cases ownership rights (e.g. tradable emission permits) have often not yet been defined and allocated.

Probably the most fruitful approach is to subdivide (the remaining issues of) sustainable development into a number of broad environmental themes or problems, for which fairly undisputed aggregate indicators can be constructed from emissions of individual pollutants (or extraction of individual resources), on the basis of their relative contribution to the problem at hand. A familiar example is the greenhouse-effect theme, with contributions by CO_2, N_2O, CH_4 and HCFCs. The relative contribution of one kilogram of each of these gases to the greenhouse effect is determined scientifically, by the Intergovernmental Panel on Climate Change (IPCC). It is quite likely that various environmental problems are shared by many, if not all, countries of the world. In addition to the greenhouse effect (which is a global problem anyway), this may apply to, e.g., acidification, water pollution and waste. Further, a suitable accounting framework should be flexible, in that it enables the incorporation of national or even regional themes. This is the essence of the NAMEA approach set out below.

5.3 THE *NAMEA* APPROACH

The NAMEA is a statistical information system that combines national (economic) accounts and environmental accounts in a single matrix (cf. Table 5.1).[4] Just like the national accounts, this matrix serves a dual purpose:

1. It yields integrated and consistent summary indicators for a quick insight into the main trends.
2. It provides an integrated and consistent *analytical* framework that serves to review or to design integrated environmental, social and economic policies, forecasts, theories, etc.

The NAMEA is a *statistical* system, that is, it contains no implicit or explicit economic modelling assumptions. As a consequence, the NAMEA's environmental accounts and indicators are in physical units. In the accounting framework, no artificial money values are imputed to flows which in reality were not coupled with a monetary settlement. The summary environmental indicators (on the greenhouse effect, ozone layer depletion, acidification, etc.) serve a more or less comparable purpose as the unemployment figure. It may be noted that nobody now seriously proposes to value the 'costs' of unemployment and to 'subtract' this from GDP.

A fundamental characteristic of the NAMEA is that a regular National Accounting Matrix is extended with two accounts.[5] one for environmental substances (pollutants, e.g. CO_2 and SO_2, and natural resources, e.g. oil) and one for environmental problems, or themes (e.g. the greenhouse effect, acidification and natural resource depletion). The former account (#11 in Table 5.1) is expressed in quantity units, such as millions of kilograms. It shows in the column the origin of each environmental substance; i.e. for each pollutant it includes its emission by industries (3,11), by household consumption (2,11) and by other domestic sources such as leakage from waste dumps (6,11), as well as its inflow from abroad (9,11). For each natural resource, the column of this account contains: gross additions to the proven reserves of subsoil assets, the natural growth of non-cultivated biological resources, and reductions of the level of natural resources other than their depletion (6,11).

The rows of the substances account show their destination. For each pollutant, this concerns its recycling or re-absorption into an economic process, such as waste processed in incineration plants (11,3), its outflow to abroad (11,9), and its accumulation into the global, national or regional environment (11,12). This accumulation is put in the column of the environ-

Table 5.1 A National Accounting Matrix including Environmental Accounts (NAMEA) for The Netherlands, 1996 (Account 1-10 in million guilders)

ACCOUNT (classification)		Goods and services (product groups) Env. cleansing services / Other goods and services		Consumption of households (purposes) Evir' ment / Other purpose		Production (industries)	Generation of income (value–added categories)
		1a	1b	2a	2b	3	4
Goods and services (product groups) Environmental Cleansing services	1a	Trade and transport margins		Consumption of households 1944		Intermediate consumption 11865	
Other goods and services	1b			539	343639	651604	
Consumption of Households (purposes) Environment	2a						
Other purposes	2b						
Production (industries)	3	Output at basic prices 15097 1271403					
Generation of income (value–added categories)	4					Net value–added at factor costs 514466	
Distribution and use of income (sectors)	5						Net national generated income at factor costs 516227
Capital	6					Consumption of fixed capital 104858	
Financial balance	7						
Taxes (types) Environmental taxes	8a	Taxes less subsidies on products 2905				Other taxes less subsidies on production 1673	
Other taxes	8b	200	66849			2034	

Table 5.1 (continued 2)

		1a	1b	2a	2b	3	4
Rest of the world, current	9	Imports (cif)					Compensation of employees to rest of the world.
			362780				1278
Rest of the world, capital	10						
Substances						Absorption by producers	
CO_2	11a						
N_2O	11b						
CH_4	11c						
CFCs and halons	11d						
NO_X	11e						
SO_2	11f						
NH_3	11g						
P	11h					22	
N	11i					117	
Waste	11j					3780	
Waste water	11k					22602	
Natural gas	11l					2868	
Crude oil	11m					95	
Environmental themes							
Greenhouse effect (CO_2-equivalents)	12a						
Ozone layer depletion (CFK11-equivalents)	12b						
Acidification (AEQ)	12c						
Eutrophication (EEQ)	12d						
Waste (kg)	12e						
Waste water (i.e.)	12f						
Changes of natural resources							
Fossil energy (p.j.)	12g						
TOTAL		Supply at purchasers' prices		Consumption of households		Input at basic prices	Destination of generated income
		15297	1703937	2483	343639	1286500	517505

Table 5.1 (continued 3)

	Distribution and use of income (sectors)	Capital	Taxes (types)		Rest of the world, current	Rest of the world, capital
			Envi-ronm'ta taxes	Other taxes		
	5	6	8a	8b	9	10
1a	Consumption of govern-ment 1488	Gross capital formation			Exports (fob)	
1b	159077	146423			402655	
2a	Consumption of households 2483					
2b	343639					
3						
4			VAT not handed over to the government 1868		Compensation of employees from rest of the world 1171	
5	Property income and current transfers 809046		Taxes less subsidies 6934	151935	Property income and current transfers from rest of the world 67451	
6	Net national savings 80712					Capital transfers from r.o.w. 2460
7		National net lending (+) or net borrowing (-) 33905				Net lending from rest of the world -33905
8a	Current taxes on income and wealth 2356	VAT on land			Current taxes on income and wealth to rest of the world	
8b	86308	1313			1130	

Table 5.1 (continued 4)

	5	6	8a	8b	9	10
9	Property income and current trans- fers to r.o.w. 66484		Current taxes on income and wealth to rest of the world 4031			Surplus of the nation on current transactions 37834
10		Capital trans- fers to r.o.w. 6389				
					Cross border pollu- tion to r.o.w.	
11a						
11b						
11c						
11d						
11e					669	
11f					196	
11g					99	
11h					20	
11i					543	
11j						
11k						
11l						
11m						
		Environmental indicators				
12a		249130				
12b		1063				
12c		119				
12d		150				
12e		11530				
12f		4562				
12g		- 649				
	Current expenditures 1551593	Capital expenditures 188030	Tax receipts (less subsidies) 6934	157834	Current receipts from rest of the world 472407	Capital receipts from rest of the world 6389

Greening the Accounts

Table 5.1 (continued 5)

	\multicolumn{13}{c|}{Substances}												
	CO$_2$	N$_2$O	CH$_4$	CFCs and halons	NO$_X$	SO$_2$	NH$_3$	P	N	Waste	Waste water	Gas	Oil
	11a	11b	11c	11d	11e	11f	11g	11h	11i	11j	11k	11l	11m
1a 1b													
	\multicolumn{13}{c|}{Emission of pollutants by consumers}												
2a 2b	39720	3	24	49	114	4	7	11	117	5160	15530		
3	\multicolumn{13}{c|}{Emission of pollutants by producers}												
	163850	62	664	911	552	205	181	94	898	10150	7233		
4													
5													
6	\multicolumn{13}{c|}{Other domestic emission of pollutants and changes of natural resources}												
	990	-	477	32				3	24			4401 2203	111
7													
8a 8b													

Table 5.1 (continued 6)

	11a	11b	11c	11d	11e	11f	11g	11h	11i	11j	11k	11l	11m
9					Cross border pollution from r.o.w.								
					118	88	19	14	322				
10													
11a													
11b													
11c													
11d													
11e													
11f													
11g													
11h													
11I													
11j													
11k													
11l													
11m													
12a													
12b													
12c													
12d													
12e													
12f													
12g													
					Origin of substances								
	204560	65	1165	992	784	296	206	122	1362	15310	27164	2203	111

Table 5.1 (continued 7)

	Environmental themes								TOTAL
	Accumulation of substances to the environment	Greenhouse effect	Ozon layer deplet'n	Acidification	Eutrophication	Waste	Waste water	Changes of natural resources Fossil energy	
	12	12a	12b	12c	12d	12e	12f	12g	
1a 1b									Use at purchasers' prices 15297 1703937
2a 2b									Consumpt'n of households 2483 343639
3									Output at basic prices 1286500
4									Origin of generated income 517505
5									Current receipts 1551593
6									Capital receipts 188030
7									
8a 8b									Tax payments (less subsidies) 6934 157834

Table 5.1 (continued 8)

	12	12a	12b	12c	12d	12e	12f	12g	
9									Current payments to the rest of the world 472407
10									Capital pay't to the r.o.w 6389
	Contribution of substances to environmental themes								Destination of sub- stances
11a	204560	204560							204560
11b	65	20110							65
11c	1165	24460							1165
11d	992		1063						992
11e	115			25					784
11f	99			31					296
11g	107			63					206
11h	80				80				122
11I	702				70				1362
11j	11530					11530			15310
11k	4562						4562		27164
11l	-665							- 665	2203
11m	16							16	111
12a									Theme equivalents 249130 1063
12b									119
12c									150
12d									11530
12e									4562
12f									
12g									-649
	Theme equivalents								
		249130	1063	119	150	11530		4562	- 649

mental themes account. For each natural resource, the row of this account shows its gross depletion by industries (11,3), and its net reduction (deple- tion) as a balancing item (11,12). This balancing item is also put in the column of the environmental themes account. Note that the above procedure ensures that the row and column totals of each substance account are equal.

The second specific account, the environmental themes account (#12 in Table 5.1), registers in the column for each theme the net accumulation of pollutants and the net depletion of resources which contribute to that theme (11,12). For instance, the accumulation of CO_2, N_2O, CH_4, and CFCs and Halons is assigned to the greenhouse effect theme, while CFCs and Halons are also assigned to the ozone layer depletion theme (11d,12b). Subsequently, the substance units are converted into theme-related units, such as global warming potential units or peta-joules (for mineral resources). The conver- sion factors are based on the relative potential harm of each substance to each problem, as estimated by scientific research. For example, the conversion of substance weights into global warming potential units is based on IPCC- conventions (11,12a).[6] After this conversion, all elements in the column can be added up, to yield a total for each environmental problem. This total serves as the macro-environmental indicator for the problem concerned, and also appears in the row of this account and in the column of the capital account (12,6).

For the rest, the NAMEA incorporates the complete system of national flow accounts.[7] Because it is closely related to a Social Accounting Matrix (SAM), it also covers distributional issues. This feature implies that a NAMEA is easily linked to (un)employment data, and more generally to labour market and human capital issues; cf. Keuning and Timmerman (1995). Moreover, the NAMEA can include environmental problems that have a current rather than a capital character (noise, stench, etc.) and to showing the current effects of environmental problems with a stock character (e.g. leakage from chemical waste dumps); refer to Keuning (1993).

In the supply and use table (or input–output table), that is an integral part of the NAMEA, environmental protection services are explicitly shown (see also Chapter 7). This may include not only purchased services (e.g. waste collection), but also own-account production within the firm (e.g. mainte- nance costs of a filter that reduces the effluent flow). The latter, internal environmental protection services are then separately recorded in the NAMEA, as output (of a by-product) which is delivered as intermediate input to the same firm that produces these services. As a consequence, both output and intermediate input of the firms concerned are higher in the NAMEA than in the regular national accounts, but their value-added is the same.

Another characteristic that serves to increase the NAMEA's policy relevance is the inclusion of a separate tax account, subdivided by type of tax. In this account, the incidence of the various taxes and subsidies is revealed. In turn, this facilitates model simulations of the consequences of a shift in the fiscal system. For a good coverage of purely local problems, a regional breakdown will be required in the future. This may involve the use of, e.g., Geographical Information Systems. Such regional NAMEAs may then also be used in comprehensive cost/benefit analyses of large infrastructural projects.

Interestingly, the NAMEA's summary indicators for five major environmental problems were originally confronted with norms set for these problems for the year 2000 (De Haan, Keuning and Bosch, 1994). These norms had been endorsed by the Dutch Parliament. Subsequently, the five theme indicators were aggregated into a single environmental 'core' policy indicator, using the distance to the norm as a weight for each theme. This procedure shows that the NAMEA's themes, and the possibility to set norms for these themes, provide the politicians with an instrument to quantify their choices (Adriaanse, 1993). This aggregation procedure was criticised by Alfieri and Bartelmus (1995), because it would give equal a priori significance to each of the themes. Of course, this depends on the way the norms are set. Their criticism does not hold if the government sets more severe norms for more serious problems. The experience with the zero-norm for ozone layer depletion may serve as an illustration of this mechanism.[8]

5.4 IMPACT OF THE *NAMEA* TO DATE

The first release of the NAMEA system in the Netherlands was the subject of an 'Economics Focus' in The Economist (1993) and also made it to the front page of a leading Dutch morning paper, under the title 'Importance of agriculture outweighed by environmental damage by this sector'. Although this headline did not do full justice to the nuances in the press release by Statistics Netherlands, it provides an indication of the kinds of message that can be conveyed by the NAMEA. Partly as a consequence of this type of information, stringent measures to reduce the phosphorus and nitrogen emissions by factory farms have been approved by the Dutch Parliament. Further, a report by the World Resources Institute had signalled that the summary environmental indicators, combined with information on the relative contribution of each industry, have played a stimulating role in reaching voluntary agreements between the Dutch government and industry representatives on a significant reduction of toxic emissions (Hammond et al., 1995, p. 7).

Meanwhile, the NAMEA has become an intrinsic part of the regular national accounts publication in the Netherlands (e.g. CBS, 1999) and this has already increased public awareness that economic development cannot be judged from GDP volume change only. For instance, a newspaper article reviewed the annual CBS publication 'The Dutch Economy' and stated:

> This study auspiciously starts with a series of core indicators which includes, apart from the well-known macro-economic figures, statistics that co-determine the measurement of welfare: income inequality, educational level of the population, criminality, life expectancy and environmental pressure. In particular with the series of data on emissions that contribute to the greenhouse effect, ozone layer depletion, acidification, eutrophication and the increase of waste dumps, the CBS provides an important contribution . . .

Moreover, the NAMEA has been applied in a range of analyses and policy studies. For example, the cumulative ecological effects per guilder of final demand have been estimated (e.g. Keuning, Van Dalen and De Haan, 1998, Table 3). In addition, a government-commissioned study (Slob et al., 1996) used the NAMEA time-series to analyse the interaction between trends in consumption patterns and in environmental pressures. Further, the NAMEA has been used in a linear programming model that produced a very rough and preliminary, yet consistent, estimate for a Green National Income (De Boer, De Haan and Voogt, 1994). In that model, the consequences of reducing pollution levels to the norms set by the Dutch Parliament have been estimated, in a situation without technological change. Bearing in mind this rather unrealistic assumption, it did not come as a surprise that the required 'optimal' reduction in economic activity was enormous and very unevenly distributed by industry.

De Haan (1996) has connected the NAMEA to a database on estimated costs and emission reductions of a range of potential energy-saving measures by industry in the Netherlands. Subsequently, he used the NAMEA-inverse to estimate, not only the direct costs and emission reductions of energy saving measures in the industries applying these measures, but also the concomitant benefits and emission changes in the rest of the economy (e.g. with the suppliers of the energy-saving devices). Assuming that the most efficient energy-saving measures are applied first, he found that up to a certain level of CO_2-emission reductions, monetary benefits would exceed monetary costs for the economy as a whole. After that level, overall economic costs would rise steeply and, moreover, the total emission reductions would be much smaller than the direct emission reductions. The main reason for these findings is that the production of energy-saving devices also causes CO_2 emissions, which gains an increasing weight once the most efficient energy-saving measures have already been implemented. At a certain stage, these indirect emission increases even surpass the direct emission reductions, so that the overall environmental effect becomes negative.

Another use of the NAMEA has been as a basic data framework in a study that has analysed sustainable economic development scenarios for the Netherlands until the year 2030 (Dellink et al., 1997). Using economic forecasts from a long-term economic development scenario without environmental indicators, four scenarios have been simulated with a NAMEA-based linear programming model: 1. 'strong together', 2. 'strong alone', 3. 'negotiated sustainability' and 4. 'weak sustainability'.

The main differences between these scenarios concern: a) the degree to which substitution among environmental, physical and human capital is allowed (cf. Serageldin and Steer, 1994), and b) the assumptions regarding the direction and the speed of technical progress. The first two scenarios are identical but for the assumption whether or not the rest of the world has a similar strong preference for sustainability. Remarkably, in each of the scenarios, it appeared feasible to reconcile sustainability with continued (albeit limited) GDP volume growth.

A few years ago, the NAMEA was extensively discussed in a letter of the Netherlands' Minister of Economic Affairs, also on behalf of the Minister of the Environment, to the Parliament (Tweede Kamer, 1996). The Ministers promised that the medium-term economic outlook of the government:

> . . . will deal more systematically than in the past with environmental indicators as well as economic developments (such as economic growth and employment) (Tweede Kamer, 1996, p. 6).

Meanwhile, this has been done in the so-called 'Economic outlook for the next cabinet period' (CPB, 1997), the model-based policy document that served as the major economic guideline to political parties preparing their programme for the 1998 general elections. The NAMEA has thus acted as a catalyst in incorporating environmental concerns into the standard macro-economic government models.

Finally, in Sweden the NAMEA framework has been used in a model that assessed the damage from sulphur depositions in Sweden (Ahlroth and Skånberg, 1995) and in a model that estimated the environmental implications of the official growth projections for Sweden up to the year 2000 (Östblom, 1998).

In addition to scenario analyses, NAMEA-based models can be used for calculating, e.g., the effects of a shift in tax incidence, from labour to energy use, say, on the environmental and economic indicators in the system. Finally, more reliable early estimates for aggregate environmental indicators can be obtained with the help of the NAMEA-framework.

5.5 TOWARDS AN INTERNATIONAL STANDARD ACCOUNTING SYSTEM FOR SUSTAINABILITY

In 1994, the Commission of the European Communities released an official communication to the Council of Ministers and the European Parliament, entitled 'Directions for the EU on Environmental Indicators and Green National Accounting: The Integration of Environmental and Economic Information Systems.' In this communication, the Commission proposed to establish:

> . . . a European System of Integrated Economic and Environmental Indices. The system – which will resemble the Dutch NAMEA system . . . – will be available to Member States and the EU in 2-3 years time. It will need permanent updating (Commission of the European Communities, 1994, p. 4).

This initiative was carried forward by Eurostat, the statistical office of the European Communities. Meanwhile, in almost all EU countries NAMEA-type tables have been compiled. Eurostat (1996) has stated its aim as follows:

> Like national accounts recommendations in general, Eurostat's approach to NAMEA is therefore top-down. NAMEA seeks to define the target concepts and tables to fill in, but leaves it to national statisticians to make the best use of all data available in their country to assign values to the entries. Initially data may be scarce but will gradually improve as various other initiatives bear fruit . . .

In addition, a Japanese NAMEA has already become available.

Because of this increasing attention on, and availability of, NAMEAs, the journal *Structural Change and Economic Dynamics* recently devoted a special issue to this accounting framework and its usefulness for modelling and policy analyses, including case-studies for Germany (Tjahjadi et al., 1999), Japan (Ike, 1999), the Netherlands (Keuning et al., 1999), Sweden (Hellsten et al., 1999) and the United Kingdom (Vaze, 1999), as well as an article comparing these case-studies (De Haan, 1999).[9] A more extensive comparison, including NAMEAs for 12 EU member states and Norway has recently been published by Eurostat (1999). In Japan, work is going on to compile a so-called bilateral NAMEA for Japan and China, in which the transfer of pollutants between these countries is taken into account.

The NAMEA has much in common with the so-called SEEA system, as laid out in an interim version of a United Nations (1993) Handbook. Apart from their joint origin in the 1993 System of National Accounts (SNA) (United Nations et al., 1993), this concerns, for example, their matrix format, their treatment of environmental protection expenditures and their objective to incorporate social issues as well.

A difference between the approaches is that the NAMEA starts from an expansion of the complete national accounts, with an environmental substances account and an environmental theme account, while the SEEA focuses on an expansion of the standard asset accounts with accounts for environmental assets (river basins, sea, air, etc.). The present SEEA also distinguishes pollutants, but does not aggregate these by environmental problem. The NAMEA's direct link to pressure indicators by type of environmental problem may be useful for two reasons: 1) environmental policies are usually formulated at that level, and 2) much more data are available for environmental pressures than for changes in the stock of environmental assets.

Another difference is that, contrary to the SEEA, the NAMEA format is ready for use in analytical applications, such as the estimation of the total (direct and indirect) pollution generated by one unit of final demand for each product group, or of the pollution embodied in foreign trade. A linkage to social policies (employment, income distribution and the like) is facilitated, because the NAMEA incorporates income distribution and use accounts. However, these accounts are lacking in the present SEEA.

The most important difference between the present version of the SEEA and the NAMEA, however, is that the NAMEA system does not contain a so-called Green National Income or Eco-Domestic Product. As stated above, a correct Green National Income is not an accounting construct, but the result of an explicit modelling exercise. At the moment, though, a new version of the SEEA is prepared, which will include the NAMEA-framework.

Concerning the further development of the NAMEA-framework, research is going on in three areas:[10]

1. Increasing its timeliness (objective: publication within seven months after the reference year).
2. Expanding its level of detail and scope (incorporating water use, the dispersion of toxic substances and the use of space).
3. Expanding the NAMEA into a comprehensive information system of environmental, economic and social accounts.

The third of these projects deals directly with sustainable development, as the heart of this policy debate gradually shifts towards the interrelations between environmental, economic and social issues. In the Netherlands, the NAMEA and a SAM have already been integrated into a so-called Social Accounting Matrix including Environmental Accounts (SAMEA); (cf. Keuning and Timmerman, 1995; Keuning and De Haan, 1997). This study has demonstrated, for instance, that women and highly educated men are typically employed in industries which burden the environment less than the industries in which most lower educated men are working. Such a finding evidently has a bearing on the expected distributional consequences of more stringent environmental policies. Similarly, it appears that the (direct) contribution of the old-aged to the environmental problems caused by household consumption exceeds their population share. The opposite applies to households that mainly depend on other transfer income (unemployment benefits and the like).

5.6 CONCLUSIONS

About five years after its initial design, the compilation of NAMEAs has been institutionalised as a regular part of Statistics Netherlands' work programme. It is increasingly used for modelling and policy analysis in the Netherlands. For instance, the official economic forecasting agency has recently taken into account NAMEA's core environmental indicators in its medium-term economic outlook. In this outlook, the expected contributions to economic and environmental objectives have also been juxtaposed by industry.

The Netherlands' Minister of Economic Affairs, in his letter to Parliament, reports on this as follows:

> At the macro-level . . . (national) income cannot be regarded as equivalent to (national) welfare. Developments in welfare are determined by many factors: not only the development of the national income, but also changes in available environmental functions, the distribution of income, employment and health. It is therefore important to have information systems at our disposal that yield an integrated picture of the connections between various aspects of welfare. Statistics Netherlands has already started setting up an integrated information system in the form of environmental accounts (NAMEA) and labour accounts (SAM) linked to the National Accounts. This should finally result in an extensive System of Economic and Social Accounting Matrices with Extensions (SESAME). (Tweede Kamer, 1996, p. 30).[11]

REFERENCES

Adriaanse, A. (1993), *Environmental Policy Performance Indicators*, The Hague: Ministry of Housing, Spatial Planning and the Environment, VROM.

Ahlroth, S. and K. Skånberg (1995), 'The sulphur project', in *The Second Meeting of the London Group on Natural Resources and Environmental Accounting, Proceeding Volume*, Washington DC: US Bureau of Economic Analysis.

Alfieri, A. and P. Bartelmus (1995), 'Valuation of the environment and natural resources – some unresolved issues', in *The Second Meeting of the London Group on Natural Resources and Environmental Accounting, Proceeding Volume*, Washington DC: US Bureau of Economic Analysis.

Brouwer, R. and M. O'Connor (1996), 'Methodological problems in the calculation of environmentally adjusted national income figures: executive summary', *Study for the European Commission Directorate General XII*, Brussels: Commission of the European Communities.

Brouwer, R., M. O'Connor and W. Rademacher (1996), 'Defining cost effective responses to environmental deterioration in a periodic accounting system', in *Third Meeting of the London Group on Natural Resource and Environmental Accounting, Proceedings Volume*, Stockholm: Statistics Sweden.

Bundesministerium für Umwelt, Naturschutz und Reaktorsicherheit (1996), *Integrated Environmental and Economic Accounting in Germany: Position of the Federal Government*, Bonn: Federal Government of Germany.

CBS [Statistics Netherlands] (1999), *National Accounts 1998*, The Hague: SDU Publishers.

Commission of the European Communities (1994), *Directions for the EU on Environmental Indicators and Green National Accounting; The Integration of Environmental and Economic Information Systems*, COM (94) 670, Brussels: Commission of the European Communities.

CPB [Netherlands Bureau for Economic Policy Analysis] (1997), *Economic Outlook for the Next Cabinet Period* [in Dutch], The Hague: SDU Publishers.

CSO [Central Statistics Office Ireland] (1999), *Pilot Environmental Accounts*, Dublin: Stationery Office.

Custance, J. and H. Hillier (1998), 'Statistical issues in developing indicators of sustainable development', *Journal of the Royal Statistical Society, Series A*, **161**, 1–10.

De Boer, B., M. De Haan and M. Voogt (1994), 'What would net domestic product have been in a sustainable economy? Preliminary views and results', in *National Accounts and the Environment*; papers and proceedings from a conference, London, England, March 16–18, 1994, Ottawa: Statistics Canada.

De Boo, A.J., P.R. Bosch, C.N. Gorter and S.J. Keuning (1993), 'An environmental module and the complete system of national accounts', in A. Franz and C. Stahmer (eds), *Approaches to Environmental Accounting*, Heidelberg: Physica-Verlag.

De Haan, M. (1996), *An Input-Output Estimation of Avoidance Costs*, paper presented at the fourth biennial meeting of the International Society for Ecological Economics, Boston, August 4–7, 1996.

De Haan M. (1999), 'On the international harmonisation of environmental accounting: comparing the NAMEAs of Sweden, Germany, the UK, Japan and the Netherlands', *Structural Change and Economic Dynamics*, **10**, 151–61.

De Haan, M. and S.J. Keuning (1996), 'Taking the environment into account: the NAMEA approach', *The Review of Income and Wealth*, **42** (2), 131–49.

De Haan, M., S.J. Keuning and P.R. Bosch (1994), 'Integrating indicators in a National Accounting Matrix including Environmental Accounts (NAMEA); an application to the Netherlands', in *National Accounts and the Environment*; papers and proceedings from a conference, London, England, March 16–18, 1994, Ottawa: Statistics Canada.

Dellink, R., M. Bennis and H. Verbruggen (1997), *Sustainable Economic Structures: Scenarios for Sustainability in the Netherlands*, Amsterdam: Institute for Environmental Studies.

Ekins, P. and S. Simon (1998), 'Determining the sustainability gap: national accounting for environmental sustainability', in P. Vaze (ed.), *UK Environmental Accounts 1998*, London: Office for National Statistics.

Eurostat (1996), 'Environmental accounting in the framework of national accounts; past, present and future work in Eurostat 1995–1996–1997', in Third Meeting of the London Group on Natural Resource and Environmental Accounting, Proceedings Volume, Stockholm: Statistics Sweden.

Eurostat (1999), *Pilot Studies on NAMEAs for Air Emissions with a Comparison at European Level*, Eurostat Studies and Research Theme 2, Luxembourg: Eurostat.

Hammond, A., A. Adriaanse, E. Rodenburg, D. Bryant and R. Woodward (1995), *Environmental Indicators: A Systematic Approach to Measuring and Reporting on Environmental Policy Performance in the Context of Sustainable Development*, Washington, DC: World Resources Institute.

Hellsten, E., S. Ribacke and G. Wickbom (1999), 'SWEEA-Swedish environmental and economic accounts', *Structural Change and Economic Dynamics*, **10**, 39-73.

Ike, T. (1999), 'A Japanese NAMEA', *Structural Change and Economic Dynamics*, **10**, 123–51.

Jensen, H.V. and O.G. Pedersen (1998), *Danish NAMEA 1980-1992*, Copenhagen: Statistics Denmark.

Jesinghaus, J. (1997), 'Approaches to valuation', in B. Moldan and S. Bilharz (eds), *Sustainability Indicators: A Report on the Project on Indicators of Sustainable Development*, Chichester: Wiley.

Keuning, S.J. (1993), 'An information system for environmental indicators in relation to the national accounts', in W.F.M. De Vries, G.P. Den Bakker, M.B.G. Gircour, S.J. Keuning and A. Lenson (eds), *The Value Added of National Accounting*, Voorburg/Heerlen: Statistics Netherlands.

Keuning, S.J. (1996), *Accounting for Economic Development and Social Change*, Amsterdam: IOS Press.

Keuning, S.J. (1997), 'SESAME: An integrated economic and social accounting system', *International Statistical Review*, **65** (1), 111–21.

Keuning, S.J. and M. De Haan (1997), 'Netherlands: what's in a NAMEA? Recent results', in K. Uno, P. Bartelmus and C. Stahmer (eds), *Environmental Accounting in Theory and Practice*, Dordrecht: Kluwer.

Keuning, S.J. and J.G. Timmerman (1995), 'An information system for economic, environmental and social statistics: integrating environmental data into the SESAME', in *The Second Meeting of the London Group on Natural Resources and Environmental Accounting, Proceeding Volume*, Washington DC: US Bureau of Economic Analysis.

Keuning, S.J., J. Van Dalen and M. De Haan (1999), 'The Netherlands NAMEA: presentation, usage and future extensions', *Structural Change and Economic Dynamics*, **10**, 15–39.

Newson, B. (1996), 'The London Group meetings so far: What have we learned and where are we going? Notes', in *Third Meeting of the London Group on Natural Resource and Environmental Accounting, Proceedings Volume*, Stockholm: Statistics Sweden.

Östblom, G. (1998), 'The environmental outcome of emissions-intensive economic growth: a critical look at official growth projections for Sweden up to the year 2000', *Economic Systems Research*, **10** (1), 19–31.

Serageldin, I. and A. Steer (eds) (1994), *Making Development Sustainable: From Concepts to Action*, Washington DC: The World Bank.

Slob, A.F.L., M.J. Bouman, M. de Haan, K. Blok and K. Vringer (1996), *Trend Analysis Consumption and the Environment* [in Dutch], The Hague: Netherlands Ministry of the Environment.

The Economist (1993), 'The price of everything, the value of nothing', *The Econo-*

mist, July 31st, London.

Tjahjadi, B., D. Schäfer, W. Radermacher and H. Höh (1999), 'Material and energy flow accounting in Germany: database for applying the NAMEA concept', *Structural Change and Economic Dynamics*, **10**, 73–99.

Tweede Kamer [Lower House of Netherlands' Parliament] (1996), *Action Plan for Green National Accounting*; letter of the Minister of Economic Affairs to the President of the Lower House of the States-General of the Netherlands, The Hague: Ministry of Economic Affairs.

United Nations (1993), *Integrated Environmental and Economic Accounting: Interim Version*, New York: United Nations.

United Nations (1998), *Handbook on Household Accounting*, New York: United Nations.

United Nations, Eurostat, International Monetary Fund, Organisation for Economic Co-operation and Development, and World Bank (1993), *System of National Accounts 1993*, Series F, No. 2, Rev. 4, New York: United Nations.

Vaze, P. (1999), 'A NAMEA for the UK', *Structural Change and Economic Dynamics*, **10**, 99–123.

NOTES

1 For instance, consider a situation in which more and more people are prepared to pay a higher price for electricity which is generated in a relatively environment-friendly way (e.g. through wind or solar energy), but which is otherwise exactly the same as the electricity that they can simultaneously buy from oil, gas, coal or nuclear power plants. In this case, the average price paid for electricity rises while the useful value of the electricity itself does not change at all. Yet, this shift in consumer preferences should be recorded as a quality improvement (in conformity with the 'revealed preference' principle) and not as a price rise, so that GDP volume growth increases while the consumer price index is not affected. Whether this principle is always correctly applied in price statistics and national accounts remains an open question.

2 This is also the consensus view of the world-wide group of national accountants and environmental statisticians who meet annually to discuss the progress in this field (the so-called London group). In a recent meeting, this has been formulated as follows:

> However the group took the view that a proper adjusted 'eco-GDP' estimating what GDP would have been *if* the economy had been on a sustainable path – in which all prices and quantities would have been different – could only be the result of an economic model, not a simple accounting deduction as has been often suggested (Newson, 1996).

3 In that case the definition of GDP itself does not change, as the model then estimates conventionally defined GDP in a situation with much less pollution.

4 The NAMEA's conceptual framework and empirical application originate from Keuning (e.g. 1993), in collaboration with Gorter, Bosch and De Boo (cf. De Boo et al., 1993). The intellectual origin of the NAMEA is rooted in the Social Accounting Matrix (cf. United Nations et al., 1993: Chapter XX), which itself is an extension of Leontief's input–output approach. The first application in The Netherlands is described in De Haan, Keuning and Bosch (1994). This application can be seen as a merger of the NAMEA's conceptual framework with the environmental themes approach developed at the Netherlands Ministry of Housing, Spatial Planning and the Environment (Adriaanse, 1993). These themes reflect the most serious environmental problems in the Netherlands, and may vary by country. In turn, the selection of themes determine which environmental substances are included in the NAMEA. Refer to Keuning, Van Dalen and De Haan (1999) or to De Haan and Keuning (1996) for a more extensive review of the NAMEA approach.

5   Refer to Section XX.B of the 1993 System of National Accounts (SNA) (United Nations et al., 1993) for the properties of a regular National Accounting Matrix.

6   According to the IPCC-conventions, 1 kg. of CO_2 equals 1 global warming potential, 1 kg. of N_2O equals 270 global warming potentials, and 1 kg. of CH_4 equals 11 global warming potentials.

7   This part of Table 4.1 is explained in, e.g., Keuning, Van Dalen and De Haan (1999).

8   An alternative approach is to quantify sustainability standards for each NAMEA-theme, based on a number of sustainability principles (Ekins and Simon, 1998). Yet another approach is advocated by Jesinghaus (1997) who wants to use panels of experts to weigh together theme indicators into a single 'pressure index'.

9   Of the available NAMEAs not included in this issue, the long NAMEA time series compiled in Denmark (Jensen and Pedersen, 1998) and the recently completed Irish NAMEA (CSO, 1999) may be mentioned.

10   Refer to Keuning et al. (1999) and the literature mentioned therein for more details on these research projects.

11   The SESAME approach is set out in Keuning (1996), while a summary can be found in Keuning (1997) and in a recent Handbook of the United Nations (1998)

6. Formal Models and Practical Measurement for Greening the Accounts

Kirk Hamilton

6.1 INTRODUCTION

Over the past 25 years the breadth of environmental and natural resource policy making has expanded from dealing with pollution incidents, such as the grounding of an oil tanker, to grappling with the new complexities of achieving 'sustainable development' and protecting the global commons. Governments everywhere have committed themselves to these new goals, whether as a product of the United Nations Conference on Environment and Development in 1992, or in response to the report of the Brundtland Commission in 1987. Policy makers need new measures of progress.

There has been corresponding innovation in information systems to guide resource and environmental policies, from the collection of physical and economic data to the development of conceptual frameworks. The OECD's 'Pressure-State-Response' framework, for instance, provides the means to interrelate complex information concerning human activities and the environment. Environmental performance indicators have taken on a key role in many countries. And natural resource and environmental accounts, with their tight coupling to *economic* accounts and indicators, promise to provide policy makers with measures of progress towards environmentally sustainable development.

The development of environmental and natural resource economics has highlighted the critical role that policy failure and market failure play in the degradation of the environment. This has put the focus squarely on policy, where it belongs. Policy failures come in many forms, from inadequate property rights regimes, to underpricing of natural resources, to subsidies on energy, fertilizers and pesticides that lead to negative impacts on the environment. Market failure exists wherever economic activities impose costs on others, in the form of pollutants carried downwind or downstream for instance, without any mechanisms for remediation.

Market failure is the prime reason that many analysts question the policy signals provided by our traditional economic indicators, in particular the Gross National Product (GNP). As codified in the UN System of National Accounts (SNA) (United Nations, 1993a), GNP measures the sum total of economic production on the basis of transactions in the marketplace. As a result, GNP masks the depletion of natural resources and presents an incomplete picture of the costs imposed by the polluting byproducts of economic activity. This has led many people to conclude, as in the case of Repetto et al. (1989, p. 3), that:

> This difference in the treatment of natural resources and other tangible assets [in the existing national accounts] reinforces the false dichotomy between the economy and 'the environment' that leads policy makers to ignore or destroy the latter in the name of economic development.

The new emphasis that governments have placed on sustainable development is another source of criticisms of the traditional national accounts. Measures such as Net National Product (NNP) and National Income account only for the depreciation of produced assets, ignoring the value of depletion of natural resources and degradation of the environment. They cannot serve, therefore, as guides for policies aimed at achieving sustainable development. 'Greener' aggregates, it is hoped, can.

In addition to these criticisms of traditional national accounting aggregates, natural resource and environmental accounting has many other antecedents. The experience of the 'oil crisis' in the 1970s led to a concern with the physical scarcity of natural resources, and the construction of natural resource accounts detailing the changing stocks and flows of physical quantities of resources was the result (Alfsen, 1993). Worries about the toxic effects of pollutants led to increasing interest in understanding the pathways that particular materials take through the economic system, with the development of material balance accounts being one of the responses (Ayres and Kneese, 1969). And the desire to analyse the connection between economic activity and pollutant flows produced models linking input–output tables to accounts of pollution emissions (Leontief, 1970; Victor, 1972; see also Chapter 7). All of these roots are still evident in what is broadly termed resource and environmental accounting.

The United Nations has attempted to bring some order to this field with the publication of interim guidelines on an integrated System of Environmental and Economic Accounts (SEEA) (United Nations, 1993b). This system aims to provide a common framework within which greener national accounting aggregates, natural resource accounts and pollution flow accounts have their appointed places.

For developing countries, the adjustments to standard national accounting aggregates that result from resource and environmental accounting are sizable, as will be seen in the empirical results below. This is obviously true for the most resource-dependent economies, but it is also likely to be of growing importance for those countries that are rapidly industrialising and urbanising; for these countries the growth in damages from pollution emissions, in terms of human health in particular, is of mounting concern.

This chapter aims to outline the variety of environmental accounts that countries and institutions are constructing, to explain the theoretical basis for environmental accounts, and to summarise what theory tells us about the mechanics of adjusting the national accounts to reflect environmental change. To show that these adjustments matter, recent empirical work from the World Bank will be presented. Finally, there will be a brief discussion of the types of policy questions raised by greening the accounts.

6.2 VARIETIES OF ENVIRONMENTAL ACCOUNTS

As noted in Section 6.1, there are several different flavours or approaches to environmental accounting. While many taxonomies are possible, the breakdown that most closely matches what countries are actually doing is the following:

- *Adjusted national accounting aggregates*, such as Eco-Domestic Product (EDP) or expanded measures of saving and wealth.
- *Natural resource accounts,* where the emphasis is on balance sheet items (the opening and closing stocks of various natural resources) and the flows that add to and subtract from the balance sheet position; these accounts are in quantities and (possibly) values, and may or may not be linked to the SNA through the National Balance Sheet Accounts.
- *Resource and pollutant flow accounts* that embody considerable sectoral detail and often are explicitly linked to the input–output accounts, a part of the SNA.
- *Environmental expenditure accounts,* which represent a breakout of existing figures in the SNA.

These are described in more detail below.

6.2.1 Adjusted National Accounting Aggregates

Hicks (1946, p. 173) defined income as:

> . . . the maximum amount which can be spent during a period if there is to be an
> expectation of maintaining intact the capital value of prospective returns . . . ; it
> equals consumption plus capital accumulation.

The notion of Hicksian income underpins most economic thinking about
income and is embodied in the System of National Accounts. The obvious
extension of Hicks into the realm of environmental accounting is to include
in 'capital accumulation' the changes in value of a wider range of economic
assets, including in particular those environmental assets that are scarce and
valued by people. Such a definition will exclude some things, such as the
value that the environment may yield for other species, but can encompass
much of what humans value in the environment.

This extended Hicksian framework provides the basis for altering the
standard SNA aggregates. The key steps in defining and measuring adjusted
national accounting aggregates are as follows:

- The starting point is simply the balance sheet account from the 1993
  revision of the SNA. In addition to the value of produced assets (buildings, machinery and equipment, infrastructure), this account includes a
  variety of tangible non-produced assets including land, subsoil assets,
  non-cultivated biological resources, and water. The key stipulations with
  regard to these assets are that they occur in nature, and that they have
  ownership regimes that are enforced and may be transferred (this limits,
  for instance, which water resources may be valued in the balance sheet
  accounts).
- Changes in wealth over the accounting period serve to define an adjusted
  savings measure, termed 'genuine' saving in recent literature.[1] This is
  measured as gross saving, less depreciation of produced assets, less the
  depletion of natural resources, less damage to tangible assets (both produced and non-produced, for example, acid rain damages to soil fertility), less damage to human health. The latter should be valued on the basis of willingness-to-pay, and should exclude any productivity losses that
  may already be reflected in the national accounts.
- Adjusted income or EDP is measured as the sum of consumption (from
  the standard SNA) and genuine saving. This is the Hicksian 'consumption plus capital accumulation'.

6.2.2 Natural Resource Accounts

As previously noted, natural resource accounts generally have a balance sheet
flavour, with their emphasis on opening and closing stocks, in quantities and
values, of natural resources including both commercial natural resources and
non-commercial or environmental resources. As such, resource accounts

form the basis of the expanded national balance sheet accounts in the revised SNA. The principal policy and analytical uses of these accounts include:

- Measuring physical scarcity.
- Providing information for resource management.
- Productivity measurement; valuing the natural assets upon which the resource sectors depend can help to refine measures of national productivity.
- Valuing depletion.
- Measuring the economic impact of pollution on living natural resources such as forests and fisheries.

Natural resource accounts, and their counterparts in the national balance sheet accounts, can therefore have wide use with regard to resource management policies and broader environmental policies.

6.2.3 Resource and Pollutant Flow Accounts

Resource and pollutant flow accounts are generally conceived as physical extensions to the (monetary) input–output (I–O) accounts. For each production and final demand sector in the I–O tables, these accounts associate a physical flow of natural resources, typically as inputs such as energy to production processes, and a physical flow of wastes and emissions in the form of SO_2, NO_X, BOD, etc. With links to the I–O tables these accounts lend themselves naturally to policy modelling. Examples of policy uses include:

- Measuring the incidence of environmental regulations and taxes.
- Estimating emission tax rates in conjuction with computable general equilibrium models.
- Measuring the efficiency of resource use.
- Macro-modelling; tying resource and pollutant flow accounts to the standard macroeconomic models governments use for projections permits the reporting of environmental effects (in terms of resource throughput and pollution emissions) as a standard component of the output from such models.
- Dispersion and impact models; the estimation of pollution emissions is a required input for 'downstream' models of dispersion and impact.

Of the *physical* accounts under consideration, resource and pollutant flow accounts clearly have links to the widest variety of policy issues. Construction of extended physical flow accounts has been pursued with particular vigour in Europe, under the heading of 'National Accounting Matrices with Environmental Accounts' (NAMEA) (see De Haan et al., 1993).

6.2.4 Environmental Expenditure Accounts

Environmental expenditure accounts generally consist of detailed data on capital and operating expenditures by economic sectors, for the protection and enhancement of the environment. The accounts may or may not include detail on the type of pollutant controlled, or the environmental medium being protected. The prospective uses of these accounts are fairly straightforward:

- Measurement of the total economic burden of environmental protection.
- Measurement of the sectoral distribution of abatement and protection costs.
- Measurement of unit abatement costs; if the survey vehicles used to collect data on environmental expenditures also collect data on the amount of abatement achieved, it is possible to estimate average unit abatement costs.

It should be noted, however, that measuring environmental expenditures is a subject fraught with definitional and measurement problems. To give just one example, manufacturers now often introduce new production technologies that jointly increase productivity and decrease emissions. In such a case, there is no meaningful way to establish what is the cost of protecting the environment.

The exposition in the balance of this chapter will focus on the construction of 'greener' environmental accounting aggregates. This topic presents both the greatest challenge to environmental analysts and the greatest opportunity for impacts on policy.

6.3 THE THEORETICAL BASIS FOR ENVIRONMENTAL ACCOUNTS

Weitzman (1976) posed a fundamental question about economic accounting: why, if the economic goal is to maximise consumption, do we measure national income as the sum of consumption and investment? One way to answer this question is to note that the sum of consumption and investment is what one would choose to maximise at each point in time if the economic goal were to maximise the *present value* of consumption along the optimal path for the economy. The Weitzman paper suggests that there is a profound linkage between national income accounting and growth theory.[2]

The notion of Hicksian income was introduced above, and a straightforward extension of this concept leads to a generalised definition of national income. It is traditional in growth theory to define total wealth to be the present value of consumption along the optimal path; in certain simple growth models this can be shown to be equal to the current value of the capital stock. If instead we define total wealth to equal the present value of *welfare* along the optimal path, then extended Hicksian income can be defined as the maximum amount of produced output that could be consumed, while leaving total wealth instantaneously unchanged.

These ideas can be made more concrete by presenting a fairly general model of an economy with natural resource stocks, and stocks of pollution associated with levels of production activity.

Assume a simple closed economy with a single resource used as an input to the production of a composite good that may be consumed, invested in produced assets or human capital, or used to abate pollution, so that $F(K, R, N) = C + \dot{K} + a + m$, where R is resource use, a is pollution abatement expenditures, N is human capital, and m is investment in human capital (current education expenditures). Function $q(m)$ transforms education expenditures into human capital that does not depreciate (it can be considered to be a form of disembodied knowledge), so that $N = q(m)$.[3] Labour is fixed and is therefore factored out of the production function.

Pollution emissions are a function of production and abatement, $e = e(F, a)$, and pollutants accumulate in a stock X such that $\dot{X} = e - d(X)$ where d is the quantity of natural dissipation of the pollution stock. The flow of environmental services, B, is negatively related to the size of the pollution stock, so that $B = a(X)$, $a_X < 0$. Resource stocks, S, grow by an amount g and are depleted by extraction, R, so that $\dot{S} = -R + g$, and resources are assumed to be costless to produce. The utility of consumers is assumed to be a function of consumption and environmental services, $U = U(C, B)$. There is a fixed pure rate of time preference r.

Wealth, V, is defined to be the present value of utility on the optimal path. It is assumed that a social planner wishes to maximise wealth as follows:

$$\max_{C} \int_{t}^{\infty} U(C, B)e^{-rs} ds$$

subject to:
$$\dot{K} = F - C - a - m$$
$$\dot{X} = e = d$$
$$\dot{S} = -R + g$$
$$\dot{N} = q(M).$$

The current value Hamiltonian function, which is maximised at each point in time, is given by:

$$H = U + \gamma_K \dot{K} + \gamma_X \dot{X} + \gamma_S \dot{S} + \gamma_N \dot{N} . \tag{1}$$

where γ_K, γ_X, γ_S and γ_N are respectively the shadow prices in utils of capital, pollution, resources and human capital. Deriving the static first-order conditions for a maximum, the Hamiltonian function may be written as:

$$H = U(C, B) + U_C (\dot{K} - (1 - be_F) F_R (R - g) - b(e - d) + q/q') .$$

Note that b is the marginal cost of pollution abatement. It is shown in Hamilton (1996) that this is precisely equal to the marginal social cost of pollution emissions, and that this in turn is equal to the level of a tax (the Pigovian tax required to maximise welfare) on emissions. These equalities hold because the economy is at the optimum. The term be_F is the effective tax rate on production as a result of the emissions tax. Therefore, although we have started with an optimal growth problem, the prices that result are those that would prevail in a competitive economy with a Pigovian tax on pollution. Note as well that $1/q'$ is the marginal cost of creating a unit of human capital.

Since $\dot{S} = -R+g$, $\dot{X} = e-d$ and $\dot{N} = q$, the parenthesised expression in the second term of this expression is equal to the change in the real value of assets in this simple economy, where human capital is valued at its marginal creation cost, pollution stocks are valued at marginal abatement costs and natural resources at the resource rental rate, F_R, net of the effective tax rate on production associated with pollution emissions. This expression serves to define genuine saving, G:

$$G = \dot{K} - (1 - be_F) F_R (R - g) - b(e - d) + q/q' . \tag{2}$$

For non-living resources the term in growth, g, can be dropped from expression (2), while for cumulative pollutants the term in dissipation, d, can be discarded.

Genuine saving therefore consists of investment in produced assets and human capital, less the value of depletion of natural resources and the value of accumulation of pollutants. It is straightforward to show that:

$$U_C G = \dot{W} = rW - U. \tag{3}$$

Expression (3) entails the following property: measuring negative genuine saving at a point in time implies that future utility is less than current utility over some period of time on the optimal path. Negative genuine saving therefore serves as an indicator of non-sustainability by Pezzey's (1989) definition (this will be discussed below).

This expression also implies that Hicksian income, the maximum amount of produced output that could be consumed while leaving total wealth instantaneously constant, is given by:

$$NNP = C + \dot{K} - (1 - be_F)F_R(R - g) - b(e - d) + q / q' . \tag{4}$$

The treatment of current education expenditures and pollution abatement expenditures requires more elaboration. Hamilton (1994) essentially argues that current education expenditures are not consumption, and therefore should be included in saving. Defining net marginal resource rents as $n \equiv (1 - be_F)F_R$, NNP be can be defined as:

$$NNP = GNP - a - m - n(R - g) - b(e - d) + q / q'$$
$$= GNP - a - n(R - g) - b(e - d) + \left(\frac{1/q'}{m/q} - 1\right)m. \tag{5}$$

where $1/q'$ is the marginal cost of creating a unit of human capital and m/q is the average cost. Assuming increasing marginal education costs, expression (5) suggests that the value of investments in human capital should be greater than current education expenditures; these current expenditures can therefore serve as a lower-bound estimate of the investment in human capital.

6.4 WHAT THEORY TELLS US

The growth model just presented is clearly far too aggregate and simple to be used in real-world problems. Its value, when combined with the Hicksian framework, is to give clear guidance on two critical questions for green national accountants: what should be subtracted (and what added) in constructing measures of income and saving? and how should these subtractions and additions be valued?

While many of the lessons from theory highlighted below are derived from the model just presented, others arise in the recent literature on environmental accounting. The lessons from theory fall under three headings: natural resources, pollution, and other issues.

6.4.1 Natural Resources

For living natural resources, expression (4) gives clear guidance: net depletion (harvest minus growth) should be deducted from NNP. If growth exceeds harvest, then there is an argument for actually increasing NNP to reflect the growth of this stock. However, it is important to count only growth in the economic portion of the total living stock (i.e. that portion with positive economic rents).[4] The basis of valuation is the unit scarcity rent, attenuated by the share of pollution damages in GNP.

Deforestation is not covered by expression (4). This represents a change in land value associated with a change in land use. Hamilton et al. (1998) show that *excess* deforestation should be deducted from NNP; this excess is determined by the number of hectares cleared for which the total economic value (TEV) of standing trees exceeds the TEV of the new land use (typically farmland). TEV for forested land includes both local and global willingness to pay for the services provided by standing forest, sustainable off-take of timber and non-timber products, production externalities (the value of upland forests to lowland agriculture, for example), and any carbon sequestration benefits.

For non-living resources, this expression suggests that depletion should be measured as the quantity of resource extracted, valued at the unit scarcity rent (i.e. the marginal rent). Because very strong assumptions concerning the optimality of the resource extraction program are required to support this valuation, and since marginal rents are typically not easily measured, the literature generally favours two valuation methods which arguably span a reasonable value for depletion: the simple present-value approach (El Serafy, 1989), which values depletion as the present value of current total resource rents (the reserves to production ratio defines the time period for the present value), or the total-rent approach (as defined, for example, in Repetto et al., 1989) which values depletion as quantity extracted times the average unit resource rent.[5]

6.4.2 Pollution

Expression (5) says that pollution abatement expenditures, a, are essentially intermediate in character and therefore any *final* abatement expenditures should be deducted in measuring Hicksian income and genuine saving. In practice, most current abatement expenditures are already in fact intermediate inputs in standard national accounting.

Two further issues arise in accounting for pollution: how to deal with abatement expenditures and how to value damages. Abatement expenditures were discussed at the end of the preceding section; any final expenditures on pollution abatement should be deducted from GNP, thereby treating them as intermediate in nature.

On valuing pollution damages, there is a strand of the literature (for example, the UN SEEA (United Nations, 1993)) which argues for a 'maintenance cost' approach. This is the cost of reducing pollution emissions to a given level as defined by a legislative standard or a scientifically determined threshold. Expressions (4) and (5) suggest that there is no theoretical basis for this approach. Moreover, maintenance costs may seriously understate the required adjustment to GNP, given that in an over-polluted economy, marginal pollution damages will be greater that marginal abatement costs. Maintenance cost calculations do answer a key policy question, however, namely what is the likely cost of meeting a given target for pollution reduction.

Expression (4) suggests that the deduction from NNP for pollution emissions should equal marginal damages times the net accumulation of the pollutant. Deriving the efficient path for marginal pollution damages in the model of the preceding section yields the following result:

$$b = \frac{\dot{b} - U_X / U_C}{(1 - be_F)F_K + d'}.$$

(6)

It is simplest to interpret this expression in the steady state (as $\dot{b} \to 0$). Then it can be seen that marginal pollution damages represent the present value of willingness to pay to avoid the pollution over the lifetime of the pollutant in the stock. The numerator is the willingness to pay expression (recall that the marginal utility of pollution is negative), while the denominator is the interest rate (the marginal product of capital adjusted for pollution damages) plus the marginal rate of dissipation of the pollution stock. For long-lived pollutants the marginal rate of dissipation will be very small; it is about 0.5 per cent per annum for CO_2, for example.

This is a good model of stock pollution, or even pollution with cumulative effects, in which case all the terms in d fall out of the preceding expressions. For important pollutants with relatively short atmospheric lifetimes, such as PM10 or acid emissions, the accounting should deal with the effects of these pollutants on other economic assets. Empirically, it turns out that the most important of these assets is human health. For health assets, the change in the stock is measured by the number of excess deaths or the number of symptom days, while the unit value of these changes is measure by marginal willingness to pay. Marginal willingness to pay in turn is measured by the 'value of a statistical life'[6] in the case of excess deaths, or the willingness to pay to avoid a marginal symptom day in the case of morbidity.

Avoiding double-counting is an important issue in pollution valuation. For example, many studies of the economic value of pollution damage measure lost productivity as a result of pollution-induced illness as an important component of the damage, which makes perfect sense. But in adjusting the national accounts, it should be remembered that the accounts already reflect the lost production owing to such illness (GNP is lower than it would otherwise be) and so no further adjustment for lost production should be made. To the extent that studies can measure individuals' willingness to pay to avoid the pain and suffering of pollution-induced illness, independent of any lost wages, this can be used in adjusting the accounts as a measure of the change in a notional stock of healthfulness. In general, adjustments to the accounts for pollution health damage should aim to measure welfare losses, rather than productivity losses.

Double-counting can be an issue for other pollution damages as well. For example, acid emissions may damage crops, but this damage is already reflected in lower GNP measures. To the extent that these emissions damage soil fertility over an extended number of years, however, this should be measured in green NNP, since it represents a loss in asset value.

6.4.3 Other Assets

As the formal model of the preceding section makes clear, there are assets other than purely environmental assets that can be brought into an extended set of national accounts. In the case of the formal model, the key non-manufactured, non-environmental asset is human capital, whose creation should arguably be measured in any set of accounts concerned with broader development outcomes. One other example bears mentioning in this context: exogenous resource price changes.

To the extent that a given resource-producing nation is a small player in total world supply of a natural resource, it must operate as a price-taker when it exports its natural resources. The resource price path is therefore exogenous for this nation and this implies that the present value of changes in the resource export value needs to be accounted in any extended measures of income and savings (see Vincent et al. (1997) for details). This makes intuitive sense: if the price path for a given resource can be assumed to be upwards independent of any production decisions by the small resource exporter, then there is a type of capital gain (or positive change in the terms of trade) that the exporter will enjoy, and the present value of these gains should be measured in income as a change in asset value. Of course, the opposite implication holds for an assumed declining resource price path.

While there is a clear logic to making such adjustments to the accounts of small resource exporters, the empirical facts suggest there may be little practical significance to this insight. The long-term time trend of most natural resources is, in fact, flat to slightly declining, making any such adjustments to the accounts negligible.

Many other extensions to the accounting system have been explored. Weitzman and Löfgren (1997) argue for an adjustment reflecting the value of exogenous technological change. Aronsson et al. (1994) examine the broader accounting issues concerning health.

The question of which assets should be treated in an extended accounting system is, to some extent, a question of the policy issues of concern. If the primary focus is on pollution and natural resources policy, then the sorts of adjustments outlined above probably suffice. If there is a concern with broader development outcomes, however, then there is an argument for dealing not only with natural resources and pollution, but with human capital creation, investments in health, and technological change as well.

6.5 SUSTAINABILITY AND GREEN ACCOUNTING

While it is generally assumed that achieving sustainable development requires a combination of economic, ecological and social sustainability, economists simplify matters by adopting definitions such as that of Pezzey (1989): a development path is sustainable as long as welfare does not decline along the path. As long as welfare is assumed to depend on a wide variety of 'goods' (consumption, environmental amenity, social harmony, and so on), then this definition is capable of capturing important aspects of sustainable development.

One of the appealing properties of the extended Hicksian measure of income, derived above, is that it leads to a simple test of sustainability: if consumption exceeds Hicksian income, then the economy is not on a sustainable path. Of course, this is just another way of saying that negative genuine saving implies non-sustainability.

Expression (3) provides the theoretical justification for genuine saving as a sustainability indicator and, while it is derived for an economy on the optimal development path, a recent paper by Dasgupta and Mäler (forthcoming) shows that this relationship holds for any development path as long as the accounting prices of different assets follow efficient paths. In the real world, we would not expect a point measure of negative genuine saving to imply an unsustainable future, but it is certainly true that a policy mix leading to persistently negative genuine saving is unsustainable.

At first glance, the genuine saving indicator would appear to be limited to questions of *weak* sustainability (i.e. the assumption that there are substitutes for all assets). Pearce et al. (1989) introduce the important idea of *strong* sustainability, which treats certain natural assets as non-substitutable; a strongly sustainable development path is one which preserves this critical natural capital.

In principle, the genuine saving indicator can deal with strong as well as weak sustainability. Closer examination of expression (6) makes this clear.

Suppose that there is some critical quantity of pollution stock $\overline{X}$, beyond which there are catastrophic consequences for welfare.[7] The notion of a catastrophic welfare loss would be manifest as extremely large and increasing values of U_X as the critical limit is approached, and a correspondingly large value of marginal willingness to pay, U_X / U_C. This, in turn, implies that the marginal damage of a unit of pollution, b, will also attain elevated values as the limit is approached, which will quickly drive the genuine saving rate to negative values.

As long as there is a well-understood and appropriately steep marginal damage curve for loss of critical assets, the genuine saving measure can capture the phenomenon of strong sustainability. Unfortunately, the nature of many environmental problems is that precise knowledge of the marginal damage curve is not available; this is certainly true for issues such as biodiversity. Under these circumstances, Pearce et al. (1996) argue for a precautionary approach, using two indicators: the first is the ratio of the current extent of the critical asset to its threshold value; the second is the genuine saving measure for those elements of nature deemed non-critical and therefore exploitable.

The final point regarding sustainability indicators concerns the role of population growth. The theoretical model presented above is explicitly a fixed population model. If population is growing, then it is possible that genuine saving could be positive, while total wealth per capita is declining. A simple formula makes this clear. Assuming that total wealth is not explicitly a function of population,[8] then for total wealth W and population P it follows that,

$$\Delta\left(\frac{W}{P}\right) = \frac{W}{P}\left(\frac{\Delta W}{W} - \frac{\Delta P}{P}\right) \tag{7}$$

where Δ represents the change in a variable over the accounting period (ΔW is therefore genuine saving, while ΔP is the total change in population). If the percentage change in total wealth is less than the percentage growth in population, total wealth per capita will fall.

While expression (7) is simple to derive, measuring it presents significant challenges. Population growth rates are widely available, but measures of total wealth are not. Balance sheet accounts are published by relatively few countries, and are limited to the value of produced assets and commercial land (although the 1993 SNA suggests expanding this to include the value of living and non-living natural resources that have an economic value). To be useful in assessing progress towards sustainability, total wealth should include not only produced assets, land and natural resources, but human capital, social capital and intangible assets such as creativity as well. *Expand-*

ing the Measure of Wealth (World Bank, 1997) represents a first step towards total wealth measurement.

6.6 SELECTED EMPIRICAL MEASURES OF GENUINE SAVING

As just noted, genuine saving is a useful indicator of sustainable development. Rather than looking more broadly at other green accounting indicators or types of environmental accounts, therefore, the examples of empirical results will be limited to the savings indicator.

Broad trends in the savings figures can be seen in Table 6.1, which summarises genuine saving for regional and income-level aggregations of countries. These figures are derived from *World Development Indicators* (World Bank, 1999), where a brief description of the methodology is given. More detailed methodological notes appear in Kunte et al. (1998).

Comparing low and middle income countries in Table 6.1, the 10.2 per cent difference in genuine savings is largely explained by a 9.2 per cent difference in the gross saving rate. However, depletion is significantly higher in low income countries, at 6.6 per cent of GDP as compared with 4.5 per cent in middle income. Much of this difference in turn is a function of the 1.8 per cent of GDP that net forest depletion represents in low income countries. In high income countries, depletion is only 0.5 per cent of GDP and education expenditures are 2 per cent higher than in low and middle income countries.

Turning to regional comparisons, East Asia and the Pacific exhibits high gross and genuine savings rates, with depletion amounting to 2.1 per cent. As the events of 1997/1998 have made clear, however, high savings rates are not synonymous with financial and macroeconomic stability, however advantageous they may be for rapid wealth accumulation. In Latin America and the Caribbean, the average genuine saving effort is fairly robust, although this masks some individual examples of poor performance, as in the case of Venezuela. Other regions exhibit a weak genuine saving effort, particularly in the oil states of the Middle East and North Africa,[9] and in Sub-Saharan Africa, where depletion is a substantial 7.8 per cent of GDP.

Country-level results for genuine saving in Sub-Saharan Africa in 1997 are presented in Table 6.2. As this table indicates, negative genuine saving is more than a theoretical possibility. It is important to note several issues with regard to these figures. First, as mentioned earlier, a point measure of genuine saving does not necessarily imply that the country in question is fated for an unsustainable development path; it does imply, however, that continuing the current policy mix is unsustainable. Second, it may be perfectly rational

Table 6.1 Genuine saving as percentage of GDP, 1997

	Gross Domestic savings	Consumption of fixed capital	Net domestic savings	Education expenditure	Energy depletion	Mineral depletion	Net forest depletion	Carbon dioxide damage	Genuine domestic savings
World	22.2	11.7	10.5	5.0	1.2	0.1	0.1	0.4	13.6
Low income	17.0	8.0	9.1	3.4	4.2	0.6	1.8	1.2	4.8
Middle income	26.2	9.2	17.0	3.5	3.8	0.5	0.2	1.1	15.0
High income	21.4	12.4	9.0	5.3	0.5	0.0	0.0	0.3	13.5
East Asia & Pacific	38.3	6.9	31.4	2.1	0.9	0.5	0.7	1.7	29.7
Europe & Central Asia	21.4	13.7	7.9	4.2	4.9	0.1	0.0	1.6	5.6
Latin America & Carib.	20.5	8.3	12.2	3.6	2.7	0.7	0.0	0.3	12.1
Middle East & N. Africa	24.1	8.8	15.3	5.2	19.7	0.1	0.0	0.9	-0.3
South Asia	18.2	9.1	9.1	3.8	2.1	0.4	2.0	1.3	7.1
Sub-Saharan Africa	16.8	9.1	7.8	4.5	5.9	1.4	0.5	0.9	3.4

Source: World Development Indicators (World Bank, 1999)

Table 6.2 Genuine saving and its components in Sub-Saharan Africa: percentage of GDP, 1997

	Gross Domestic savings	Consumption of fixed capital	Net domestic savings	Education expenditure	Energy depletion	Mineral depletion	Net forest depletion	Carbon dioxide damage	Genuine domestic savings
Angola	27.3	6.0	21.2	2.6	20.7	0.0	0.0	0.4	2.7
Benin	10.8	5.4	5.4	0.0	0.0	0.0	0.0	0.2	5.2
Botswana	44.7	13.3	31.4	6.9	0.0	0.8	0.0	0.3	37.2
Burkina Faso	9.2	4.6	4.6	2.8	0.0	0.0	0.0	0.2	7.1
Burundi	2.6	4.4	-1.8	3.0	0.0	0.0	8.5	0.1	-7.4
Cameroon	20.6	7.5	13.1	2.3	7.4	0.0	0.0	0.3	7.7
C. African Rep.	6.7	5.2	1.5	3.8	0.0	0.0	0.0	0.1	5.1
Chad	1.2	4.6	-3.4	0.0	0.0	0.0	0.0	0.0	-3.5
Congo, Dem. Rep.	9.0	5.0	4.0	0.7	0.0	0.6	0.0	0.2	3.8
Congo, Rep.	34.8	9.2	25.6	4.3	23.9	0.0	0.0	0.4	5.6
Côte d'Ivoire	23.1	7.0	16.0	5.7	1.5	0.0	0.0	0.7	19.6
Eritrea	-17.4	4.1	-21.5	-	0.0	0.0	0.0	-	-
Ethiopia	8.7	-	-	2.9	0.0	0.0	0.0	0.3	-
Gabon	48.3	15.2	33.1	3.1	15.8	0.0	0.0	0.4	20.0
Gambia, The	3.8	12.3	-8.6	3.3	0.0	0.0	0.0	0.3	-5.6
Ghana	9.8	4.3	5.5	2.4	0.0	2.5	0.0	0.4	5.0
Guinea	18.7	6.1	12.6	2.3	0.0	18.8	0.0	0.2	-4.1
Guinea-Bissau	5.0	4.8	0.3	1.8	0.0	0.0	0.0	0.5	1.5
Kenya	11.4	6.7	4.7	5.9	0.0	0.0	8.0	0.4	2.1
Lesotho	-9.8	8.3	-18.1	4.8	0.0	0.0	0.0	-	-13.3
Madagascar	3.6	4.9	-1.3	2.3	0.0	0.0	0.0	0.2	0.8
Malawi	2.1	6.4	-4.3	3.2	0.0	0.0	5.4	0.2	-6.7
Mali	13.6	5.8	7.8	2.8	0.0	0.0	0.0	0.1	10.5

Table 6.2 (continued)

	Gross Domestic savings	Consumption of fixed capital	Net domestic savings	Education expenditure	Energy depletion	Mineral depletion	Net forest depletion	Carbon dioxide damage	Genuine domestic savings
Mauritania	8.5	8.6	-0.1	4.9	0.0	14.6	0.0	1.7	-11.5
Mauritius	24.1	7.7	16.4	3.1	0.0	0.0	0.0	0.2	19.3
Mozambique	13.6	3.6	10.0	3.9	0.0	0.0	3.7	0.2	9.9
Namibia	14.2	13.8	0.4	1.7	0.0	0.6	0.0	-	1.5
Niger	3.3	4.5	-1.2	1.9	0.1	0.0	0.0	0.4	0.2
Nigeria	21.9	2.4	19.5	0.8	30.7	0.0	0.0	1.5	-12.0
Rwanda	-7.5	5.6	-13.1	3.2	0.0	0.1	0.0	0.2	-10.2
Senegal	13.2	5.3	7.9	4.1	0.0	0.4	0.0	0.4	11.1
Sierra Leone	-8.0	5.7	-13.8	2.5	0.0	3.6	0.0	0.2	-15.1
South Africa	17.0	13.8	3.2	6.6	2.1	1.9	0.1	1.4	4.4
Tanzania	3.4	2.8	0.6	2.9	0.0	0.0	0.0	0.2	3.2
Togo	9.8	5.1	4.7	5.3	0.0	2.4	0.0	0.3	7.4
Uganda	7.5	5.0	2.5	2.6	0.0	0.0	3.4	0.1	1.6
Zambia	9.8	9.9	-0.1	3.8	0.1	1.3	0.0	0.4	1.9
Zimbabwe	11.9	6.0	5.9	8.2	0.8	9.9	0.4	1.0	2.0

Source: World Development Indicators (World Bank, 1999)

for either extremely poor or extremely rich countries to consume wealth in the short run – in the former case to hold off starvation, in the latter because consuming a very small proportion of wealth entails a low loss of welfare over time. Finally, negative genuine savings rates represent an opportunity not taken: resource endowments represent a type of stored development finance, and some countries choose not to benefit from this natural advantage.

The estimates in Tables 6.1 and 6.2 include the depletion of timber, coal, oil, natural gas, zinc, iron ore, phosphate rock, bauxite, copper, tin, lead, nickel, gold, and silver. Data problems led to the exclusion of diamonds. The only pollutant considered is CO_2, which is valued at \$20 per ton of carbon (see Fankhauser, 1995); as suggested by expression (6), this represents the present value of global warming damages over the roughly 200-year residence time of a unit of carbon in the atmosphere. Note that as long as it is assumed that other countries have the right not to be damaged by their neighbour's pollution emissions, then it is correct to adjust the national accounts of the emitting country. The fact that local pollutants are excluded from Tables 6.1 and 6.2, for lack of data, implies that in some regions of the world the savings estimates are overstated by several per cent of GDP. This is true for air and especially water pollution in South Asia, and for air pollution in East Asia.

The genuine saving estimates in the *World Development Indicators 1999* can be the starting point for a range of analytical investigations. For example, of the six countries with notably negative savings rates in Table 6.2, three (Burundi, Rwanda and Sierra Leone) are countries facing civil unrest and violence, and another three (Guinea, Mauritania, and Nigeria) are highly dependent on mineral or crude oil resources.

6.7 POLICY ISSUES

Achieving sustainable development will require a range of policy actions, spanning economics, ecology and the social sciences. Greener national accounts can play a role in providing the information base for better policy. The sorts of issues explored below are all concerned with the use of the genuine saving indicator, to the extent that it provides a rough measure of whether an economy is on a sustainable path; the next questions concern the range of policies that can influence this indicator.

It is abundantly clear that monetary and fiscal policies are the biggest levers for boosting savings rates. The first policy issue is, therefore, a classic macroeconomic one: to what extent do monetary and fiscal policies encourage strong domestic savings?

While natural resource exports boost foreign savings and therefore the overall savings effort, the analysis of genuine savings suggests a further question: to what extent do exports of *exhaustible* resources boost the genuine rate of saving?[10] The answer to this lies in netting out the value of resource depletion from gross export values.

More optimal natural resource extraction paths will, other things being equal, boost the value of genuine savings. The policy question for natural resource management is therefore: to what extent can stronger resource policies (royalty regimes, tenure) boost the genuine rate of saving?

Similarly, reducing pollution emissions to socially optimal levels will boost the value of genuine savings. The policy issue with respect to pollution is: to what extent can more optimal pollution control policies increase the rate of genuine saving?

Note that the policy prescriptions for boosting genuine savings should never be to stop extracting resources or emitting pollutants altogether. Rather, pricing resources and pollutants correctly, and enforcing property rights, will lead to efficient levels of exploitation of the environment, reducing incentives to 'high-grade' resources or pollute indiscriminately. Optimal resource and environmental policies will maximise genuine savings, subject to the macroeconomic policy regime in place. However, the sorts of issues raised by Gelb (1988), about the nature and effects of oil windfalls in developing countries, are particularly relevant to the policy issues just raised: without sound macroeconomic policies and prudent allocation of public resources, the effects of reliance upon large resource endowments can be negative for many countries.

6.8 CONCLUSIONS

Still in its development phase, natural resource and environmental accounting is a field with important implications for policies for sustainable development. As governments attempt to match their actions to their rhetoric on achieving sustainability, the importance of environmental accounting will grow.

The development and use of environmental accounting will not be a uniform process across countries. Many developed countries have sophisticated models, that permit the integration of resource and environmental information into macroeconomic analysis. For these countries, the usefulness of adjusting national accounts aggregates may be limited, largely because policy simulations can be carried out directly. The physical natural resource and environmental accounts described above support the implementation of these models.

Building complex policy models may be an expensive luxury in many developing countries, however. For these countries, rapid assessments of resource depletion and the value of environmental degradation, placed in the savings and wealth framework presented above, will guide policy makers aiming for sustainable development. Green national accounting aggregates, including Hicksian income (EDP) and genuine savings, place natural resources and the environment in an economic context that is otherwise lacking in developing countries.

Growth theory provides the intellectual underpinning for expanded national accounting and, through the measure of genuine saving, an indicator of when economies are on an unsustainable development path. This theory points in useful directions for countries concerned with sustainable development.

Far from being a mere theoretical possibility, there is abundant evidence for countries whose policy mix results in negative genuine saving rates. While the World Bank estimates for 1997 are emphasised here, previous studies such as Hamilton and Clemens (1999) and Atkinson et al. (1997) have shown this to be true over decades as well.

The evidence suggests that, while resource-dependent economies are potentially sustainable if resource rents are invested in other productive assets (including human capital), many of these economies have not chosen this path. The results presented here show distinctive patterns of genuine savings across regions and country income groups.

However, as the example of Southeast Asia in 1997/98 shows, robust genuine savings do not necessarily lead to a smooth development path. Some of the broader lessons from the financial crisis in Southeast Asia concern the rates of return that were achieved with these savings; many savings investments were yielding zero or exceedingly small returns. So the lessons to be drawn from the analysis of genuine saving must go beyond the level of saving, to a concern with the quality of the investments that are made with these savings.

The genuine savings analysis raises an important set of policy questions that goes beyond the traditional concern with the macro and microeconomic determinants of savings effort. The questions of rent capture, public investments of resource revenues, resource tenure policies, and the social costs of pollution emissions, are equally germane in determining the overall level of saving, although it is clear that monetary and fiscal policy remain the big levers.

This analysis also provides a practical way for natural resource and environmental issues to be discussed in the language that Ministries of Finance understand. This may prove to be an important advantage as many resource-dependent economies struggle to achieve their development goals.

REFERENCES

Alfsen, K.H. (1993), *Natural Resource Accounting and Analysis in Norway*, Conference on Medium-Term Economic Assessment, Oslo, 2–4 June.

Aronsson, T., P.O. Johansson and K.G. Löfgren (1994), 'Welfare measurement and the health environment', *Annals of Operations Research*, **54**, 203–15.

Atkinson, G., R. Dubourg, K. Hamilton, M. Munasinghe, D.W. Pearce and C. Young (1997), *Measuring Sustainable Development: Macroeconomics and the Environment*, Cheltenham: Edward Elgar.

Ayres, R.U. and A. Kneese (1969), 'Production, consumption and externality', *American Economic Review*, **59**, 282–97.

Dasgupta, P., and K.-G. Mäler (forthcoming), 'Decentralization schemes, cost benefit analysis, and Net National Product as a measure of social well-being', *Environment and Development Economics*.

de Haan, M., S.J. Keuning and P. Bosch (1993), *Integrating Indicators in a National Accounting Matrix Including Environmental Accounts* (NAMEA), NA 060, 1993, Voorburg: Central Bureau of Statistics.

El Serafy, S. (1989), 'The proper calculation of income from depletable natural resources', in Y.J. Ahmad, S. El Serafy and E. Lutz (eds), *Environmental Accounting for Sustainable Development*, Washington: The World Bank.

Fankhauser, S. (1995), *Valuing Climate Change: The Economics of the Greenhouse*, London: Earthscan.

Gelb, A.H. (1988), *Oil Windfalls: Blessing or Curse?* New York: Oxford University Press.

Hamilton, K. (1994), 'Green adjustments to GDP', *Resources Policy*, **20** (3), 155–68.

Hamilton, K. (1996), 'Pollution and pollution abatement in the national accounts', *Review of Income and Wealth*, **42** (1), 13–33.

Hamilton, K., G. Atkinson and D.W. Pearce (1998), 'Savings rules and sustainability: selected extensions'. Presented to the World Congress on Environmental and Resource Economics, Venice, June.

Hamilton, K., and M. Clemens (1999), 'Genuine savings rates in developing countries, *World Bank Economic Review*, **13** (2), 333–56.

Hartwick, J.M. (1990), 'Natural resources, national accounting and economic depreciation', *Journal of Public Economics*, **43**, 291–304.

Hicks, J.R. (1946), *Value and Capital*, 2nd Ed., Oxford: Oxford University Press.

Kunte, A., K. Hamilton, J. Dixon and M. Clemens (1998), 'Estimating national wealth: methodology and results', Environment Department Papers, Environmental Economics Series No. 57, Washington: The World Bank.

Leontief, W. (1970), 'Environmental repercussions and the economic structure: an input–output approach', *Review of Economics and Statistics*, **52**, 262–71.

Mäler, K.-G. (1991), 'National accounts and environmental resources', *Environmental and Resource Economics*, **1**, 1–15.

Pearce, D.W., and G. Atkinson (1993), 'Capital theory and the measurement of sustainable development: an indicator of weak sustainability', *Ecological Economics*, **8**, 103–8.

Pearce, D.W., A. Markandya and E. Barbier (1989), *Blueprint for a Green Economy*, London: Earthscan Publications.

Pearce, D.W., K. Hamilton and G. Atkinson (1996), 'Measuring sustainable development: progress on indicators', *Environment and Development Economics*, **1**, 85–101.

Pezzey, J. (1989), 'Economic analysis of sustainable growth and sustainable development', Environment Dept. Working Paper No. 15, Washington: The World Bank.

Repetto, R., W. Magrath, M. Wells, C. Beer and F. Rossini (1989), *Wasting Assets: Natural Resources in the National Accounts*, Washington, World Resources Institute.

United Nations (1993a), *System of National Accounts 1993*, New York: United Nations.

United Nations (1993b), *Integrated Environmental and Economic Accounting*, Series F No. 61, New York: United Nations.

Victor, P.A. (1972), *Pollution, Economy and Environment*, London: Allen and Unwin.

Vincent, J., T. Panayotou and J.M. Hartwick (1997), 'Resource depletion and sustainability in small open economies', *Journal of Environmental Economics and Management*, **33**, 274–86.

Vincent, J. (forthcoming), 'Net accumulation of timber resources', *Review of Income and Wealth*.

Weitzman, M.L. (1976), 'On the welfare significance of national product in a dynamic economy', *Quarterly Journal of Economics*, **90**, 156–62.

Weitzman, M.L. and K.-G. Löfgren (1997), 'On the welfare significance of green accounting as taught by parable', *Journal of Environmental Economics and Management*, **32**, 139–53.

World Bank (1997), *Expanding the Measure of Wealth: Indicators of Environmentally Sustainable Development*, Environmentally Sustainable Development Studies and Monographs Series No. 17, Washington: The World Bank.

World Bank (1999), *World Development Indicators 1999*. Washington: The World Bank.

NOTES

1   Pearce and Atkinson (1993) presented the first cross-country empirical work on adjusted savings measures.

2   Hartwick (1990) and Mäler (1991) extended the growth-theoretic approach to national accounting to deal with environment and natural resource issues, while Hamilton (1996) looked in detail at accounting for pollution.

3   Human capital provides a type of endogenous technical progress. Cf. Weitzman and Löfgren (1997), who deal with exogenous technical change.

4   More elaborate models, such as that of Vincent (forthcoming), deal explicitly with the rotation age of forest resources, so that for a given stand there is several years of net appreciation of the stock, followed by depreciation at the point of harvest.

5   This if often, confusingly, termed the 'net price' method, while the simple present value is, equally confusingly, termed the 'user cost' approach. Both methods can be shown to measure user costs of resource extraction under appropriate assumptions.

6   This should be termed more accurately the willingness to pay to reduce the risk of death. Most governments have an 'official' value of a statistical life that is used in establishing safety standards for public infrastructure such as highways.

7   While strong sustainability was originally formulated with critical stocks such as rainforest or the ozone layer in mind, the analytical issues associated with a critical stock of pollution are precisely the same.

8   Atkinson et al. (1997) derive the more general expression when total wealth is a function of population.

9	It must be recalled, however, that the total rent approach to measuring depletion tends to exaggerate the value of depletion, particularly for countries with very large resource endowments.
10	The question is also germane for unsustainable forest harvest programs.

7. The Magic Triangle of Input–Output Tables

Carsten Stahmer

7.1 INTRODUCTION

The discussion on sustainable development has focused on three dimensions of the problem; a successful strategy has to integrate the social, environmental and economic aspects of sustainability. Such an approach can be symbolized by a triangle with these three dimensions of sustainability as corners. The meeting point of economists, environmentalists and social scientists has to be found in a process of stepwise bargaining and compromising in the central area of this triangle. Each specialist has to leave his corner to consider other opinions and to find a common strategy for achieving sustainability.

Input–Output (I–O) tables can play an important role in delivering a suitable database for studying sustainable development. I–O tables can be used not only for economic analysis, but also for ecological and social studies. Experience during recent years has shown that it might be useful to use I–O tables with differing units of presentation to facilitate special studies on different aspects of sustainability:

- I–O tables in monetary units are especially useful for analysing economic problems.
- I–O tables in physical units (tonnes etc.) could be used for ecological studies.
- I–O tables in time units might serve as a database for social studies.

From my point of view, a comprehensive analysis of sustainability can only be successful if all three types of I–O tables are used separately, as well as in combination. In the following, a detailed description of the advantages and disadvantages of the three types of units for presenting I–O data will be presented. As an example, comparable I–O tables using the above mentioned different types of units are shown describing the German economy for the year 1990.

7.2 GENERAL CONCEPTUAL CONSIDERATIONS

Two concepts of the production boundary of an economy are distinguished in the System of National Accounts (SNA): the traditional approach which mainly includes production for other economic units and a broader concept, also taking into account that part of household production which could be done by third parties (United Nations, 1993, par. 6.14–6.36).

7.2.1 Beyond the Narrow Concept of Production

These concepts seem to be too narrow for analysing social, economic and environmental problems in a comprehensive way. For describing the social dimension of sustainability, all activities of the population have to be considered. On the average of the whole population including all ages from babies up to retired persons, employment activities comprise only two of the twenty-four hours per day, whereas all other activities are normally neglected in traditional economic analysis.

It was shown in the 1960s that a useful general activity analysis can be introduced which interprets all household activities as the production of services (Becker, 1964; Lancaster, 1966). Such a concept is useful for social as well as for environmental studies. Households are producing not only goods (services) but also 'bads', such as wastes and air pollutants.

According to such a comprehensive activity concept, the production boundary as well as the corresponding concept of capital have to be extended. All purchases of consumer durables become part of capital formation, and the depreciation of these goods is part of household costs.

7.2.2 Beyond the Economic Concept of Transactions

In national accounting, the description of transactions focuses on transactions which are actually carried out in monetary units. In special cases such as barter transactions, non-monetary transactions are valued using comparable market values (United Nations, 1993, par. 3.34–3.49).

Such an approach cannot be sufficient if a comprehensive activity analysis is aimed at. The physical flows of materials from nature to the economy have to be described, as well as all transformation processes within the economy and the material flows back to nature. In the traditional framework, only about one twelfth of the material flows are valued in monetary units, while all other transactions are neglected.

Furthermore, even all service flows within the household sector are not taken into account. The following paragraphs will discuss the possibility of extending this narrow economic concept of transactions, to achieve a comprehensive database for sustainability studies.

7.2.3 Limits of Monetarization

In the 1960s and 1970s, many economists hoped to describe economic activities in a comprehensive way using the concept of economic welfare (Nordhaus and Tobin, 1972; NNW Measurement Committee, 1973; Uno, 1995; Diefenbacher, 1995; Reich and Stahmer, 1993). The measure of economic welfare not only included the traditional economic transactions, but also a comprehensive valuation of all household activities, as well as of the environmental costs of economic activities.

Further stimulation for comprehensive monetarisation was given in the 1980s by the discussions on environmentally adjusted gross domestic product. The aim of these approaches was to calculate a sustainable level of economic activity. Different versions of this measure were presented in the System for Integrating Environmental and Economic Accounting (SEEA) of the United Nations (United Nations, 1993; van Dieren, 1995). The concepts discussed revealed fundamental differences in comparison to the welfare measures presented in the 1970s. The aim of economic activities cannot only be defined as the maximisation of present welfare of the population, but rather as a path of development which takes into account the welfare in other countries and the needs of future generations too. It was *A Long Goodbye* (Raymond Chandler) to the dream of overall welfare measurement (Radermacher and Stahmer, 1996).

The debate on possibilities of calculating a sustainable level of economic activities has also shown that an approach dealing with sustainability in a national accounting framework has severe drawbacks. Sustainability paths could often be only reached after a longer period of adjusting economic processes. Thus, modelling of future scenarios seems to be unavoidable, which cannot be adequately reflected in the backward-oriented national accounting system. Furthermore, the international interrelationships, especially the global impacts of economic activities and the indirect environmental impacts of imported goods and services abroad, have to be taken into account (Ewerhart and Stahmer, 1998; Radermacher, 1999). Proops (1991) made a good point in his comments to the World Bank on the SEEA when he proposed the used of the term 'global modelling' instead of 'national accounting'.

Considering this discussion, national accountants may arrive at a more modest approach of additional monetarisation. In any case, it seems to be useful to value those non-monetary flows which might have similarities to market transactions and, thus, could be monetarised by using comparable market values. Examples of such imputations are estimates at market values for the flows of natural resources from nature to the economy, and for the services provided by households as far as they could also be delivered by third persons. This concept is described as version V.1 in the SEEA (United Nations, 1993, pp. 124–8;. Stahmer, 1995).

Of course, such a limited concept of imputed monetary values cannot be sufficient for an extensive description of the social, environmental and economic dimensions of human activities. Household activities not following the third-person criterion, as well as the impacts of economic activities on the natural environment (like climatic changes), cannot adequately be analysed. In the following paragraphs, some other types of input–output tables are discussed which might play a complementary role.

7.2.4 Uses of Physical Accounting

A complete description of the interactions between nature and human beings can only be given by using physical units, such as tonnes, joules, etc. Such physical accounting can show the material flows from nature to the economy, the different steps of transformation within the economy and, finally, the material flows back to nature. Physical accounting also allows consistent balancing of all metabolic processes of living beings, such as plants, animals and human beings. A concept for treating human beings as an integral part of nature seems to be urgently needed (Ayres and Simonis, 1994; Strassert, 1993, 1998).

These considerations have already led to physical accounting as an integral part of the SEEA (United Nations, 1993, part III). Similar concepts have been used to compile physical input–output tables in Germany, Denmark and Italy (Stahmer et al., 1997; Gravgard, 1998; Nebbia, 1999; de Boer et al., 1996). In the case of the German physical input–output tables, units of weight (tonnes) have been used supplemented by a description of energy flows in thermal values (joule).

The physical I–O tables also shows physical changes connected with household activities. Of course, these physical processes are mainly trans-formations of goods into residuals which are stored, treated or disposed of into nature.

The difficulty of taking into account qualitative aspects of material flows is a severe disadvantage of physical accounting. Poisonous and innocuous materials are 'valued' only by their weights, but not according to their impacts, e.g. on living beings. Such analysis has to be made in a second step, using suitable weighting schemes. Nevertheless, consistent material balances of all metabolic processes in units of weight are indispensable as a database for all further studies of the physical world.

Another shortcoming of physical accounting is the insufficient description of the production of services. These activities have an increasing importance in all countries. Hence, additional information on services has to be given by I–O tables in other units, e.g. in monetary units or units of time.

7.2.5 Uses of Time Accounting

It is an old dream of economic science to describe economic activities by using non-monetary units. It has been discussed over and over again whether it is possible to break through the appearance of revealed monetary values and to discover the hidden mystery of the substance of economic production (Reich, 1981, 1989).

In classical economic science, such analysis was carried out by using the necessary labour time for producing goods and services as indicator of their true values. Unfortunately, this approach again raises problems. In which way should skilled labour be weighted in comparison to simple work? Could the contribution of machines, buildings, etc., for producing goods and services be neglected?

These problems could only be solved by introducing the concept of the 'frozen' labour time used for producing education services as well as investment goods in the past. Such labour time 'melts' in the described present when skilled labour or fixed capital goods are used. Following this concept, depreciation of both education (human) capital and fixed assets can be calculated in time units (cf. Austrian capital theory: Böhm-Bawerk (1889/91); Faber and Proops (1990, especially Chapter 3)). In this case, the time of skilled labour is composed of both the actual working hours and the depreciation of the accumulated hours of educational services necessary to achieve the respective level of labour.

The transformation of monetary values into time values has to take into account not only direct inputs of working time, but also the labour inputs on preceding stages of production. Such analysis can only be done by using input–output models. The time directly and indirectly necessary to produce goods and services can be calculated in the following way (Ewerhart and Stahmer, 1999):

$$\mathbf{p} = \mathbf{s}'(\mathbf{I} - \mathbf{A} - \mathbf{D})^{-1} \tag{1}$$

Here: $\mathbf{p}$ – total labour 'cost' of production (vector).

s – coefficients of direct labour inputs (related to gross output) (vector).

A – coefficients of intermediate inputs including imported intermediate products (related to gross output) (matrix).

D – coefficients of depreciation by investment good and branch (related to gross output) (matrix).

The Leontief-inverse coefficients in formula (1) also include the coefficients of depreciation **D**. This extension of the normally used inverse coefficients allows an endogenisation of the use of capital goods (including the depreciation of human capital). Thus, the time values of products comprise both current and capital costs. (For an extensive introduction to input–output analysis, see Miller and Blair (1985).)

As already discussed in Section 7.2.1, a suitable concept of economic activities would comprise all human activities. According to this approach, the inputs of time contain not only the labour hours of occupied persons but also the 24-hour day of the whole population. Such comprehensive description of all activities in an input–output framework has been completed for Germany in spring 1999 (Ewerhart and Stahmer, 1999; Aslaksen et al., 1995). For facilitating comparisons with the physical I–O table 1990, the same reporting year has been chosen. The time I–O table is especially based on the results of a time budget study which has been conducted for the years 1991/92 (Blanke et al., 1996; Franz, 1998; Schäfer and Schwarz, 1994). Special emphasis has been laid on a detailed description of teaching and studying activities, which improve the educational level of the population.

The values of products according to an I–O table in units of time cannot reflect an ideal concept of true values even if the depreciation of human capital and produced fixed assets are taken into account. It seems to be impossible to include all important factors of production. As an example, the infrastructure of organisation and knowledge documented in books and other media cannot be adequately represented in units of time. The present situation is determined by activities which reach back to the preceding decades and even centuries. It seems impossible to transform this influence into data on time use. Furthermore, all environmental problems connected with human activities are neglected in a time I–O table.

Nevertheless, the comprehensive valuation of human activities in units of time has huge advantages. While physical I–O tables can give a complete description of all interrelationships between human activities and their natural environment, the time I–O tables can present a complete picture of all human activities. Furthermore, it allows linkages to quantitative as well as qualitative data on the whole population. Such linked analysis of economic, environmental and demographic aspects of the society has been widely neglected in the past.

This brief presentation of the advantages and disadvantages of the three types of units within an I–O framework has shown the necessity of combining their advantages for achieving a comprehensive description of human activities. The old debate on suitable units of presenting economic activities might be closed by admitting that no approach can be regarded as loser or winner. Instead of fighting against each other, cooperation seems to have a higher priority. The next part of my contribution will discuss similarities and differences between the three types of I–O tables for describing primary and intermediate inputs, gross output and final uses of the economy in the different quadrants of the tables. 1990 data of Germany are taken as numerical example. For comparing the extended versions of I–O tables with the traditional concept, the original monetary I–O table 1990 is additionally presented (Statistisches Bundesamt, 1994).

7.3. COMPARISON OF THE CONCEPTS OF THE THREE TYPES OF I–O TABLES

As preparation for a thorough description of the three types of table it is first necessary to discuss the concepts used in their preparation.

7.3.1 Classification of Activities

A common activity classification has been used for facilitating a comparison between the three types of I–O tables. This classification comprises the breakdown of activities by 58 branches and 30 additional branches normally applied in I–O tables. The activities shown in addition are 2 branches of environmental protection services (waste water treatment, waste disposal), ten branches of education services (from the level of kindergarten up to university level) and 18 branches of household services containing 10 activities related to studying (corresponding with the 10 branches of education services).

In the traditional 1990 classification, the environmental protection services and the education services were not separate, but included in the respective branches of enterprises, non-profit institutions serving households and government. The classification used in this chapter is already similar to NACE rev. 1 (see code no. 80: Education services, code no. 90: Sewage and refuse disposal services, sanitation and similar services). The activities of environmental protection and education have been separated from their institutional background and shown in branches comprising all activities of the same kind.

The branches of household services are additional branches. In the traditional context, purchases of households are only shown as part of private consumption. It should be stressed that all activities are included comprising the household production activities (following the third-person criterion) as well as other activities, such as services related to employment (e.g. driving to the work place), study activities, activities of media consumption, social contacts and physiological regeneration.

The I–O tables presented in Section 7.4 of this paper are aggregated to 12 branches: agriculture, forestry, fishing; mining, water and energy supply; manufacturing; construction; market services (except environmental and education services); household production services; household services related to employment; household services related to studying; other household services.

7.3.2 Primary Inputs

Table 7.1 gives an overview of the different types of primary inputs presented in the monetary, physical and time I–O tables. In the case of monetary I–O tables, the traditional one is shown in addition to the extended version.

Primary inputs represent a fresh impetus given to economic circulation. In this sense, primary inputs are treated as external factors whereas intermediate inputs already contain primary inputs of preceding production stages. Thus, they are shown as endogenous part of the economic circulation. In the I–O tables, primary inputs are presented in the third quadrant of the table, whereas intermediate inputs are items of the first quadrant.

In the traditional monetary I–O tables (Table 7.1, column 1), three types of primary inputs play prominent roles:

- The production factor of labour measured with its income flows.
- The production factor of fixed capital measured with its depreciation.
- The flow of imports of goods and services used for domestic production.

In addition, the government revenues on products (like non-deductible value-added tax and production taxes) are treated as primary inputs.

In the extended monetary I–O tables (Table 7.1, column 2) the same types of primary inputs are used, but the contents of the different items are substantially extended.

In the case of labour inputs, imputed values of time spent on household production, according to the third-person criterion, are included. Furthermore, a margin of labour and education is included which balances the depreciation of education (human) capital, as well as additional intermediate inputs regarding household services related to employment. It is assumed that labour income includes components corresponding to the depreciation of education capital, recorded as part of the consumption of fixed produced assets and with the additional costs of households related to employment. To avoiding double counting, the income flow has to be corrected by using the mentioned margin.

Table 7.1 Primary inputs in the German monetary, physical and time input–output tables (IOT), 1990

Ser.	Description	Monetary IOT		Physical IOT	Time IOT
		Tradi-tional	extended		
No.		million DM		1 000 tons	million hours
		(1)	(2)	(3)	(4)
1	**1. Labour inputs**	1 868 800	2 584 225		554 096
2	Employment	1 868 800	1 866 887		46 268
3	margin of labour and education		- 135 814		
4	household activities		853 152		507 828
5	*household production*		*853 152*		*82 312*
6	*Activities related to employment*				*12 255*
7	*Activities related to education*				*15 430*
8	*other household activities*				*397 831*
9	**2. Revenues on products**	101 680	179 391		
10	non-deductible value-added tax	28 240	105 951		
11	taxes less subsidies on products	73 440	73 440		
12	**3. Consumption of fixed produced capital**	303 010	572 542	42 216	36 012
13	fixed assets (except consumer durables)	303 010	307 874	38 106	9 451
14	consumer durables		126 030	4 110	3 907
15	education (human) capital		138 638		22 654
16	**4. Withdrawal from the non-produced natural capital**			49 510 759	
17	Water			46 427 665	
18	other raw material			3 083 094	
19	*Oxygen*			*810 171*	
20	*carbon dioxide, other air emissions*			*311 838*	
21	*soil excavation*			*1 151 818*	
22	*energy carriers*			*193 347*	
23	*other solid materials*			*615 920*	
24	**5. Imports from the rest of the world**	342 179	502 842	387 100	16 741
25	goods (without private consumption goods)	301 892	301 892	342 904	9 441
26	services (without private consumption services)	40 287	40 287	46	1 268
27	private consumption goods and services		160 662	44 150	6 032
28	**Total primary inputs**	**2 615 669**	**3 839 000**	**49 940 075**	**606 849**

The extension of the production boundary also influences the other primary inputs of the extended monetary I–O table. Purchases of private consumption products are now treated as intermediate inputs. This concept implies that the non-deductible value-added tax on private consumption products, as well as the imported part of private consumption, are now treated as primary inputs and therefore they are increasing the respective items.

The purchase of consumer durables is part of capital formation in the extended monetary I–O tables. According to this concept, depreciation of consumer durables is treated as a primary input.

Monetary data on economic uses of the natural environment are missing in the extended monetary I–O table of 1990. This compilation work will hopefully be done by the Wuppertal Institute for Climate, Environment and Energy.

Market valuation of the raw materials extracted from nature could be used as a starting point for such an estimation. Estimates of the use of nature as a sink for economic residuals are much more difficult to obtain, because the impacts of present activities are normally only observable in the future. Furthermore, such impacts could be international, even global.

Primary inputs of physical I–O tables (see Table 7.1, column 4) can only comprise data which could be measured in physical terms. Such information is especially available in the case of raw materials which are withdrawn from nature. These materials comprise water flows, air components, such as oxygen (inputs of animals) or carbon dioxide (inputs of plants), as well as solid materials, such as sub-soil assets. Other physical flows recorded as primary inputs are imported goods from the rest of the world which are used as intermediate inputs.

In physical I–O tables, a presentation of the uses of fixed assets creates difficulties. The concept of depreciation cannot be applied, because decreasing monetary values do not necessarily correspond with decreasing physical stocks. Hence, the so-called gross concept of fixed assets has to be preferred. According to this concept, fixed assets are recorded in two different periods: in the reporting period of investment and in the period when the respective asset is leaving the production process. In this period, a physical flow is shown from final uses back to the branch which had used the asset. Such a flow is treated as a primary input, substituting for the depreciation value of the monetary tables. It increases gross output and is distributed according to the destination of the asset (e.g. being re-used, being treated as waste, or being discharged on controlled landfills).

Such a concept cannot be considered an ideal approach. From my point of view, it would be preferable to treat fixed assets at the beginning of the respective period as intermediate inputs of production processes, and assets at the end of the period as additional inputs of production (cf. the growth model of von Neumann (1945), Lancaster (1971, p. 164 ff.)). Such a procedure would allow an endogeneous treatment of assets in activity analysis and would also facilitate a description of physical flows connected with fixed assets. Further discussion is necessary to clarify the concepts which should be aimed at.

A comprehensive description of human activities as a primary factor of production can only be given by using an I–O table based on time as the unit of presentation. According to the concepts of time I–O tables (see Table 7.1, column 4), primary inputs of labour are not limited to the working hours of employed persons, or to the time spent for household production (following the third-person criterion), but comprises the complete time budget of the whole population.

The labour inputs of time (1990: 554.1 billion hours) representing the whole time spent by the population can only reflect quantitative, but not qualitative, aspects of labour. This disadvantage of time accounting can be reduced by introducing a concept of education (human) capital and calculating the depreciation of such capital stock in time units. Such an estimate could be based on information about the accumulated use of time spent for teaching and studying. In a second step, the education capital can be depreciated according to the length of life time persons are using the knowledge accumulated.

A similar procedure has been used to calculate the direct and indirect time inputs which had been necessary to produce fixed produced assets (e.g. machinery, equipment, buildings and consumer durables) used for production purposes. The monetary depreciation of fixed assets could be completely transformed into time units. Furthermore, the imported intermediate inputs are calculated in direct and indirect labour inputs, by assuming that the structures of production (input coefficients related to outputs) are the same for both domestic production and production in foreign countries.

The concept of time used in these I–O tables cannot be sufficient in the field of environmental studies; raw materials withdrawn from nature are normally not produced by human beings. Therefore, they cannot be transformed into production time of human activities. Supplementary data in physical units are necessary to give a more comprehensive picture of the economic-environmental interrelationships.

7.3.3 Intermediate Inputs

The intermediate inputs of economic activities in the different types of I–O tables are presented in Table 7.2, rows 1 to 11.

The intermediate inputs shown in the first quadrant comprise only domestic goods and services used in production processes. Imported intermediate products are treated as primary inputs and recorded in the third quadrant of the I–O tables (see Section 7.3.2).

The extended monetary I–O table (Table 7.2, column 2) differs from the traditional version (Table 7.2, column 1) with regard to the treatment of environmental protection services and household activities. Environmental protection services for housing (e.g. payments of households for waste water

Greening the Accounts

and waste treatment) are not recorded as intermediate inputs of the housing sector (as a part of the rent), but as direct inputs of household activities.

Table 7.2 Intermediate inputs and gross outputs in the German monetary, physical and time input–output tables (IOT), 1990

Ser. No.	Description	Monetary IOT		Physical IOT	Time IOT
		traditional	extended		
		million DM		1 000 tons	million hours
		(1)	(2)	(3)	(4)
		Intermediate Inputs			
1	**1. Product inputs**	**2 041 341**	**4 040 240**	**8 437 839**	**203 487**
2	goods (except water and private consumption goods)	1 031 867	1 031 867	1 565 100	33 915
3	water	8 953	8 953	6 654 051	220
4	services (incl. re-used products, without private consumption services)	1 000 521	992 090	73 872	40 166
5	private consumption goods and services (except water)		879 173	109 279	27 262
6	services related to employment		58 372		14 685
7	Intermediate uses of household Production services		1 069 784	35 537	87 239
8	**2. Residual inputs**			**4 536 634**	
9	wastes for economic re-use and treatment			140 468	
10	waste water for treatment			4 396 166	
11	**Total intermediate inputs**	**2 041 341**	**4 040 240**	**12 974 473**	**203 487**
		+ Primary inputs			
12	**Total primary inputs**	**2 615 669**	**3 839 000**	**49 940 075**	**606 849**
		= Gross outputs			
13	**1. Product outputs**	**4 657 010**	**7 879 240**	**9 266 130**	**810 336**
14	goods (except water)	2 380 859	2 380 859	2 452 146	77 769
15	Water	8 972	8 972	6 661 841	220
16	services (incl. re-used products, except household services)	2 267 179	2 261 702	116 606	83 011
17	household services		3 227 707	35 537	649 336
18	*household production services*		*1 351 755*	*35 537*	*111 302*
19	*services related to employment*		*58 372*		*14 685*
20	*services related to education*		*42 215*		*18 255*
21	*other household services*		*1 775 365*		*505 094*
22	**2. Residual outputs**			**53 648 418**	
23	waste water			49 246 503	
24	water vaporised			1 566 597	
25	other residuals			2 835 318	
26	*oxygen*			*226 052*	
27	*carbon dioxide, other air emissions*			*811 944*	
28	*soil disposal, other solid materials*			*1 507 635*	
29	*wastes*			*289 687*	
30	**Total outputs**	**4 657 010**	**7 879 240**	**62 914 548**	**810 336**

The purchases of household consumption goods and services are (except for consumer durables) intermediate inputs of household activities. An additional increase of intermediate inputs of household activities is caused by internal flows of household services which are used as intermediate inputs of other household activities.

In physical I–O tables (Table 7.2, column 3), intermediate inputs consist of domestic products and of residuals of domestic production which are recycled or treated in environmental protection facilities. Intermediate flows of services are not recorded in the physical table (exceptions are, e.g., some equipment for defence purposes or meals prepared in restaurants).

In time I–O tables, the product flows of the extended monetary I–O tables are transformed into the hours directly and indirectly necessary to produce the respective products. In contrast to the physical version, both goods and service flows can be valued in time units.

7.3.4 Outputs

The outputs of the different activities (see Table 7.2, rows 13 to 30) are identical with the totals of intermediate and primary inputs.

In traditional monetary I–O tables (Table 7.2, column 1), outputs comprise products sold, increases of stocks of own products and products used in the same unit for own purposes (e.g. own-account production of assets). In the case of non-market production, market values of the products are not available. Consequently, gross outputs are calculated as totals of intermediate and primary inputs.

In the extended monetary I–O tables (Table 7.2, column 2), additional outputs of household activities are shown. These outputs are compiled in the same way as non-market services in the traditional framework, by adding all intermediate and primary inputs of the respective activity. These inputs comprise private consumption goods, depreciation of both consumer durables and education (human) capital and, in the case of household production services (following the third-person criterion), monetary values of the time spent on these activities.

In physical I–O tables, outputs consist of products and residuals of production processes. The outputs of service activities (also including all household activities) normally comprise only residuals. Thus, the importance of the service sector for the whole economy cannot be adequately reflected in a physical framework.

In time I–O tables (Table 7.2, column 4), outputs are valued by the hours directly or indirectly being necessary to produce the respective goods and services. Such a concept also allows an adequate treatment of all household activities; labour inputs of these activities are valued by the hours spent. Insofar as imported products are used for domestic production, the time values of these products are calculated by using the assumption that the production processes of both domestic production and production abroad have the same input structures. Furthermore, it has already been mentioned that the depreciation of fixed assets, including consumer durables and education capital, is calculated by the time necessary to produce the respective investment goods and services in the period of investment.

7.3.5 Final Uses

Final uses are outputs of economic activities which leave the economic circulation. They are described in the second quadrant of I–O tables. An overview of the final uses presented in the different types of tables is given in Table 7.3.

In the traditional monetary I–O tables, four types of final uses are distinguished:

- Private consumption.
- Government consumption.
- Fixed capital formation (including change in stocks).
- Exports of goods and services.

Private consumption comprises purchases of private consumption products and the consumption of non-profit institutions serving households. The products purchased disappear into a 'black hole', because their further uses in household activities are not described. Furthermore, it is assumed that consumer durables are consumed in one period. This concept reveals the low priority household activities are given in traditional national accounting.

Government consumption comprises all government services which are provided for the whole community, without payment of specific users.

Fixed capital formation contains only investment goods which are used for production purposes. Thus, consumer durables are not taken into account because household activities are not treated as production in the conventional framework. Furthermore, changes of non-produced natural capital are not recorded.

The flows between the home country and the rest of the world only comprise goods and services. Flows of residuals (e.g. air emissions) which might affect the natural environment of other countries are not taken into account.

Substantial changes can be observed in the extended version of monetary I–O tables (Table 7.3, column 2).

Private consumption is now defined as the final uses of household services produced in the different branches of household activities. The aggregates could be interpreted as consumption for own use, similar to government consumption. Similar to government consumption and consumption of nonprofit institutions serving private households, private consumption is valued by the costs of household activities (intermediate consumption, depreciation, value of time spent for household activities).

Table 7.3 Final uses in the German monetary, physical and time input–output tables (IOT), 1990

Ser. No	Description	Monetary IOT		Physical IOT	Time IOT
		traditional	extended	1 000 tons	million hours
		million DM			
		(1)	(2)	(3)	(4)
1	**1. Private consumption**	**1 085 325**	**2 076 030**		**529 997**
2	Consumption products	940 548	2 057 337		529 157
3	*Goods*	*306 052*			
4	*Services*	*634 496*			
5	*Household services*		*2 057 337*		*529 157*
6	consumer durables	114 047			
7	Consumption of nonprofit institutions serving Households	30 730	18 693		840
8	**2. Government consumption**	**444 070**	**361 944**		**13 761**
9	except education services	358 994	361 944		13 761
10	education services	85 076			
11	**3. Fixed capital formation**	**425 577**	**685 408**	**733 007**	**40 041**
12	produced natural assets			28 699	
13	machinery and equipment	176 928	176 928	8 554	5 605
14	Buildings	248 248	248 248	553 052	8 339
15	consumer durables		114 047	4 403	4 040
16	education (human) capital		145 784	20 949	22 006
17	change in stocks	401	401	117 350	51
18	controlled landfills				
19	**4. Disposal into the non-produced natural capital**			**48 994 384**	
20	waste water			44 846 589	
21	water vaporised			1 565 925	
22	other residuals			2 581 870	
23	*oxygen*			*226 052*	
24	*carbon dioxide, other air emissions*			*811 655*	
25	*soil disposal, other solid materials*			*1 507 577*	
26	*wastes*			*36 586*	
27	**5. Exports to the rest of the world**	**660 697**	**715 618**	**212 684**	**23 051**
28	goods	577 696	602 226	192 591	19 119
29	services	83 001	113 392	17 950	3 932
30	wastes for treatment			2 143	
31	**Total final uses**	**2 615 669**	**3 839 000**	**49 940 075**	**606 850**

The concept of government consumption has not been substantially modified. The treatment of education services as investment is the only conceptual change.

The concept of fixed capital formation shows more important changes in the extended monetary I–O tables. Apart from the treatment of consumer durables as investment goods, the education services and the household services related to studying are treated as fixed capital formation which increases the education (human) capital. The household services related to studying comprise all costs of pupils and students directly associated with their studies (e.g. travelling costs, costs of teaching aids, part of dwelling costs). Further changes of fixed capital formation would be necessary if changes of natural capital were taken into account.

The final uses of physical I–O tables (Table 7.3, column 3) do not comprise private and government consumption, because all physical inputs of government and private activities are treated as intermediate inputs. The outputs of these activities are services without material counterpart, as well as residuals which partly increase the flows back into the nature. Fixed capital formation and disposal into non-produced natural capital are the most important aggregates of final uses in the physical I–O tables. As far as exports comprise physical goods, physical flows to the rest of the world are shown.

The concept of final uses in the time I–O tables (Table 7.3, column 4) is very similar to that of the extended monetary I–O tables. The value of private consumption, also comprising most of the time spent for household activities, dominates all other aggregates. In the context of fixed capital formation, the increase of education (human) capital also contains the time of pupils and students for studying.

7.4 DESCRIPTION OF THE THREE TYPES OF I–O TABLES

We now move to the three types of tables discussed above, and offer a description of each in turn.

7.4.1 General Comments

In the following paragraphs, there is a brief description of the three types of I–O tables showing German economic activities in the year 1990 (see Tables 7.4 to 7.6). Comments will focus on the twelve activities which are presented in the highly aggregated tables. It has already been mentioned that the I–O tables have been compiled from 91 activities (see Section 7.3.1). It is planned to publish the tables in this detailed classification to allow special studies, e.g. on household activities or on education services.

It is not possible to describe all supplementary tables which have been compiled in the context of the three extended I–O tables. It should be mentioned that import matrices are available for all types of I–O tables, showing the imports in a breakdown by product group as well as by using branch and final use, respectively. In Tables 7.4.1 to 7.4.3, the column totals of the import matrices are only presented as primary inputs of the respective using branches.

Several additional tables are available in the case of physical I–O tables. The data comprise detailed information on the material inputs and outputs of economic activities, which can be further subdivided into complete material balances of energy uses, water uses and other materials. Furthermore, special balances of biological metabolism of animals plants and human beings are estimated.

In the case of physical I–O tables, it might be useful to reduce material flows for some specific analyses. There are throughput materials which do not enter economic circulation, but are only treated as primary inputs (withdrawal from non-produced natural assets) and final uses (disposal into the non-produced natural assets). Most important examples are water flows, like cooling water, which enter the natural sphere again without any further treatment. Other examples are soil materials only moved in the context of construction activities. In Table 7.4, throughput materials are shown in row 20. They comprise about three-quarters of all material flows without having an important economic or ecological influence. Thus, it could be considered to remove them before analysing the physical flows of economic activities in the context of physical I–O tables.

In the case of time I–O tables, additional information on the qualification structures of employed persons by branch are available. Furthermore, data on the qualification levels of the whole population can be combined with the complete range of household activities.

7.4.2 Extended Monetary I–O Table

The activities shown in columns 1 to 5 and 8 of Table 7.4 represent the traditional classification of production activities. Special emphasis is given to environmental protection activities which are explicitly presented in column/row 6. The environmental protection activities only comprise services which are delivered to third parties (external protection activities) whereas internal protection activities, like water treatment plants for own purposes, are not taken into account (Schäfer and Stahmer, 1988; Kuhn, 1996). It might be possible to 'externalise' their costs by establishing separate production units, but it would be very difficult to estimate the corresponding physical flows, e.g. of waste and air pollution.

In column/row 7, there is a description of education services of government institutions, enterprises and nonprofit institutions serving households.

Table 7.4 Extended monetary input–output table: Germany, 1990 (Billion Deutsche marks)

Row No.	Uses / Supply	Agriculture, forestry, fishing 1	Mining, water and energy supply 2	Manuf'ring 3	Construction 4	Market services 5
	Product output by product group					
1	Products of agriculture, forestry, fishing	7.5	0.1	43.4	0.1	5.9
2	Products of mining. water and energy supply	1.8	30.8	45.0	0.5	20.7
3	Products of manufacturing	14.8	13.1	571.1	72.0	109.0
4	Construction work	0.7	3.9	7.1	4.2	23.4
5	Market services	8.2	15.9	288.6	39.6	424.5
6	Environmental protection services	0.1	0.9	5.2	2.0	1.8
7	Education services	-	-	-	-	-
8	Non-market services	0.4	0.5	5.8	0.7	4.9
9	Household production services	-	-	-	-	-
10	Household services related to employment	0.5	1.0	17.5	4.0	22.7
11	Household services related to education	-	-	-	-	-
12	Other household services	-	-	-	-	-
13	**Product and residual inputs. totals**	**34.0**	**66.1**	**983.5**	**123.1**	**612.8**
14	Labour inputs	28.9	47.8	581.1	120.0	793.8
15	Margin of labour and education	- 1.8	- 1.5	- 27.8	- 6.4	- 37.0
	Revenues on products					
16	Non-deductible value-added tax	-	-	-	-	11.6
17	Taxes less subsidies on products	- 4.5	- 2.6	54.5	2.3	23.3
	Consumption of fixed produced assets					
18	Assets incl. consumer durables	11.8	20.3	72.9	5.4	170.7
19	Education (human) capital	1.3	0.6	10.3	2.4	14.3
	Withdrawal from the non-produced natural capital					
20	Throughput materials	-	-	-	-	-
21	Other materials	-	-	-	-	-
	Imports					
22	Goods	5.9	13.4	225.2	13.0	29.5
23	Services	0.4	0.7	8.6	1.0	22.9
24	**Primary inputs. Totals**	**42.0**	**78.6**	**924.8**	**137.7**	**1 029.1**
25	**Gross output. balancing items**	**76.0**	**144.7**	**1 908.3**	**260.8**	**1 642.0**

Input of branches

Table 7.4 (continued)

Env'mental protection services	Education services	Non-market services	Household production	Services related to employment	Services related to studying	Other services	Totals	Row No.
				Household services				
6	7	8	9	10	11	12	13	
-	0.1	1.1	6.0	0.1	0.0	3.2	**67.3**	1
0.7	1.6	5.7	15.4	0.4	0.2	18.4	**141.3**	2
2.4	2.7	41.3	109.1	7.6	1.5	116.1	**1 060.6**	3
1.8	1.3	7.2	1.0	0.1	-	2.4	**53.1**	4
1.7	7.8	109.1	127.9	20.1	10.1	403.4	**1 457.1**	5
4.9	0.5	1.1	2.5	0.2	0.1	7.2	**26.5**	6
-	-	-	-	-	-	-	-	7
1.3	0.1	66.5	2.8	0.3	2.2	20.7	**106.2**	8
-	-	-	130.3	-	17.4	922.1	**1 069.8**	9
-	3.0	9.6	-	-	-	-	**58.4**	10
-	-	-	-	-	-	-	-	11
-	-	-	-	-	-	-	-	12
12.9	**17.1**	**241.8**	**395.0**	**28.7**	**31.6**	**1 493.6**	**4 040.2**	13
5.4	78.2	211.6	853.2	-	-	-	**2 720.0**	14
- 0.2	- 6.1	- 15.4	- 39.5	-	-	-	**-135.8**	15
1.0	1.3	14.3	23.3	3.0	1.1	50.3	**106.0**	16
-	0.2	0.3	-	-	-	-	**73.4**	17
6.5	8.3	12.0	33.3	14.0	2.5	76.1	**433.9**	18
0.2	3.1	5.7	39.5	5.4	4.7	51.1	**138.6**	19
-	-	-	-	-	-	-	-	20
-	-	-	-	-	-	-	-	21
0.7	0.6	13.6	42.1	5.0	1.0	70.2	**420.1**	22
0.0	0.9	5.7	4.8	2.2	1.4	34.0	**82.7**	23
13.6	**86.5**	**247.8**	**956.7**	**29.6**	**10.7**	**281.7**	**3 839.0**	24
26.6	**103.6**	**489.6**	**1 351.8**	**58.4**	**42.2**	**1 775.4**	**7 879.2**	25

Table 7.4 (continued)

Private cons'ption	Gov'ment cons'ption	Fixed assets	Consumer durables	Education capital	Disposal	Exports	Totals	Total uses	Row No.
		Final uses							
		Fixed capital formation							
14	15	16	17	18	19	20	21	22	
-	-	2.8	-	-	-	5.9	8.7	76.0	1
-	-	-0.7	-	-	-	4.1	3.4	144.7	2
-	-	184.7	73.3	-	-	589.7	847.7	1 908.3	3
-	-	205.1	-	-	-	2.5	207.7	260.8	4
-	-	32.6	40.7	-	-	111.6	184.9	1 642.0	5
-	0.1	-	-	-	-	-	0.1	26.6	6
-	-	-	-	103.6	-	-	103.6	103.6	7
18.7	361.9	1.1	-	-	-	1.8	383.4	489.6	8
282.0	-	-	-	-	-	-	282.0	1 351.8	9
-	-	-	-	-	-	-	-	58.4	10
-	-	-	-	42.2	-	-	42.2	42.2	11
1 775.4	-	-	-	-	-	-	1 775.4	1 775.4	12
2 076.0	361.9	425.6	114.0	145.8	-	715.6	3 839.0	7 879.2	13
-2 720.0	-	-	-	-	-	-	-2 720.0	-	14
135.8	-	-	-	-	-	-	135.8	-	15
-	-155.0	27.7	17.9	-	-	3.4	-106.0	-	16
-	-73.4	-	-	-	-	-	-73.4	-	17
-	-	-307.9	-126.0	-	-	-	-433.9	-	18
-	-	-	-	-38.6	-	-	-138.6	-	19
-	-	-	-	-	-	-	-	-	20
-	-	-	-	-	-	-	-	-	21
-	-	66.3	31.9	-	-	-518.3	-420.1	-	22
-	-	0.1	0.1	-	-	-82.9	-82.7	-	23
-2 584.2	-228.4	-213.7	-76.1	-138.6	-	-597.8	-3 839.0	-	24
-508.2	133.5	211.8	37.9	7.1	-	117.8	-	7 879.2	25

The gross output of these activities is treated as fixed capital formation and increases the stock of education (human) capital (row 7, column 18). The consumption of education capital is associated with those activities which use the accumulated knowledge of people (row 19). As far as labour inputs have monetary values (row 14), it is assumed that the value of depreciation of education capital is part of these revenues. To avoid double counting, a (negative) margin of labour and education has been introduced (row 15) which also counterbalances the intermediate inputs of household services related to employment (row 10).

It is assumed that all household activities are productive. Nevertheless, the use of the term 'household production' is limited to the case of household activities which meet the third-person criterion (column/row 9). The gross output of household production is compiled as the total of the value of intermediate consumption products, depreciation of consumer durables and the value of the time spent for household production. The depreciation of education capital is counterbalanced by the mentioned margin (row 15, column 9). Household production services are partly used as intermediate inputs of other household activities (row 9, columns 9, 11 and 12). The remaining values leave the economic circulation and are treated as private consumption (row 9, column 14).

The household services (except household production) (columns/rows 10 to 12) represent household activities for own purposes which cannot be carried out by third persons. Thus, a suitable valuation of the time spent for these activities seems to be impossible. The gross output of these services comprise only intermediate inputs and consumption of fixed produced assets, including the depreciation of education capital which has not to be counterbalanced in this case. Household services related to employment (column/row 10) are used by the branches employing the respective persons. Household services related to studying (column/row 11) comprise learning activities of pupils and students. The costs of these activities are treated as investment in education capital (row 11, column 18). All other household services (column/row 12) are used for consumption purposes only (row 12, column 14). These activities comprise, e.g., social activities and activities for physiological regeneration (eating, sleeping, etc.).

7.4.3 Physical I–O Table

The physical I–O table (Table 7.5) shows a completely different picture of the economy. The activities producing material goods play a much more important role, while service branches, with their immaterial outputs, have a relatively low importance.

The production activities of agriculture, forestry and fishing (column/row

1) also comprise balances of plants and animals as far as they belong to the controlled economy. Thus, an analysis of the biological metabolism of living beings is possible.

The production activities of mining, water and energy supply (column/row 2) especially contain the withdrawal of raw materials from nature and their transformation into marketable goods. In comparison to the other flows of materials, water inputs and outputs dominate the description of these activities. As mentioned already, it seems to be preferable to allow a suitable reduction of these flows to facilitate the analysis of material flows. In row 20/column 2, most of the water flows are shown as throughput materials (e.g. cooling water) which represents about a half of all material flows of the economy.

In manufacturing and construction (columns/rows 3 and 4), the transformation of material goods into other material goods is described. Of course, these transformation processes require further inputs of raw materials withdrawn from nature, and they produce not only goods but also residuals. Insofar as soil is only moved but not used as material input of buildings etc., the respective material flow (row 20, column 4) is shown as throughput material.

In the case of market services (column/row 5), education services (column/row 7) and non-market services (column/row 8), material product inputs are normally transformed into residuals only. Apart from some exceptions (e.g. preparing meals in restaurants), the product output of services is immaterial.

Important material flows can be observed in environmental protection activities (column/row 6). Wastes and waste-water of other branches are treated and transformed into other types of residuals, which could be safely stored in controlled landfills, or which could be disposed of into nature without severe damage to ecosystems.

The material balances of household activities (columns/rows 9 to 12) are similar to those of the other service branches. Apart from preparing meals, no material product output is shown. The output of household services normally consists of residuals only. Some raw materials (e.g. oxygen and water) are taken into account in the case of the biological metabolism of human beings.

7.4.4 Time I–O Table

The comments given to the extended monetary I–O table (Section 7.4.2) could be applied for the interpretation of the time I–O table (Table 7.5) to a great extent.

Table 7.5 Physical input–output table: Germany, 1990 (Million tonnes)

Row No.	Uses / Supply	Agriculture, forestry, fishing	Mining, water and energy supply	Manuf'ring	Construction	Market services
		1	2	3	4	5
	Product output by product group					
1	Products of agriculture, forestry, fishing	98.3	0.2	80.3	0.8	0.8
2	Products of mining, water and energy supply	64.5	2 084.7	1 343.9		109.9
3	Products of manufacturing	20.7	6.7	494.5	550.8	84.5
4	Construction work	-	-	-	0.0	28.5
5	Market services	4.7	-	47.8	20.7	1.8
6	Environmental protection services	-	0.4	-	-	6.0
7	Education services	-	-	-	-	0.1
8	Non-market services	-	-	-	-	0.5
9	Household production services	-	-	-	-	2.6
10	Household services related to employment	-	-	-	-	0.3
11	Household services related to education	-	-	-	-	0.1
12	Other household services	-	-	-	-	3.6
13	**Product and residual inputs, totals**	**188.2**	**2 091.9**	**1 966.5**	**589.7**	**238.7**
14	Labour inputs	-	-	-	-	-
15	Margin of labour and education	-	-	-	-	-
	Revenues on products					
16	Non-deductible value-added tax	-	-	-	-	-
17	Taxes less subsidies on products	-	-	-	-	-
	Consumption of fixed produced Assets					
18	Assets incl. consumer durables	-	1.9	15.1	21.0	0.0
19	Education (human) capital	-	-	-	-	-
	Withdrawal from the non-produced natural capital					
20	Throughput materials	-	31 428.0	5 346.1	113.2	-
21	Other materials	606.9	6 797.1	1 138.5	67.9	118.0
	Imports					
22	Goods	10.4	49.2	238.9	28.1	13.3
23	Services	-	-	0.0	0.0	0.0
24	**Primary inputs, totals**	**617.4**	**38 276.2**	**6 738.6**	**230.2**	**131.4**
25	**Gross output, balancing items**	**805.6**	**40 368.1**	**8 705.1**	**819.9**	**370.1**
	Supplementary information					
26	Product outputs	251.4	6 961.0	1 361.4	540.3	99.4
27	Residual outputs	554.2	33 407.2	7 343.7	279.6	270.7

Table 7.5 (continued)

Input of branches				Household services				
Env'mental protection services	Education services	Non-market services	Household production	Services related to employment	Services related to studying	Other services	Totals	Row No.
6	7	8	9	10	11	12	13	
27.3	0.0	0.1	8.5	0.1	0.0	4.8	221.3	1
111.4	51.2	310.5	741.5	66.7	35.7	2 099.0	7 036.3	2
1 180.2	0.5	14.2	32.7	4.5	0.7	34.6	2 424.5	3
21.7	0.0	6.0	-	-	-	-	56.3	4
112.1	0.0	0.1	0.5	0.0	0.0	5.7	193.5	5
4.7	-	-	-	-	-	-	11.1	6
49.1	-	-	-	-	-	-	49.1	7
298.6	-	-	-	-	0.0	0.2	299.3	8
652.2	-	-	-	-	-	35.5	690.3	9
59.8	-	-	-	-	-	-	60.1	10
32.0	-	-	-	-	-	-	32.0	11
1 897.0	-	-	-	-	-	-	1 900.6	12
4 446.0	51.8	330.9	783.2	71.4	36.4	2 179.8	12 974.5	13
-	-	-	-	-	-	-	-	14
-	-	-	-	-	-	-	-	15
-	-	-	-	-	-	-	-	16
-	-	-	-	-	-	-	-	17
-	0.0	0.0	1.1	0.5	0.1	2.5	42.2	18
-	-	-	-	-	-	-	-	19
3 500.0	-	-	-	-	-	-	40 387.3	20
9.8	14.8	89.7	62.3	6.9	3.4	208.2	9 123.5	21
0.2	0.3	2.4	18.5	4.0	0.6	17.0	383.0	22
-	0.0	0.0	0.3	0.0	0.0	3.8	4.1	23
3 510.0	15.1	92.1	82.2	11.3	4.0	231.6	49 940.1	24
7 956.0	66.9	423.0	865.3	82.7	40.5	2 411.3	62 914.5	25
0.4	-	16.8	35.5	-	-	-	9 266.1	26
7 955.6	66.9	406.3	829.8	82.7	40.5	2 411.3	53 648.4	27

Table 7.5 (continued)

Private cons'ption	Gov'ment cons'ption	Fixed assets	Consumer durables	Education capital	Disposal	Exports	Totals	Total uses	Row No.
		Fixed capital formation							
14	15	16	17	18	19	20	21	22	
-	-	47.1	-	-	526.9	10.2	**584.3**	**805.6**	1
-	-	- 0.3	-	-	33 305.6	26.5	**33 331.8**	**40 368.1**	2
-	-	13.9	4.4	-	6 106.4	155.9	**6 280.6**	**8 705.1**	3
-	-	534.2	-	-	229.4	0.0	**763.6**	**819.9**	4
-	-	- 0.3	-	-	163.8	13.2	**176.7**	**370.1**	5
-	-	-	-	-	7 942.8	2.1	**7 945.0**	**7 956.0**	6
-	-	-	-	-	17.7	-	**17.7**	**66.9**	7
-	-	16.6	-	-	107.1	-	**123.7**	**423.0**	8
-	-	-	-	-	173.2	1.8	**175.0**	**865.3**	9
-	-	-	-	-	22.5	0.1	**22.6**	**82.7**	10
-	-	-	-	-	8.4	0.0	**8.5**	**40.5**	11
-	-	-	-	-	507.9	2.8	**5 10.7**	**2 411.3**	12
-	-	**611.3**	**4.4**	-	**49 111.7**	**212.7**	**49 940.1**	**62 914.5**	13
-	-	-	-	-	-	-	-	-	14
-	-	-	-	-	-	-	-	-	15
-	-	-	-	-	-	-	-	-	16
-	-	-	-	-	-	-	-	-	17
-	-	- 40.8	- 4.1	-	2.7	-	**- 42.2**	-	18
-	-	-	-	-	-	-	-	-	19
-	-	-	-	-	-40387.3	-	**-40387.3**	-	20
-	-	-	-	-	- 9 123.5	-	**- 9 123.5**	-	21
-	-	7.4	2.7	-	-	- 393.1	**- 383.0**	-	22
-	-	-	-	-	-	- 4.1	**- 4.1**	-	23
-	-	- 33.4	- 1.4	-	-49508.1	- 397.2	**-49940.1**	-	24
-	-	**577.9**	**3.0**	-	**- 396.4**	**- 184.5**	-	**62 914.5**	25
									26
									27

Table 7.6 Time input–output table: Germany, 1990 (Billion hours)

Row No.	Uses / Supply	Agriculture, forestry, fishing	Mining, water and energy supply	Manuf'ring	Construction	Market services
		1	2	3	4	5
	Product output by product group					
1	Products of agriculture, forestry, fishing	0.44	0.00	2.50	0.00	0.27
2	Products of mining, water and energy supply	0.05	1.09	1.29	0.01	0.55
3	Products of manufacturing	0.50	0.40	17.97	2.20	3.39
4	Construction work	0.02	0.13	0.24	0.14	0.80
5	Market services	0.26	0.49	8.68	1.18	21.71
6	Environmental protection services	0.00	0.03	0.15	0.06	0.11
7	Education services	-	-	-	-	-
8	Non-market services	0.02	0.02	0.25	0.03	0.20
9	Household production services	-	-	-	-	-
10	Household services related to employment	0.13	0.24	4.41	1.01	5.71
11	Household services related to education	-	-	-	-	-
12	Other household services	-	-	-	-	-
13	**Product and residual inputs, totals**	**1.43**	**2.41**	**35.50**	**4.64**	**32.75**
14	Labour inputs	2.04	0.74	13.82	3.33	17.40
15	Margin of labour and education	-	-	-	-	-
	Revenues on products					
16	Non-deductible value- added tax	-	-	-	-	-
17	Taxes less subsidies on products	-	-	-	-	-
	Consumption of fixed produced assets					
18	Assets incl. consumer durables	0.38	0.65	2.31	0.17	5.24
19	Education (human) capital	0.20	0.08	1.52	0.35	2.10
	Withdrawal from the non-prod. natural capital					
20	Throughput materials	-	-	-	-	-
21	Other materials	-	-	-	-	-
	Imports					
22	Goods	0.22	0.33	7.12	0.41	0.90
23	Services	0.01	0.02	0.27	0.03	0.72
24	**Primary inputs, totals**	**2.84**	**1.83**	**25.05**	**4.29**	**26.36**
25	**Gross output, balancing items**	**4.27**	**4.24**	**60.55**	**8.93**	**59.11**

Table 7.6 (continued)

			Input of branches					
				Household services			Totals	Row No.
Env'mental protection services	Education services	Non-market services	Household production	Services related to employment	Services related to studying	Other services		
6	7	8	9	10	11	12	13	
-	0.00	0.06	0.35	0.00	0.00	0.18	**3.82**	1
+0.03	0.04	0.14	0.41	0.01	0.01	0.48	**4.12**	2
0.09	0.09	1.29	4.21	0.15	0.04	3.38	**33.71**	3
0.08	0.04	0.23	0.04	0.00	-	0.08	**1.83**	4
0.06	0.21	3.58	3.65	0.71	0.32	11.80	**52.65**	5
0.13	0.01	0.03	0.10	0.01	0.00	0.28	**0.90**	6
-	-	-	-	-	-	-	-	7
0.08	0.01	2.87	0.12	0.01	0.10	0.83	**4.54**	8
-	-	-	10.56	-	1.41	75.27	**87.24**	9
0.00	0.76	2.43	0.00	-	-	-	**14.69**	10
-	-	-	-	-	-	-	-	11
-	-	-	-	-	-	-	-	12
0.47	**1.16**	**10.62**	**19.43**	**0.90**	**1.87**	**92.30**	**203.49**	13
0.26	1.83	6.84	82.31	12.25	15.43	397.83	**554.10**	14
-	-	-	-	-	-	-	-	15
-	-	-	-	-	-	-	-	16
-	-	-	-	-	-	-	-	17
0.11	0.28	0.32	1.02	0.41	0.07	2.40	**13.36**	18
0.04	0.44	0.86	6.67	0.93	0.79	8.67	**22.65**	19
-	-	-	-	-	-	-	-	20
-	-	-	-	-	-	-	-	21
0.02	0.02	0.43	1.67	0.11	0.03	2.39	**13.64**	22
0.00	0.03	0.18	0.20	0.09	0.05	1.50	**3.10**	23
0.43	**2.59**	**8.63**	**91.87**	**13.79**	**16.38**	**412.79**	**606.85**	24
0.90	**3.75**	**19.25**	**111.30**	**14.69**	**18.25**	**505.09**	**810.34**	25

Table 7.6 (continued)

Private cons'ption	Gov'ment cons'ption	Fixed assets	Con-sumer durables	Education capital	Dis-posal	Exports	Totals	Total uses	Row No.
14	15	16	17	18	19	20	21	22	
-	-	0.12	-	-	-	0.33	0.45	4.27	1
-	-	- 0.03	-	-	-	0.15	0.11	4.24	2
-	-	5.86	2.43	-	-	18.56	26.84	60.55	3
-	-	7.02	-	-	-	0.09	7.10	8.93	4
-	-	0.99	1.61	-	-	3.86	6.46	59.11	5
-	-	-	-	-	-	-	-	0.90	6
-	-	-	-	3.75	-	-	3.75	3.75	7
0.84	13.76	0.04	-	-	-	0.07	14.72	19.25	8
24.06	-	-	-	-	-	-	24.06	111.30	9
-	-	-	-	-	-	-	-	14.69	10
-	-	-	-	18.25	-	-	18.25	18.25	11
505.09	-	-	-	-	-	-	505.09	505.09	12
530.00	**13.76**	**13.99**	**4.04**	**22.01**	-	**23.05**	**606.85**	**810.34**	13
- 554.10	-	-	-	-	-	-	- 554.10	-	14
-	-	-	-	-	-	-	-	-	15
-	-	-	-	-	-	-	-	-	16
-	-	-	-	-	-	-	-	-	17
-	-	- 9.45	- 3.91	-	-	-	- 13.36	-	18
-	-	-	-	- 22.65	-	-	- 22.65	-	19
-	-	-	-	-	-	-	-	-	20
-	-	-	-	-	-	-	-	-	21
-	-	2.06	1.03	-	-	- 16.73	- 13.64	-	22
-	-	0.00	0.01	-	-	- 3.11	- 3.10	-	23
- 554.10	-	**- 7.39**	**- 2.87**	**- 22.65**	-	**- 19.84**	**- 606.85**	-	24
- 24.10	**13.76**	**6.60**	**1.17**	**- 0.65**	-	**3.21**		**810.34**	25

All values of the monetary table have been transformed into time values by the labour inputs directly or indirectly necessary to produce the respective products.

The additional primary inputs of household services (except household production) (columns/rows 10 to 12) cause the only major difference between the time and the monetary I–O table. In the extended monetary tables, the direct inputs of time of these activities have not been valued. Thus, the output is compiled only as the sum of intermediate inputs and depreciation. In the time I–O table, the direct inputs of time of all household services are taken into account. These amount to more than half of the value of time of all outputs of the whole economy (425 billion hours in comparison to 810 billion hours).

In the case of services related to employment (column/row 10), the additional inputs of time are linked with the traditional branches of the economy. The time spent travelling to the workplace is now an additional intermediate input of the branches where the commuting persons are employed. These additional inputs are not counterbalanced, but are treated as part of the gross output of the traditional branches.

According to the extended concept of inputs of time, the hours spent by pupils and students for studying are now an important part of the outputs of the household services related to studying (column/row 11). In comparison to the outputs of education services (column 7), the household activities have now a substantially increased importance as part of the investment in education capital (see column 18: 18 billion hours in comparison to 4 billion hours of education services).

The other household services (column/row 12) have a higher value of gross output than all other activities shown in the time I–O table (505 billion hours in comparison to 305 billion hours). This output (e.g. social and leisure activities, physiological regeneration) can be interpreted as a final goal of all activities. The outputs are treated as private consumption (row 12, column 14) amounting to five-sixths of all final use.

7.5. OUTLOOK

This chapter has presented three different types of I–O tables, using differing units of presentation. For facilitating comparisons, the same concepts of production and capital have been applied. Furthermore, the same classifications of activities, primary inputs and final use have been used. The presentation sought to give good arguments for a combined use of these tables. Each type can show only specific aspects of economic activities, while all three types together can achieve a nearly comprehensive overview. For analysing the very general concept of sustainability, it seems to be urgently needed to describe human activities with their social, economic and ecological aspects by this magic triangle of I–O data.

Further research work is necessary to develop suitable I–O models using not only one type of table, but combining data for two or three types of I–O tables. Using monetary I–O tables and linking physical data with the results of monetary I–O analysis is a relatively simple case of linking the different types. Furthermore, it is possible to merge parts of the three types to produce new artificial tables which might be more useful for I–O analysis. Examples of such merging procedures are energy I–O tables with both physical and monetary data (Beutel and Stahmer, 1982). In more sophisticated econometric models, simultaneous use of different units of presentation could be introduced. Such models could define relationships between the elements of the different types of I–O tables (see, e.g., the Osnabrück model in Meyer et al. (1999)).

REFERENCES

Aslaksen, I., T. Fagerli and A.A. Gravningsmyhr (1995), 'Measuring household production in an input–output framework: the Norwegian experience', *Statistical Journal of the United Nations*, **12**, 111–31.

Ayres, R.U. and U.E. Simonis (eds) (1994), *Industrial Metabolism. Restructuring for Sustainable Development*, New York: United Nations.

Becker, G.S. (1964), *Human Capital*, Chicago: Chicago University Press.

Beutel, J. and C. Stahmer (1982), 'Input–Output-Analyse der Energieströme 1980', *Allgemeines Statistisches Archiv*, **3**, 309–39.

Blanke, K., M. Ehling and N. Schwarz (1996), 'Zeit im Blickfeld. Ergebnisse einer repräsentativen Zeitbudgeterhebung', *Schriftenreihe des Bundesministeriums für Familie, Senioren, Frauen und Jugend*, 121, Stuttgart: Verlag W. Kohlhammer.

Böhm-Bawerk, E.V. (1889/1891), *Kapital und Kapitalzins. Zweite Abteilung: Positive Theorie das Kapitals*, Innsbruck. Trans. W. Smart (1891), London: Macmillan.

de Boer, S., J. van Dalen and P.J.A. Konijn (1996), 'Input–output analysis of material flows: the Dutch experience', in Statistics Sweden (ed.), *Third Meeting of the London Group on Natural Resource and Environmental Accounting, Proceedings Volume*, Stockholm, May.

Diefenbacher, H. (1995), 'The Index of Sustainable Economic Welfare', *Fallstudie für die Bundesrepublik Deutschland*, Heidelberg: FEST.

Ewerhart, G. and C. Stahmer (1998), 'Zukunftsentwürfe statt Vergangenheitsbewältigung: Paradigmenwechsel in der umweltökonomischen Berichterstattung', in U.-P. Reich, C. Stahmer and K. Voy (eds), *Kategorien der Volkswirtschaftlichen Gesamtrechnungen, Zeit und Risiko*, Marburg: Metropolis-Verlag.

Ewerhart, G. and C. Stahmer (1999), 'Ökonomie, in Zeit aufgelöst', *3. Berliner Kolloquium zur Weiterentwicklung der Volkswirtschaftlichen Gesamtrechnungen*, Berlin: unpublished paper.

Faber, M. and J. Proops (1990), *Evolution, Time, Production and the Environment*, Heidelberg: Springer-Verlag.

Franz, A. (1998), 'SNA-Zeit, Non-SNA-Zeit, Zeit-SNA: Unzeitgemäße Überlegungen zu einer existentiellen Taxinomie', in U.-P. Reich, C. Stahmer and K. Voy (eds), *Kategorien der Volkswirtschaftlichen Gesamtrechnungen', Zeit und Risiko*, Marburg: Metropolis-Verlag.

Gravgard, O. (1998), 'Physical input–output tables for Denmark, 1990', *Statistics Denmark*, Copenhagen: Statistics Denmark.

Kuhn, M. (1996), *Umwelt-Input–Output-Tabelle für Deutschland, 1990*, Auftrag von Eurostat erstellt, Dok. Eco-Ind/97/3, Luxembourg: Eurostat.

Lancaster, K. (1966), 'A new approach to consumer theory', *Journal of Political Economy*, **74**, 132–57.

Lancaster, K. (1971), *Mathematical Economics*, London: Macmillan.

Meyer, B., A. Bockermann, G. Ewerhart and C. Lutz (1999), *Marktkonforme Umweltpolitik - Wirkungen auf Luftschadstoffemissionen, Wachstum und Struktur der Wirtschaft*, Heidelberg: Physica Verlag.

Miller, R.E. and P.D. Blair (1985), *Input–Output Analysis: Foundations and Extensions*, Englewood Cliffs: Prentice-Hall.

Nebbia, G. (1999), *Contabilità monetaria e contabilità ambientale*. Lictio doctoralis, Laurea honoris causa in Economia e Commercia, University di Bari.

NNW Measurement Committee (1973), *Measuring Net National Welfare of Japan*, Tokyo: Economic Council of Japan.

Nordhaus, W.D. and J. Tobin (1972), 'Is growth obsolete?', in *National Bureau of Economic Research, Economic Growth*, 50th Anniversary Colloquium, General Series No. 96, New York: National Bureau of Economic Research.

Proops, J. (1991) *National Accounting and the Environment*, Report to the World Bank, Keele University.

Radermacher, W. (1999), 'Green Stamp report on an EU research project', in European Commission (ed.), *Proceedings from a Workshop*, Luxembourg, 28–29, September 1998.

Radermacher, W. and C. Stahmer (1996), 'Abschied vom Wohlfahrtsmaß: Monetäre Bewertung in den Umweltökonomischen Gesamtrechnungen', in Statistisches Bundesamt (eds), *Wohlfahrtsmessung - Aufgabe der Statistik im gesellschaftlichen Wandel*, Band 29 der Schriftenreihe Forum der Bundesstatistik, Stuttgart: Statistisches Bundesamt.

Reich, U.-P. (1981), 'Moderne Deflationierungsmethoden und klassische Wertthorie', in U.-P. Reich and C. Stahmer (eds), *Input–Output-Rechnung: Energiemodelle und Methoden der Preisbereinigung*, Frankfurt: Campus Verlag.

Reich, U.-P. (1989), 'Essence and appearance: reflections on input–output methodology in terms of a classical paradigm', *Economic Systems Research*, **1** (4), 417–28.

Reich, U.-P. and C. Stahmer (1993), *Gesamtwirtschaftliche Wohlfahrtsmessung und Umweltqualität. Beiträge zur Weiterentwicklung der Volkswirtschaftlichen Gesamtrechnungen*, Frankfurt: Campus Verlag.

Schäfer, D. and N. Schwarz (1994), 'Wert der Haushaltsproduktion', *Wirtschaft und Statistik*, **8**, 597–612.

Schäfer, D. and C. Stahmer (1989), 'Input–Output model for the analysis of environmental protection activities', *Economic Systems Research*, **1** (2), 203-28.

Stahmer, C. (1995), 'Satellitensystem für Aktivitäten der privaten Haushalte', in B. Seel and C. Stahmer (eds), *Haushaltsproduktion und Umweltbelastung. Ansätze einer Ökobilanzierung für den privaten Haushalt*, Frankfurt am Main: Campus Verlag.

Stahmer, C., M. Kuhn and N. Braun (1997), *Physische Input–Output-Tabellen, Beiträge zu den Umweltökonomischen Gesamtrechnungen*, Band 1, Stuttgart: Metzler-Poesch Verlag.

Stahmer, C., M. Kuhn and N. Braun (1998), *Physical Input–Output Tables for Germany 1990*, Eurostat Working Papers 2/1998/b/1, Luxemburg: Eurostat.

Statistisches Bundesamt (1994), *Fachserie 18 Volkswirtschaftliche Gesamtrechnungen, Reihe 2 Input–Output-Tabellen 1986, 1988, 1990*, Wiesbaden: Statistisches Bundesamt.

Strassert, G. (1993), 'Towards an ecological-economic accounting of the provision-transformation-restitution cycle, in *Entropy and Bioeconomics*, Proceedings of the First International Conference of the E.A.B.S., Rome: Nogard Publisher.

Strassert, G. (1998), 'The German throughput economy: lessons from the first Physical Input–Output Table (PIOT) for Germany', *International Joint Conference of the E.A.B.S.*, Palma de Mallorca, Spain: unpublished paper.

United Nations (1993), *Integrated Environmental and Economic Accounting, Handbook of National Accounting, Studies in Methods*, Series F, No. 61, New York: United Nations.

Uno, K. (1995), *Environmental Options: Accounting for Sustainability*, Dordrecht: Kluwer.

van Dieren, W. (ed.) (1995), *Mit der Natur rechnen. Der neue Club-of-Rome-Bericht: Vom Bruttosozialprodukt zum Ökosozialprodukt*, Basel: Birhäuser Verlag.

von Neumann, J. (1945), 'A model of general economic equilibrium', *Review of Economic Studies*, **13**, 1–9.

8. Alternative Green Accounting Methodologies

Fulai Sheng and Sandrine Simon

8.1 INTRODUCTION

In this chapter we shall discuss some of the numerous methodologies that have been adopted, and are still being formulated, in research on green accounting. The variety of these approaches reflects the wide range of understandings and interpretations of green accounting; that methodologies are still being developed illustrates the constant evolution in this area. We note that the disparities, sometimes incompatibilities, between approaches are being reduced, and that some complementarity between certain approaches is possible.

Numerous categorisations of green accounting methodologies have been adopted, themselves representative of a certain understanding of the rationale for environmental accounting (Sheng, 1995).

In this chapter, we shall focus first on the original distinction between 'satellite accounts' and 'aggregate economic indicators'. This will then lead us to a discussion of green accounts expressed in physical units and those expressed in monetary units. We then present the construction of accounting 'frameworks' as a consequence of the debates on 'indicators of sustainability' and 'environmental indicators', and of their importance in environmental policy making. Finally, we mention some new developments that relate 'green accounting' to modelling and simulation exercises, as well as the revival of input–output analysis in accounting construction and implementation.

The discussion presented in this chapter on these various methodologies aims at raising questions concerning:

- The (practical or conceptual) motives driving the formulation of a certain green accounting methodology.
- The trends in research in green accounting.

- The pros and cons of having a range of environmental accounting approaches, as opposed to a single, universal approach.

8.2 AGGREGATE INDICATORS AND SATELLITE ACCOUNTS

When research on 'green accounting' started, a little more than 25 years ago, the main rationale was to correct the shortcomings that had been identified in the System of National Accounts (SNA). The aim of reforming the already existing accounting tool resulted in the adoption of various approaches that differed in their 'radicalism'; i.e. how far we needed to go in order to correct these shortcomings and reform the SNA.

The first difference in green accounting approaches was observed between:

- those who felt that correcting the shortcomings of the SNA required the adding of what was missing, and the subtracting of what was not supposed to appear in the national accounts, in the calculation of GDP, in order to construct a green adjusted GDP, and

- those who identified shortcomings in the SNA, not only with regard to the non-inclusion of environmental considerations, but also in relation to how the interrelations between the environment and our economic activities were represented in the structure of the accounts.

This fundamental distinction resulted in the construction of two very different sets of 'accounting tools'. It can also be interpreted as a more fundamental disagreement concerning the way in which we should analyse our relationship to, and dependency upon, the environment and, consequently, the way in which we should conduct economic analysis and policy making. It is mainly these differing views on the economic paradigm that allow us to distinguish environmental economics from ecological economics.

8.2.1 Reformed SNA as a Provider of a Single Aggregate Green Indicator

The 'green GDP' approach stipulates that there is nothing wrong with the way in which economic functioning is being envisaged, carried out and also illustrated in our national accounts.[1] However, it stresses that economic results would be considerably improved if environmental considerations were better represented and taken into account within the SNA. Thus, this school of thought suggests that the depletion of natural capital (DNC) should be calculated and subtracted from GDP, in the same way as the depreciation of human-made capital. Similarly, residual pollution and defensive expenditures (necessary to defend ourselves from the unwanted side effects of our aggregate production and consumption) should be taken out of the GDP measure in order to further correct this indicator (Leipert, 1989). This approach therefore introduced the idea that the environment can, and should, be treated as (natural) capital, since it contributes (greatly) to economic production and welfare. Since we are interested in its overall maintenance, as we are interested in the maintenance of human-made capital, we should keep track of its depreciation and signal it to policy makers by integrating it in the economic signals they use, primarily GDP

This approach was originally developed and promoted by Pearce et al. (1989), who defined 'sustainable income' as measured income, *minus* households' defensive expenditures, *minus* the depreciation of human-made capital, *minus* the depreciation of environmental capital. He also suggested the definition of 'current welfare' in society as the measured consumption, *minus* the households' defensive expenditures, *minus* the monetary value of residual pollution damage.

In his adjustment of GDP, Daly (1990, p. 8). based his calculation of a corrected aggregate on the Net National Product since:

> . . . the production of NNP requires supporting activities that are not biophysically sustainable, and the measurement of NNP overestimates the maximum net product available for consumption.

Daly's 'Sustainable Social Net National Product' (SSNNP) was therefore calculated as NNP, *minus* Defensive Expenditures, *minus* Depreciation of Natural Capital.

Peskin (1990) calculated a 'Consolidated National Income' by adding to GNP a measure of environmental services, and subtracting from it a measure of environmental damage.

Numerous other methods could be quoted that all focus on the construction on aggregate adjusted indicator. Bartlemus et al. (1993) developed a Sustainable Net National Expenditure and an 'environmentally adjusted NDP'; Hueting et al. (1995) based their calculation of a 'Sustainable Income' on the subtraction from GNP of the costs to meet sustainability standards; etc.). This aggregate measure is either regarded as a measure of sustainable development, a better measure of welfare, or a proper measure of value added in the economy.

These methods are now regarded as dated, because of the development of criticisms concerning the construction of a single aggregate. The above approach is known as 'monetarisation'.[2] i.e. the 'measurement' of environmental depreciation and services are carried out in monetary terms, in order to be commensurable with units used to calculate GDP. The problems identified by those who are not in favour of the use of this approach to develop a green GDP also relate to its aggregate character (Aaheim and Nyborg, 1993; Faucheux et al., 1994; Hammond et al., 1995). Focusing on an aggregate stops us from observing the dynamic interrelations between ecosystems and economic functioning in detail, which is what is needed if our policies are to be more respectful of the natural life-support system upon which our activities and welfare depend. Other critical debates have focused on the fact that it is impossible to encapsulate the dynamic and broad concept of sustainability in a single measure. Consequently, the interpretation of green GDP as a measure of sustainable income, or even as a measure of sustainability in general, is highly dubious. Neumayer (1998) expressed the view that sustainability cannot be measured, and used this argument to suggest that calculating a green GNP measure is not a relevant exercise. Viederman (1994) insisted that it is the systemic dimension of sustainability which makes it impossible to reduce it to a meaningful 'figure'. We will discuss later, however, how several research exercises have reached conclusions concerning how to represent sustainability, notably in accounting frameworks, rather than as single measures. Rennings and Wiggering (1997) argued that a representation of sustainability needs to take account, simultaneously, of its economic, social and ecological dimensions. They suggested that measures of green GNP do not adopt this holistic view because, by definition, the calculation uses the market sphere as the context in which environmental assets are being valued. Many environmental and social considerations are therefore ignored and excluded from the aggregate (semi-) 'adjusted' indicator. Finally, Brouwer et al. (1997) have reviewed the numerous methodological problems in the calculation of environmentally adjusted national income figures and give special attention to four considerations: scientific adequacy, social adequacy, economic rationality, and statistical adequacy.

8.2.2 Satellite Accounts

The recognition of the SNA's shortcomings stimulated the exploration of 'natural environment functions', and how we not only interact with these but also impact upon them through our various economic activities, be they based on the exploitation of resources or source of pollution. These studies suggested that the way to 'reform' the SNA was, first of all, to represent what happens within the environment in a separate 'satellite' accounting framework. This is then linked to the SNA, in order to identify the interactions and impacts between economic activities and ecosystem functioning.

The creation of satellite accounts acknowledged the fact that economic analysis[3] had ignored environmental considerations, and had not properly considered the economic sphere as being a sub-system of the environment upon which we depend. This opening of the economic discipline to environmental science accompanied important conceptual shifts, such as those initiating the development of 'ecological economics'.

Perhaps the best known examples of satellite accounts are the French Patrimony accounts and the Material Flow accounts in Norway.

8.2.2.1 The French Patrimony Accounts
In 1978 the French government established the Interministerial Committee on Natural Resource Accounts (Commission Interministerielle Des Comptes Du Patrimoine Naturel) and decided to design a Natural Patrimony Account (NPA, Les Comptes du Patrimoine Naturel) within its overall environmental information framework 'to assess both quantitatively and qualitatively the state and the development of the natural patrimony, as well as the causes and effects of its evolution' (Theys, 1990, p. 42). Natural patrimony includes 'all that can be quantitatively or qualitatively changed by human activity'.

The NPAs describe the natural environment in terms of its three basic functions: economic, ecological and social. They are based on a system of stock and flow accounts, the latter describing the flows which allow one to understand how initial stocks have been transformed into the final stock. The Patrimony Accounts are intended to support both environmental and economic models. To serve this role, they are divided into different sub-accounts (Costantino, 1996), which can be related to each other. The 'accounts of elements' describe how the stock of individual resources evolve and by what factor (natural and or human) it is affected. The 'ecozone accounts' describe the functioning of ecosystems and the pressure which affects their homeostasis (equilibrium). These two sets of accounts are expressed in physical units. The 'agents accounts' establish the link between the ecozone accounts and the accounts of elements and the SNA by listing the impacts of economic actions on the natural patrimony. The NPA originally included accounts of inland water management, waste disposal and recovery, protected natural areas, protection of marine waters and hunting. An INSEE (1986) publication provided some further NPAs on flora and fauna, forests and inland waters.

Although monetary units can be applied, the French framework focuses on physical units. As Theys (1990) noted, the success of patrimony accounts depends on the quality of their connection with the SNA, which has the tremendous advantage of having a homogenous and consistent framework and of being re-appraised annually in most countries.

A comprehensive and visionary framework as it is, the NPA's complexity and limited budgetary resources (merely US$100,000 of original funding) have prevented the system from being fully implemented and from having much policy impact. In 1991, the newly established French Institute of the Environment under the Ministry of the Environment initiated a programme to continue the work on the NPA. Being prepared are new accounts for water quantity and quality, ecozone accounts concerning land use and land cover, and satellite accounts of environmental expenditures. The French Statistical Office (INSEE) has been involved in these efforts at a conceptual level.

8.2.2.2 The Norwegian Natural Resource Accounting system (NRA)

Norway has the longest history of physical environmental accounting. The Central Bureau of Statistics (CBS, subordinate to the Ministry of Finance) compiled accounts for forests in 1970 and accounts for fish in 1974. In 1974, the Ministry of Environment initiated a programme in response to a request from the Parliament for the establishment of Norwegian Resource Accounting System (NRA) (Lone et al., 1993). The primary focus was on resource budgeting, reflecting the prevailing concern about oil price shocks and the possible exhaustion of depletable resources. The Ministry prepared a preliminary conceptual report in that year, and proceeded to compile pilot accounts for energy, land use, and fish resources.

In 1978, the CBS formally assumed the responsibility for the NRA in cooperation with the Ministry of Finance and the Ministry of Environment. Accounts have been compiled and published for petroleum, minerals, and hydropower, land use, selected air and water pollutants. These natural resources or environmental aspects were considered as strategically important. These accounts are inputs into medium and long-term economic models and 'are viewed as a tool to help policy makers better manage the natural environment' (Peskin and Lutz, 1993, p. 167). Initial results were reported in 1980.

The CBS has published an annual report on the changes and status of natural resources and environment, which contain 'Resource Accounts and Analysis' (Central Bureau of Statistics of Norway, 1993). More attention is now being paid to air pollution and energy, largely reflecting the current emphasis on environmental degradation, in comparison with fisheries, minerals, and forests. The land use account is no longer compiled, due to the limited use of the account. These changes in priority sectors reflect the user-driven, issue-oriented approach of the CBS.

In preparing an environment-adjusted domestic product as an aid to an integration of economic and environmental policies, the persons preparing the statistics have to make a long series of subjective assessments of values. This implies that the statistics may contain a number of political evaluations, which will not necessarily be obvious to those who are to use the data. Thus it is possible that conditions which require a balance of different considerations may become obscure. On the basis of the above considerations, CBS has chosen not to recommend the preparation of an environment-adjusted domestic product (Aaheim and Nyborg, 1993; Alfsen, 1994).

8.2.2.3 Other countries' experience in satellite accounting

A few countries have decided to develop satellite accounts on the basis that they both provide useful information on 'strategic natural resources' and assist policy makers in taking account of environmental consideration, even though a complete integrated reform of the structure of the SNA has not taken place.

Thus, the UK Office for National Statistics has developed satellite accounts for resources such as oil and gas, atmospheric emissions of greenhouse gases, forests and water (Vaze, 1996; Vaze, 1999; see also Chapter 10). Satellite accounts have also been developed in Canada (physical accounts of sub-soil assets and forest accounts (Born, 1998; Anielski, 1992)). In Germany the Federal Statistical Office started working on Natural Resource Accounts at the beginning of the 1990s and seemed to support a satellite approach with a prime interest in wastes issues and CO_2 emissions (Radermacher and Stahmer, 1998).

It is noticeable that, in many cases where satellite accounts were developed, research has evolved and now links satellite accounting to other output from research in green accounting (modelling, input–output analysis, etc.), which will be discussed later in this chapter (and is addressed in Chapters 6 and 7).

8.3 ENVIRONMENTAL RESOURCE ACCOUNTING EXPRESSED IN PHYSICAL AND MONETARY UNITS

Research in 'green accounting' soon established a fundamental distinction between satellite accounts and aggregate adjusted indicators. This distinction was not only seen as based on different interpretations concerning the ways in which to reform the SNA. It was also related to 'policy language' and issues of commensurability. For some time, the defence of exercises focused on the adjustment of economic aggregates was based on the fact that policy makers' language is based on 'money': they would take environmental considerations into account only if these were introduced in the policy debates in the same way as other issues;[4] i.e. through indicators and measures expressed in monetary units.

This led to controversy and debate on the issue of 'environmental valuation'. It became clear that the issue of green accounting was very closely related to that of valuation, and of how to communicate the fact that a society puts value on its natural environment to the policy makers in charge of its management. The adjusted aggregates, expressed in monetary terms, were portrayed as 'understandable' for policy makers, while satellite accounts, expressed in physical terms and based on biological information, seemed too complex and 'incompatible', although linked to the SNA.

Research in green accounting became progressively bifurcated between the physical and monetary approaches, rather than the satellite accounts versus aggregate indicators approaches, as indicated by the following sections.

8.3.1 Physical Accounting

The UNSD's handbook on SEEA describes two prototypes of the physical environmental accounting approach (henceforth 'physical approach'). One is called 'material/energy balances' (MEB), which describes 'the material input of an economy delivered by the natural environment, the transformation and use of that input in economic processes (extraction, conversion, manufacturing, consumption) and its return to the natural environment as residuals (wastes and so on)' (United Nations, 1993, p. 67). As Bartelmus (1990, pp. 80-1) noted, MEB seeks to trace the extraction and transformation of materials and energy from natural resources through various successive stages of processing, to final use, and thence back to the environment as waste or, alternatively, to secondary use.

Compatibility with the SNA is achieved by using its standard categories (domestic output and consumption, imports and exports and its classification of economic activities). Contrary to the concepts of monetary accounting, physical stocks and flows and materials/energy transformation processes are presented in such balances. Transformation processes *within* the environment are not included. Bartelmus stressed that, in focusing on processes of resources flows through the economic system, the MEB can also be considered as a physical extension of the input–output tables of national accounting.

Material and energy flow analysis is, for instance, being carried out in Germany. Radermacher and Stahmer (1998) noted that the German Environmental-Economic Accounting (GEEA) approach has selected MEB as an appropriate way of approaching the interrelationship between the environment and the economy at a macroscopic level, amongst the broad spectrum of existing methods including material balance sheets, eco-balance sheets and product line analysis. The authors provided a material flow account for Germany in the years 1960 and 1990. The left-hand side of the matrix describes the material withdrawn by the economy from nature and the rest of the world, and the right-hand side describes the material discharged by the economy into nature and the rest of the world. The balancing item comprises materials remaining in the economy and statistical differences. This approach requires the quantities of unused raw material withdrawals (overburden, slag, etc.) to be counted as well. Bringezu et al. (1998) also commented on the fact that the Wuppertal Institute has contributed to the development of an overall material flow account and that one major objective of this exercise was the indication of progress or regress with respect to environmental sustainability. They have presented this approach as being in complete agreement with, and contributing significantly to, the international programmes on integrated environmental and economic accounting (United Nations, 1993).

Another prototype of the physical approach is called 'natural resource accounting', which describes stocks and stock changes of natural assets, which comprise biological assets (produced or wild), sub-soil assets (proven reserves), water, air, and land areas (including water areas) within their terrestrial and aquatic ecosystems (ecozones). It includes changes that take place within the environment. This physical accounting approach encompasses the various types of satellite accounts described in the previous section.

The physical approach is valid in its own right. It aims to provide environmental information in physical units and at different geographical locations and levels. Such information is indispensable for environmental management. To devise technical solutions to the problem of water pollution, for example, we must first know where the pollution occurs, what the pollutants are, how much water is polluted and by whom, etc. This approach does not have to be linked with monetary valuation or SNA in order to prove its usefulness. But if it were linked to the SNA, the physical approach would provide useful input for annualising the impact of various economic policies and activities on the environment and natural resource base (Commission for Environmental Accounting, 1991).

8.3.2 Monetary Green Accounting

The monetary environmental accounting approach (henceforth 'monetary approach') in essence belongs to an economic accounting system. It estimates the monetary costs and benefits of environmental changes related to economic activities. Its purpose is to provide a better basis for making economic decisions that involve financial outlays, on the one hand, and affect the environment on the other. It has been used, on an experimental basis, for devising economic instruments such as pollution charges for the conservation of nature and natural resources. Economic decision, rather than technical solution, is the main objective of this approach.

The monetary approach usually has greater attention from policy makers (Bartelmus, 1994). This is because decisions to deal with environmental problems often have to involve the associated monetary benefits and costs.

Although benefits and costs cannot, and should not, all be presented in monetary terms only, a decision to improve the environment does imply measures that involve financial outlays which often, in practice, have to be justified by the prospective benefits or by potential environmental costs to be avoided. However, excessive reliance on monetary analysis is not justified. But in view of the serious flaws in conventional monetary analysis, and the prevailing obsession with this type of analysis, an immediate effort should be made at least to reduce the distortions in the existing system while increasing the weight of other information systems in the decision making process.

Much effort has been put into improving the way in which monetarisation is being carried out in environmental policy making and more specifically in green accounting exercises (Radermacher et al., 1997; Federal Statistical Office of Germany and Statistics Netherlands, 1996; Jackson, 1991). Thus, a growing literature on abatement, avoidance, prevention and restoration costs, as well as work on cost-efficient measures, present some alternative ways of putting monetary figures on issues related to the environment. These alternative approaches seek to help the policy making process and shift the attribution of monetary measurements to the cost of economic activities, rather than to 'environmental values' *per se*. This research has also been related to research in green accounting.

8.3.3 Physical Versus Monetary Approaches

The physical and monetary approaches have overlapping, but different, scopes. Although both take the environment as the object for their respective accounting, the physical approach has a broader coverage than the monetary. For one thing, the monetary approach cannot encompass all of the environmental aspects described through the physical approach, particularly those that are within the environment and have no direct and immediate interactions with the economy. Bartelmus et al. (1993) noted that physical resource accounts cover the total stock or reserves of natural resources and the changes therein, even if these resources are not (yet) affected by the economic system. But this is not necessarily a shortcoming of the monetary approach. We cannot monetarise everything. As for those environmental aspects that are covered by both approaches, the monetary approach depends on the physical approach; the latter provides the prerequisite information to enable the monetarisation process to take place. In order to assess the monetary costs of deforestation, for example, we must first know how many trees have been cut in a given period, at a given location. The physical approach is, therefore, the first step for the monetary approach. But this does not mean that the physical approach exists just for the purpose of the monetary approach. As mentioned above, the physical approach is much broader and serves a different purpose.

Both the physical and monetary approaches are important for decision making. Thus, Born (1998) argued that Canada needs both physical and monetary accounts to measure its natural wealth and numerous authors have suggested that the two approaches, considered and used in specific ways, can be complementary. There is an argument that the physical approach does not provide aggregated information due to its use of different physical units. But aggregation can be deceptive as it may conceal vitally important, locally specific yet disaggregated, information. Further, non-monetary measures used in some green accounting procedures have been shown to be useful in policy making (Faucheux, 1994). The monetary approach is useful because it provides an economic rationale for environmental actions. But over-reliance on the monetary approach can mislead environmental efforts, because this approach typically fails to capture non-monetary factors, such as the human pressure on ecosystems (Common et al., 1993).

The environmental valuation methods, mentioned at the beginning of this section, have moved from being closely and directly related to the green accounting debate, to having an agenda and message in themselves. Numerous alternative valuation methods are now being developed and present some very radical views on who should value the environment and, by extension, who should take part in the policy making process (Foster, 1997; Bartelmus and Parikh, 1998; Hamilton and Ward, 1998). These new positions[5] hence embrace an ecological institutional approach and question not only the policy making process, but also the policy tools currently used in policy making. It therefore seems reasonable that they carry on being linked to research in green accounting. That this is currently not the case clearly highlights the difficulty in shifting research in green accounting, from an exercise that is perceived as technical to one that is mainly political and institutional.

In the making of economy-wide policy, both physical and monetary approaches should be considered. Neither should be promoted to the exclusion of the other.

The next section shows how, in view of what has been said so far, research in green accounting has moved a step further towards new approaches that we describe here under the term of 'accounting frameworks'.

8.4 ACCOUNTING FRAMEWORKS

The development of green accounts in the form of a *framework* is not new. One can immediately refer to at least two famous examples that used such an approach. One is the Social Accounting Framework developed by Bulmer-Thomas (1982) and implemented in Less Developed Countries. The second is

the Framework for the Development of Environmental Statistics, constructed
by the United Nations Statistical Office (United Nations, 1984).

In both cases, the methodologies developed acknowledged that constructing environmental accounts requires a great deal of information, which is
itself of different types. If green accounts are to be useful in policy making,
and related to the complex concept of sustainability, they have to cover the
numerous dimensions of the concept. The construction of the accounts
therefore involves the use of environmental information in the form of
indicators of various types, and these need to be integrated in a consistent
framework in order to be meaningful.

The relevance of an accounting *framework* can related to the interest
currently shown in 'indicators of sustainability' and 'environmental indicators'. The development of indicators *per se* has been perceived as a first step
towards the operationalisation of the complex concept of sustainability.
However, it has become progressively clear that these indicators need to be
related to each other, and need to illustrate the interrelationships between
economic activities and ecosystem functioning. Only then can they represent
sustainability, or give a useful message to policy makers concerning progress
towards sustainability. The indicators therefore need to be integrated into a
framework.

The following examples illustrate a range of research in green accounting
which support the construction of such 'accounting frameworks'.

8.4.1 The SEEA

In 1993 the UN handbook on the SEEA was launched in New York. It is a
UN satellite system linked to the SNA. It uses the same asset boundary as the
SNA, and expands asset classification within that boundary. In addition to
valuing produced natural assets, it also covers near-market and non-market
non-produced natural assets using non-market prices (Lutz, 1993). The SEEA
therefore integrates the environment and natural resources into the key
concepts and accounts of the SNA and leads to adjustment of GDP and
national income. It does not attempt to replace the existing SNA *per se*,
hence the use of the term 'satellite system'. However, it is not a satellite
system purely expressed in physical terms and, instead, seeks to offer a
compromise between satellite versus aggregate indicators, and also between
physical versus monetary accounts.

The SEEA uses both the physical and monetary approaches and synthe-
sises various valuation methodologies into a flexible framework that integrates sets of environmental data with the information existing in national
accounts while maintaining SNA concepts and principles. It provides a menu
of alternative versions, which are built upon each other within the frame-

work, but can also be used separately at different levels of sophistication. This building-block approach allows SEEA users to choose among different approaches according to their priorities and statistical capacities (Bartlemus, 1994). Apart from a collection of approaches and methodologies, the SEEA provides useful guidelines for environmental data classification, accounting standards, and linkages with the SNA. There are five major objectives of the SEEA, quoted in Bartelmus (1994):

- Segregation and elaboration of all environmentally related flows and stocks of traditional accounts: this segregation allows the estimation of environmental protection expenditures. Those expenditures have been considered part of the costs necessary to compensate for the negative impacts of economic growth, in other words, defensive expenditures.
- Linkage of physical accounts with monetary environmental accounts and balance sheets: physical resource accounts comprehensively cover the total stock or reserves of natural resources and changes therein, even if those resources are not (yet) affected by the economic system. Natural resource accounts thus provide the physical counterpart of the SEEA's monetary asset and flow accounts. They were pioneered by Norway and further developed by France in its natural patrimony accounts.
- Assessment of environmental costs and benefits: the SEEA expands and complements the SNA with regard to costing the use (depletion) of natural resources in production and final demand, and the changes in environmental quality resulting from pollution and other impacts of production, consumption, and natural events on the one hand, and environmental protection and enhancement on the other.
- Accounting for the maintenance of tangible wealth: the SEEA extends the concept of capital to cover not only human-made but also natural capital. Natural capital includes scarce renewable resources such as marine resources or tropical forests, non-renewable resources of land, soil and subsoil assets (mainly deposits), and cyclical resources of air and water. Capital formation is correspondingly changed into a broader concept of capital formation.
- Elaboration and measurement of indicators of environmentally adjusted product and income: the consideration of the costs of depletion of natural resources and changes in environmental quality allows the calculation of modified macroeconomic aggregates in different SEEA version. It includes, in particular, the compilation of an Environmentally adjusted net Domestic Product.

The basic flaws in the SNA that the SEEA tries to address are the omission of costs from depleting and degrading non-produced natural assets, and the consequently inaccurate presentation of benefits due to misattribution of environmentally defensive expenditures. Looking from another angle, the SEEA is addressing the depletion and degradation of non-produced natural assets. The cost of both depletion and degradation is deducted from the conventional NDP, to arrive at an environmentally adjusted net domestic product, often abbreviated as EDP.

The SEEA framework suggests two major methodologies for estimating the monetary values of depletion of marketable resources: the user-cost method and the net price method.[6] The user-cost is calculated in such a way that, if it is invested year after year, it would generate a perpetual stream of income that, together with the true income from any remaining resource, would provide the same level of true income both during the life of the resource and after the resource has been exhausted. In the net-price method (net-rent method, or depreciation method), the consumption of natural capital, both quantitatively and qualitatively, is treated the same as the depreciation of human-made (or produced) capital. As a resource is extracted, the capacity of the remaining stock of the resource to generate future income is weakened. For environmental degradation or depletion of non-marketed resources, the maintenance cost method (avoidance cost method or replacement cost method) is used. This is to value the costs that would have been necessary to keep the natural capital intact during the accounting period. The maintenance cost method can be applied where market or near-market prices do not exist for depleted resources.[7]

At present the SEEA represents the only green accounting framework that carries an international authority. It is based on research, experiments, case studies, and discussions over the last two decades. It is, of necessity, a compromise among various valuation methodologies, given the divergent technical ways of handling such a complex matter as the estimation of environmental values. But at least, the SEEA has confirmed an international consensus that the conventional SNA is flawed and that environmental value must be incorporated into the SNA. The SEEA could well serve as a starting point for governments and international organisations to be involved in this work. In 1999 UNSD released (at www.un.org/unsd/enviro/) an operational manual on the SEEA. It has incorporated developments of concepts and methods of green accounting since the publication of the 1993 handbook on the SEEA and provides hands-on guidance for the implementation of the SEEA. The manual is accompanied by a user-friendly software package, consisting of a sequence of worksheets through a set of automatic formulae.

8.4.2 The European Environmental Pressure Indices Project

At the European level, a European System of Environmental Pressure Indices

(ESEPI) and a European System of Integration of Economic and Environmental Indices (ESI) have been developed by the Commission of the European Communities (1996). The former requires the formulation of relevant indicators by a Scientific Advisory Group and these indicators are then compiled into a coherent framework. The latter focuses on themes that are policy relevant and therefore requires the collection and development of indicators that are directly related to these issues.

The construction of these frameworks started with an assessment of the ongoing projects at national and international levels, such as the Pressure-State-Response indicator model promoted by the OECD's State of the Environment group, or the above-discussed UN SEEA handbook. Interestingly, the participants to the formulation of the framework realised that they could not reach a consensus on a common monetary valuation procedure that would lead them to the construction of a green GDP. As a consequence, the group opted for the adoption of a satellite accounting approach, alongside the national accounts and closely linked to them, some in physical and some in monetary units. It also agreed on the utility of calculating physical indicators and indices related to the pressures of human and economic activities on the environment. Eurostat was in charge of the project and the research developments were supported politically and financially by the Commission.

The work carried out by Eurostat illustrates very well the framework dimension and the relevance of this research in green accounting. The 1996 publication from the Commission explains in detail the procedure concerning the difficulty in classifying the indicators and organising the information in a framework that would be meaningful and helpful for environmental policy makers. Numerous types of classification of such indicators exist (by environmental media, by source of problems, by type of political instruments, by reversibility, etc.) and Eurostat opted for a classification that would respect the list of ten policy fields related to the themes of the Fifth Environmental Action Plan Programme.[8]

Although this approach did not favour the calculation of an aggregate indicator, it is clear that some 'headline' indicators had to be selected in order to represent the theme under which a variety of more detailed indicators were used. The 60 environmental pressure indicators will be aggregated into 10 indices, one for each policy field. The importance was stressed of linking the indicators, to each other, in order to represent better sustainability as a whole, and also to indicators such as GDP.

This framework is to be used at regional and local levels for specific needs (at the city level for instance) and, at a micro level, the pressure indices are related to issues such as eco-efficiency.

Other European research projects, such as ExternE[9] (Externalities of Energy cycles) and GARP[10] (Green Accounting Research Project), that both contribute to the calculation of damage costs, as well as the GreenStamp project, which focuses on avoidance costs, can be related to the framework of pressure indices.

8.4.3 The SERIEE[11]

Eurostat (1994) has carried out useful work on accounting of environmental expenditures. A well-developed scheme is the European System for the Collection of Economic Information on the Environment known as the SERIEE framework, which collects information on actual expenditures made by industries, households, and governments for environmental protection. SERIEE consists of an Environmental Protection Expenditure Account (EPEA) which is consistent with the satellite approach described in the 1993 SNA. The list of classification for SERIEE was developed jointly by Eurostat and UNECE.

On the question of environmental accounting, Eurostat believed that at least in the short run a green GDP will not be adequate to indicate what would be an optimal policy for the benefit of the environment and what would be the cost of such a policy. Eurostat sees these two questions as being at the heart of any environmental policy. It therefore suggested a dual approach: an extension of GDP to focus on the costs of environmental policy (through accounting of environmental expenditures), and the development of indicators and indices to focus on the benefits.

The SERIEE developed by Eurostat is seen as a module of a satellite system, which extends the SNA. It provides information on environmental expenditures, a reflection of the cost of environmental policy. To assess the benefit of environmental policy, the use was suggested of a system of environmental indicators and indices based on the PSR (pressure-state-response) model to give aggregate information about the reduction of total environmental pressure as a result of environmental policy. Various environmental pressures are suggested to be weighted by willingness to pay (WTP), expert assessments, and compliance with EC's policy goals.

Eurostat suggests two priorities for action. One is the improvement of basic data, which are needed for both the satellite approach and the index approach. Another is research on valuation methods, focusing on market valuation for the satellite approach, and internalised valuation for the index approach. Co-operation with EEA is stressed because the valuation of environmental damages requires the information on the state of the environment, for which EEA is supposed to monitor and collect data. Support from natural science is also seen as important for understanding the dose-response relationships.

8.4.4 The NAMEA[12] and the SAMEA[13]

The NAMEA approach was presented for the first time in 1991, following the conceptual design by Keuning (De Haan et al., 1993; also see Chapter 5). The original design contained a complete system of national flow accounts, including a full set of income distribution and use accounts, accumulation accounts and changes in balance sheet accounts. Not only emissions of pollutants and extraction of natural resources are represented, but also their effects.

The present NAMEA has largely maintained the same format. It is represented as a conventional national accounting matrix that is extended by three accounts on the environment: a substances account (account 11), an account for global environmental themes (account 12) and an account for national environmental themes (account 13). These accounts present information on the environment in physical units. The environmental themes are consistent with that determined by the National Environment Policy Plan. Global environmental themes include the greenhouse effect and the ozone layer depletion, while national environmental themes cover acidification, eutrophication, wastes and loss of natural resources. A number of environmental themes will be expended when new information becomes available (e.g. on dispersion of toxic substances, or noise nuisance).

As Keuning and De Haan (1998, p. 144) note, for each of these themes, a single indicator has been designed by weighing together the emissions that contribute to each theme. The conversion of emissions into theme equivalents was based on the expected contribution of each polluting agent to a particular environmental problem. Target values for each theme in the year 2000 were also formulated, so that the accounting framework allows policy makers to assess whether or not there has been improvement towards what can be described as a more sustainable situation.

The rest of the NAMEA presents the well-known national accounts flows in a matrix format.

The analysis of the NAMEA allowed policy makers to observe the contribution of each industry to GDP and to the major environmental problems in the Netherlands. An overview of the annual changes in economics and environmental indicators for a certain period of time can also be derived from the NAMEA.

The NAMEA provides an interesting example of an accounting framework that encompasses a broad range of environmental information in both an aggregated and disaggregated forms. Its development proved to be useful for, and compatible with, national environmental plans. It is also closely related to research being carried out by the Commission of the European Communities that encouraged the development of Social Accounting Matrices (SAM). At present, both a 1990 SAM and a 1990 NAMEA are available for the Netherlands (Keuning and De Haan, 1998) and these two frameworks have been linked into a so-called 'SAMEA'. This new integrated framework includes the representation of a breakdown of the distribution-and-use-of-income account into three sub-accounts and illustrates the allocation of various value-added categories to institutional sub-sectors, including ten household groups.

The most recent research has focused on the development of a System of Economic and Social Accounting Matrix and Extensions (SESAME) and on how this could be related to the NAMEA.

8.5 LATEST ADVANCES IN GREEN ACCOUNTING

This section makes reference to new areas of research in green accounting that are presented in more detail in other chapters of this book. They are worth mentioning briefly here since they give a good representation of current developments and also a useful insight concerning how things could evolve in research in green accounting in the future.

8.5.1 Rethinking the Notion of Natural Capital

Some old considerations, even premises of research in green accounting, have been revisited on a conceptual and policy-oriented basis. Thus, the notion of the environment being a type of (natural) 'capital', supposed to make economists more at ease when presented with the possibility of introducing environmental considerations in the context of national accounts, has been discussed and questioned by various institutions and projects. We will mention here only two of them, but feel that they might have the potential to orientate research in green accounting in a policy direction that approaches 'the environment' and our interactions with it, in a new light.

The concept of natural capital has been discussed by English Nature in a document produced in collaboration with CAG Consultants, London, and called 'Environmental Capital: A New Approach' (CAG Consultants, 1997). The European research project called CRITINC (Ekins et al., 1999) (for 'Critical Natural Capital') has also discussed the notion of natural capital. It has used the output of this debate to construct an accounting framework aimed at better representing the interrelations between economic activities and ecosystem functioning, and also at helping policy makers in their assessment of economic developments in relation to environmental considerations. In both cases, the notion of natural capital is viewed as being too rigid and, as a consequence, of having resulted in us (including policy makers) understanding the environment in a very static way. Instead, these approaches advocate shifting to a more dynamic approach to the environment as capital in order to understand, represent and integrate better in our economic analysis the functioning of the environment and the dynamic nature of our interdependency with the environmental world.

The CRITINC project, for instance, integrates within an accounting framework, the notion of 'environmental functions' (De Groot, 1992), defined as 'the capacity of natural processes and components to provide goods and services that satisfy directly or indirectly human needs' (De Groot, 1992, p. 7). De Groot has identified 37 environmental functions and classified them into Regulation, Carrier, Production and Information functions. The CRITINC project seeks to offer a methodological accounting framework that will help policy makers in operationalising 'strong sustainability' (i.e. recognising the non-substitutability of natural and human-made capitals). In order to do so, the premise is that environmental sustainability has to be achieved, i.e. that environmental functions are maintained (which is different from conserving stocks of specific types of natural capital).

The CRITINC accounting framework allows one to identify what economic activities threaten environmental functions and illustrate the extent of damage to be dealt with in order to make the economic situation progress towards a sustainable situation in which economic, social and environmental sustainability are achieved. This work is the continuation of a previous research on alternative accounting approaches carried out by Ekins and Simon (1999).

This approach has the potential to give some useful insights to policy makers concerning the functioning of the environment and the dynamic dimension of our interrelationships with our environment. Consequently, it could allow a radical rethinking of how we organise environmental and conservation policies.

8.5.2 Modelling and Accounting

It is also worth noting a relatively new development in research accounting that has focused on the utility of linking modelling exercises to the construction of green accounts. This has followed a broader debate on the policy implications of green accounting in the policy making process and in the operationalisation of sustainability (see also Chapter 6).

While it was becoming clear that green accounting should help in the environmental policy making process, and hence in the operationalisation of sustainability, it also became evident that one important characteristic of national accounting frameworks constitutes an obstacle in the way of attempts to meet this objective. National Accounts are based on observations, 'facts', or actual data. They aim to answer the question 'What has actually happened' by illustrating it.

When attempting to put sustainability concepts into practice, one is looking forward and seeks to reach a certain state of economic development, respectful of certain economic-environmental conditions. The policy making process projects information into the future, simulates, models. As Vanoli (1998, p. 355) argues:

> . . . modelling is normally future oriented, and aims to forecast what will probably happen, taking into account the past and present, what can already be known about the future, or simulating the consequences of various phenomena or of economic policy measures.

Modelling tries to analyse 'what would or could happen if...?'. Vanoli argues shows that one of the main uses of (ex-post) national accounts is to serve as a basis for (ex-ante) modelling. In other words, the complementarity between (green) modelling and accounting exercises could help a progressive move towards sustainability, with green accounts illustrating the results of an environmental policy opted for despite the various remaining uncertainties. Vanoli focuses on the implementation of modelling in the context of the use of the SEEA. Other authors have examined the issue of modelling in the context of research in green accounting.

Like Aaheim and Nyborg mentioned earlier, Lange (1994; see also Chapter 9) is in favour of complementing green accounting with modelling. She explains (based on the work she conducted in Indonesia) how Natural Resource Accounts can be used to develop policies and planning to provide an improved indicator of macroeconomic performance, EDP, and a framework for monitoring specific resource variables (e.g. water pollution) and linking these variables to economic activities. She emphasises that, while drawing attention to the urgency of environmental problems, EDP itself does not provide any guidance about what actions are needed to achieve sustainability. Instead, her work demonstrates how NRA can be compiled and used with analytical models to address development issues. To anticipate the state of the environment in the future, Lange grouped various parameters in a matrix, that are used as inputs in ecological-models: they represent environmental inputs and impacts per unit of sectoral output.

Another example of modelling related to accounting exercises is the Structural Economy-Environment Simulation Modelling (SEESM) (O'Connor et al., 1996). This model is based on the assumption that focus on economic and ecological sustainability implies a shift in emphasis away from expansion of the vector of produced commodities (measures such as GDP), towards a view of qualitative improvements in life conditions, based on the delivery of produced economic goods and services and the 'judicious management promoting the reproduction and resilience of our system of natural capitals'. The objective of the SEESM is to define, in pursuit of sustainable development, an 'optimal mix' of economic and environmental goods and services, and to construct a dynamic multisectoral simulation modelling used for integrated analysis of employment, sectoral change, innovation and environmental protection. A strong emphasis is placed on defining the economic resource opportunity cost associated with the achievement of specified environmental quality goals. This approach can be given an algebraic formulation using extended input–output analysis allied to satellite accounts. The formulation of various state and pressure indicators, in whose terms policy norms for environmental sustainability are defined, can be derived from this exercise.

It is interesting to observe to what extent input–output analysis has been revived thanks to research in green accounting. The tendency to simplify the accounts and to opt for the aggregation of information has not always proved to be beneficial to the debate on sustainability and to the efforts to operationalise it. For instance, an important part of the work on material and energy flow accounting in Germany is related to the calculation of the Physical Input–Output Tables (PIOT) for the year 1990 (Radermacher and Stahmer, 1998).

Another modelling exercise has been carried out, based on the NAMEA data system, using a linear programming procedure which optimises the net domestic product with respect to environmental targets. Meyer and Ewerhart (1998) tried to use this approach to answer the question: 'What would be the avoidance costs for the West German economy, if the government started implementing now an ecological policy that would operationalise sustainability in the year 2005?'. They restricted their analysis to CO_2 emissions. The model they used was a 58-sector econometric simulation and forecasting model INFORGE (Inter-industry Forecasting Germany) that relied on an integrated input–output model. The use of this model allowed them to show that sustainable development may be possible without substantial losses in GDP, because of structural change induced by an ecological policy which raises the price of energy.

Numerous other approaches rely on modelling and/or input–output analysis, and certain new advances in research on green accounting also include a geographical dimension and use instruments such as remote sensing (e.g. Radermacher, 1998).

8.6 CONCLUSION

This chapter has discussed how research in green accounting has evolved through time and what methodologies have been formulated as a result of the observed changes of focus in environmental interests.

The original focus on the shortcomings of the SNA generated an interest in the form and structure that corrected accounts should take and resulted in the construction of, on the one hand, satellite accounts and, on the other hand, aggregate adjusted indicators. This was followed by a controversy concerning the development of environmental valuation methodologies and conceptualisations, the issue of valuation being central to that of green national accounting. The adoption of different approaches to 'valuation' was notable mainly by the physical versus monetary accounting controversy. The issue of sustainability then became central to environmental debates related to research in green accounting. While the concept of sustainability had previously been extensively discussed and defined, it was becoming relevant in the context of green accounting, as national accounting tool is mainly a policy instrument. One hoped that a reformed set of accounts would lead to an equally reformed type of economic policy, more focused on sustainability concerns. The interest in 'indicators of sustainability', perceived as the first practical step that would help policy makers in operationalising the concept of sustainability, was extended to research in green accounting. To this end, a series of accounting frameworks of indicators of sustainability was constructed. From a systemic representation of environmental information and sustainability, the research focus then moved to the use policy makers can actually make of green national accounts as a source of information. It then became necessary to move research in green accounting a further step towards being linked and used with ecological-economic modelling.

This constant evolution shows that research in green accounting is always changing and that these changes follow the improvements in our understanding of sustainability at a conceptual and also a practical level. It also shows that the actual implementation of green accounts in the policy making process is not dependent on the formulation of an 'exact, universal and finite' system of green accounts. Finally, and most importantly, it demonstrates that changes in the national accounting framework do not constitute a 'radically provocative' reform, since the structure of the accounts has always changed in response to the evolution in the economic paradigm and the new policy needs. Perhaps this time it is the reform in the structure of the accounts which will make people realise that a reform in the economic paradigm is urgently needed, if we are to manage our interrelations with the environment in a better way.

REFERENCES

Aaheim, A. and K. Nyborg (1993), 'Green National Product: good intentions, poor device?', Statistics Norway, Discussion paper No.103.

Alfsen, K.H. (1994), *Natural Resource Accounting and Analysis in Norway*, Statistics Norway Research Department, Document 94/2.

Anielski, M. (1992), 'Resource accounting: indicators of the sustainability of Alberta's forest resources', Paper presented at the ISEE conference 1992, Stockholm.

Bartelmus, P. (1990), 'Environmental accounting and the system of national accounts', in Y.J. Ahmad, S. El Serafy and E. Lutz (eds), *Environmental Accounting for Sustainable Development*, Washington DC: The World Bank.

Bartelmus, P. (1994), 'Greening National Accounts, in E&D File, Briefings on UNCED follow-up', Vol. III, No. 5, UN non governmental liaison service, Geneva: United Nations.

Bartelmus, P. and K.S. Parikh (1998), 'The value of nature: valuation and evaluation in environmental accounting', in K. Uno and P. Bartelmus (eds), *Environmental Accounting in Theory and Practice*, Dordrecht: Kluwer.

Bartelmus, P., C. Stahmer and J. van Tongeren (1993), 'Integrated environmental and economic accounting: a framework for an SNA satellite system', in E. Lutz (ed.), *Toward Improved Accounting for the Environment*, Washington DC: World Bank.

Born, A. (1998) 'Measuring Canada's natural wealth: why we need both physical and monetary accounts', in K. Uno and P. Bartelmus (eds), *Environmental Accounting in Theory and Practice*, Dordrecht: Kluwer.

Bringezu, S., R. Behrensmeier and H. Schutz (1998) 'Material flow accounts indicating environmental pressure from economic sectors', in K. Uno and P. Bartelmus (eds), *Environmental Accounting in Theory and Practice*, Dordrecht: Kluwer.

Brouwer, R., W. Radermacher, S. Faucheux, M. O'Connor, E. Seifert, and C. Leipert (1997), *Methodological Problems in the Calculation of Environmentally Adjusted National Income Figures*, Report for the European Commission Directorate General X-II.

Bulmer-Thomas, V. (1982), *Input–Output Analysis in Developing Countries: Sources, Methods and Applications*, Chichester: Wiley.

CAG Consultants (1997) *What Matters and Why? Environmental Capital: A New Approach. Provisional Guide*, A report to the Countryside Commission, English Heritage, English Nature and the Environment Agency.

Central Bureau of Statistics of Norway (1993), *Natural Resources and the Environment 1992*, Statistics Norway, Oslo.

Commission for Environmental Accounting (1991), *Taking Nature Into Accounts: Proposed Scheme of Resource and Environmental Accounting*, Stockholm: Ministry of Finance.

Commission of the European Communities (1996), *Environmental Indicators and Green Accounting*. COM (94) 670 final, Luxembourg: CEC.

Common, M., R.K. Blamey and T.W. Norton (1993), 'Sustainability and environmental valuation', *Environmental Values*, **2**, 299–334.

Costantino, C. (1996), 'Elements of environmental accounting in some European countries – a methodological and operational analysis: the cases of France, Germany and the Netherlands', in I. Musu and D. Siniscalco (eds), *National Accounts and the Environment*, Dordrecht: Kluwer.

Daly (1990) 'Toward a measure of sustainable social net national product', in Y.J. Ahmad, S. El Serafy and E. Lutz (eds), *Environmental Accounting for Sustainable Development. A UNEP: World Bank Symposium*, Washington DC: The World Bank.

Daly, H. and J. Cobb (1990), *For the Common Good*, London: Green Print.

De Groot, R. (1992) *Functions of Nature*, Groningen: Wolters-Noordhoff.

De Haan, M., S. Keuning, and P. Bosch (1993), *Integrating Indicators in a National Accounting Matrix Including Environmental Accounts (NAMEA). An Application to the Netherlands*. Central Bureau of Statistics. Nr. NA-060, Voorburg.

Ekins, P. and S. Simon (1999) 'The sustainability gap: a practical indicator of sustainability in the framework of the national accounts', *International Journal of Sustainable Development*, 2 (1), 24–58.

Ekins, P., S. Simon, L. Deutsch, C. Folke, and R. de Groot (1999) *A Framework for the Practical Application of the Concepts of Critical Natural Capital and Strong Sustainability*, A Report to the European Commission, DG XII (forthcoming).

El Serafy, S. (1989), 'The proper calculation of income from depletable natural resources', in Y.J. Ahmad, S. El Serafy and E. Lutz (eds), *Environmental Accounting for Sustainable Development*, Washington DC: The World Bank.

Eurostat (1994), *SERIEE 1994 Version; Theme Environment Series Methods. 8E*, Statistical Document, Luxembourg: Eurostat.

Faucheux, S. (1994), *Application of Non-Monetary Procedures of Economic Valuation for Managing a Sustainable Development*, Summary final report for the DG-XII Environmental Research Programme; Economic and Social Aspects of the Environment.

Faucheux, S., G. Froger and M. O'Connor (1994), *The Costs of Achieving Sustainability: The Difference Between 'Environmentally Corrected National Accounts and Sustainable National Income as Information for Sustainability Policy*, Cahier du C3ED No 94-18. C3ED, Paris.

Federal Statistical Office of Germany and Statistics Netherlands (1996), *The Construction of Abatement Cost Curves: Methodological Steps and Empirical Experiences*, Wiesbaden: Voorburg.

Foster, J. (ed.) (1997), *Valuing Nature? Economics, Ethics and the Environment*, London: Routledge.

Hamilton, K., and M. Ward (1998), 'Greening the national accounts: valuation issues and policy issues', in K. Uno and P. Bartelmus (eds), *Environmental Accounting in Theory and Practice*, Dordrecht: Kluwer.

Hammond, A., A. Adriaanse, E. Rodenburg, D. Bryant, and R. Woodward (1995), *Environmental Indicators: A Systematic Approach to Measuring and Reporting on Environmental Policy Performance in the Context of Sustainable Development*, Baltimore: World Resource Institute.

Hueting, R., P. Bosh and B. de Boer (1995), *The Calculation of Sustainable National Income*, Indo-Dutch Programme on Alternatives in Development IDPAD 1995-2, New Delhi, The Hague.

INSEE (1986), *Les Comptes de Patrimoine Naturel*, Collection C137–138, Paris.

Jackson, T. (1991), 'Least cost greenhouse planning: supply curves for global warming abatement', *Energy Policy*, 23, 117–38.

Keuning, S. and M. De Haan (1998), 'Netherlands: What's in a NAMEA? Recent results', in K. Uno and P. Bartelmus (eds), *Environmental Accounting in Theory and Practice*, Dordrecht: Kluwer.

Lange, G.M. (1994), *Strategic Planning for Sustainable Development Using Natural Resource Accounts. The Case of Indonesia*, Paper presented at the Third Biennial

Conference of the International Society for Ecological Economics, October, San Jose, Costa Rica.

Leipert, C. (1989) 'Social costs of the economic process and national accounts: the example of defensive expenditures', *Journal of Interdisciplinary Economics*, **3**, 27–46.

Lone, O., K. Nyborg and A. Aaheim (1993), 'Natural resource accounting: the Norwegian experience', in A. Franz and C. Stahmer (eds), *Approaches to Environmental Accounting: Proceedings of the IARIW Conference on Environmental Accounting*. Baden, May 1991, Heidelberg: Physica-Verlag.

Lutz, E. (ed.) (1993), *Towards Improved Accounting for the Environment*, Washington DC: World Bank.

Meyer, B., and G. Ewerhart (1998), 'Multisectoral policy modelling for environmental analysis', in K. Uno and P. Bartelmus (eds), *Environmental Accounting in Theory and Practice*, Dordrecht: Kluwer.

Neumayer, E. (1998) 'Why sustainability cannot be measured in practice: a critique of green Net National Product', Working Paper, LSE, London.

O'Connor, M. (1998), *The Green Stamp Methodology. An Analytical Overview*, Prepared for the Green Stamp European project, Paris: M3ED/C3ED.

O'Connor, M., S. Faucheux, G. Froger, S. Funtowicz and G. Munda (1996), 'Emergent complexity and procedural rationality: post normal science for sustainability', in R. Costanza, O. Segura and J. Martinez-Alier (eds), *Getting Down to Earth*, Washington DC: Island Press.

Pearce, D., K. Hamilton and G. Atkinson (1996), 'Measuring sustainable development: progress on indicators', *Environment and Development Economics* **1**, 85–101.

Pearce, D., A. Markandya and E. Barbier (1989), *Blueprint for a Green Economy*, London: Earthscan.

Peskin, H.M. (1990), 'A proposed environmental accounts framework', in Y.J. Ahmad, S. El Serafy and E. Lutz (eds), *Environmental Accounting for Sustainable Development*, Washington DC: The World Bank.

Peskin, H.M with E. Lutz (1993), 'A survey of resources and environmental accounting approaches in industrialised countries', in E. Lutz (ed.), *Towards Improved Accounting for the Environment*, Washington DC: The World Bank, pp. 144–76.

Radermacher, W. (1998), 'Land use accounting – pressure indicators for economic activities', in K. Uno and P. Bartelmus (eds), *Environmental Accounting in Theory and Practice*, Dordrecht: Kluwer.

Radermacher, W. and C. Stahmer (1998), 'Material and energy flow analysis in Germany: accounting framework, information system, applications', in K. Uno and P. Bartelmus (eds), *Environmental Accounting in Theory and Practice*, Dordrecht: Kluwer.

Radermacher, W., W. Riege-Wcislo and A. Steurer (1997), 'Environmental cost and environmental accounting: a review of concepts in the light of recent developments', Paper presented at the 4th Annual London Group Meeting, June 17-20 1997, Ottawa.

Rennings, K. and H. Wiggering (1997), 'Steps towards indicators of sustainable development: linking economic and ecological concepts', *Ecological Economics*, **20**, 25–36.

Sheng, F. (1995), *Real Value for Nature: An Overview of Global Efforts to Achieve True Measures of Economic Progress*, Gland, Switzerland: World Wide Fund for Nature International.

Theys, J. (1990) 'Environmental accounting in development policy: the French experience', in Y.J. Ahmad, S. El Serafy and E. Lutz (eds), *Environmental Accounting for Sustainable Development*, Washington DC: The World Bank.

United Nations (1984), *A Framework for the Development of Environment Statistics*, Statistical Papers, series M, No.78, New York: United Nations Statistical Office.

United Nations (1993), *Handbook of National Accounting. Integrated Environmental and Economic Accounting*, Studies in Methods. Series F, No. 61, New York: United Nations Statistical Office.

Vanoli, A. (1998), 'Modelling and accounting work in national and environmental accounts', in K. Uno, K. and P. Bartelmus (eds), *Environmental Accounting in Theory and Practice*, Dordrecht: Kluwer.

Vaze, P. (1996), 'Environmental accounts: valuing the depletion of oil and gas reserves', *Economic Trends*, **510**, 36–44.

Vaze, P. (ed.) (1999), *UK Environmental Accounts 1998*, London: Office for National Statistics.

Viederman, S. (1994), *The Economics of Sustainability: Challenges*, prepared for the workshop: The economics of sustainability, under the auspices of the Fundacao Joaquim Nabuco, Recife, Brazil. Sept. 13–15.

NOTES

1 Note that the framework of national accounts (grouping and typology of activities, contemporary understanding of the notion of production as being market-centred and focused on exchanges that involve monetary payment, etc.), is an illustration of the way in which we view and understand economic functioning. In other words, national accounts give a picture of our 'economic paradigm'.

2 This will be discussed in more detail the next section on monetary versus physical environmental accounts.

3 Here, by 'economic analysis' we mean 'chrematistics'; i.e. modern, neoclassical understanding of economic analysis, focused on a market economy. For more information about the notion of chrematistics and the evolution of the economic paradigm, see Daly and Cobb (1990).

4 Hence the term 'commensurability'.

5 They include methods such as 'deliberative democracy' or 'multi-criteria analysis'.

6 For more detail, see El Serafy (1989).

7 GreenStamp approach developed by O'Connor (1998).

8 These themes are: air pollution; climate change; loss of biodiversity; marine environment and coastal zones; ozone layer depletion; resources depletion; dispersion of toxic substances; urban environmental problems; wastes; and water pollution and water resources.

9 ExternE aims at a systematic description of damages caused by fossil, renewable and nuclear fuel cycles.

10 GARP is an extension of the ExternE project to a wider range of pressures.

11 Système Europeen de Rassemblement de l'Information Economique sur l'Environnement.

12 National Accounting Matrix including Environmental Accounts.

13 Social Accounting Matrix including Environmental Accounts.

PART THREE

Uses of Green Accounting

9. Case Studies: Uses of Green Accounting

Glenn-Marie Lange

9.1 INTRODUCTION: USES OF ENVIRONMENTAL ACCOUNTS FOR ENVIRONMENTAL POLICY

Environmental and natural resource accounts (ENRA) contribute to improved policy making in two fundamental ways. First, ENRA provide essential technical information for monitoring and analysis. ENRA differ from other systems of information such as environmental statistics because of a) the direct linkage with economic information in the System of National Accounts (SNA), and b) the comprehensive coverage of the environment. Secondly, the ENRA framework promotes more effective policy dialogue in several ways, outlined below.

ENRA promote a new way of thinking about resource management, which has two components. First, ENRA are based on a systems approach in which the key feature is to understand the interdependence of the economy and the environment. Secondly, the use of ENRA is based on a proactive approach to policy-making rather than a reactive one, an approach to policy based on anticipation of possible future situations through a series of 'what if?' scenario simulations.

ENRA also improve policy dialogue by providing a transparent system of information about the state of the environment and relationships between human activities and the environment. The power of the SNA for economic information stems from the fact that it has become an information system to which all parties agree (despite recognized limitations). The ENRA organizing framework plays a similar role in searching for common ground to describe the environment and environment-economic linkages in a potentially conflict-ridden situation. Also, by making the environment-economy interactions more transparent to non-specialists, it improves the role the public can meaningfully play in policy dialogue.

Finally, ENRA bring environmental considerations into *macro-level economic policy analysis* in a formal and consistent way which, in turn, provides a concrete basis for productive dialogue in government about alternative, cross-sectoral development strategies and the associated policy trade-offs. While this chapter will concentrate primarily on the technical contributions of ENRA to policy analysis, the potential for ENRA to transform the policy-making landscape should not be underestimated.

This chapter begins with a review of conceptual and implementation issues as they affect the usefulness of ENRA for policy. The remaining part of this chapter discusses specific examples of policy applications. At this point in time, countries are still learning how to best make use of ENRA to address their domestic environmental concerns and so applications vary among countries. The intent is to show the breadth of applications, rather than to provide a comprehensive survey of every use in every country.

9.2 CONCEPTS AND IMPLEMENTATION

The challenge of creating and effectively using ENRA arises from trying to fit together two very different systems, environment and economy, in a single unified framework. Practitioners have developed different classification systems, spatial and time units, and units of measurement appropriate for each system. Because its primary objective is to link environmental information with the SNA, where conflict arises between the two systems, the economic system takes precedence.

9.2.1 Conceptual Issues

This section explores how some basic concepts of the ENRA and the way in which the concepts are implemented may limit the uses of ENRA. In the last part of this section, an important aspect is discussed: progress toward harmonisation which would allow international comparisons.

9.2.1.1 Time and spatial scales
One set of problems imposed on the environmental data within the ENRA arises from the spatial and time dimensions of the SNA. Following the SNA, ENRA also use national boundaries to set geographical limits and use a year as its time frame. In some instances, the adherence to national boundaries can limit the usefulness of ENRA because the geographic classifications appropriate for the environment do not always not coincide with national boundaries. Some pollutants or resources have a very localised effect and, consequently, require a much smaller spatial scale. For example, relatively low

national levels of air pollution can mask unacceptably high local concentrations, especially in urban areas (Lange, 1998).

In theory, this problem can be handled by the construction of ENRA for disaggregated spatial units within a country. Implementation may be difficult, however, because most countries collect economic data according to administrative spatial classifications, which are only by coincidence the spatial units that are useful for environmental management, such as water catchment areas.

At the other extreme, a spatial scale much larger than the nation state is required where pollutants affect countries other than their source of origin, or several countries share a common resource, such as water. For certain pollutants, such as greenhouse gases and chlorofluorocarbons (CFCs), the global concentration of these pollutants is important, not the national concentration. For regionally mobile pollutants, like those associated with acidification, transboundary flows are extremely important; the construction of 'trade' accounts for the transboundary flows of pollutants into or out of a country has been proposed to handle this problem (Keuning et al., 1999). Internationally shared resources, like migratory fish stocks, also pose challenges to the concept of national accounts. Sustainable use can only be determined in a regional context; the sustainability of the fish stock does not depend on a single country's catch rates (Danielsson, 1999).

These difficulties arise from the attempt to address sustainability on a national basis when sustainability is increasingly a regional and global issue. Despite this limitation, national-level ENRA are indispensable for addressing environmental issues because, ultimately, policy decisions affecting the environment will be taken within the national context, even if such decisions arise from regional agreements.

Similarly, the annual time frame of national accounts can be too long to adequately capture significant seasonal fluctuations of pollution concentration or of water availability within a year. The annual time frame may also be too short for phenomena whose effects are only felt in periods longer than a year. For example, constructing asset accounts for groundwater on an annual basis may not be meaningful in cases where the natural cycle of depletion and recharge may be much longer than one year, as is often the case in arid and semi-arid lands (Lange, 1998).

9.2.1.2 Valuation of environmental degradation

A second set of conceptual problems concern monetary valuation. The two major systems of environmental accounting, the UN's SEEA (United Nations, 1993) and the NAMEA developed by Statistics Netherlands (Keuning et al., 1999), take fundamentally opposed positions with regard to valuation. There are many problems with valuation techniques, whether they are implemented as part of the ENRA as advocated by the SEEA, or whether they are implemented outside the ENRA as part of the policy analysis of the ENRA as advocated by the NAMEA. This issue is discussed elsewhere in the book; this chapter raises only the aspects of the valuation issue that affect the usefulness of ENRA for policy makers:

- Can the ENRA assign a unique, meaningful value to each form of environmental degradation?
- Is the aggregate figure derived from summing up all forms of environmental degradation useful for policy makers?

The major problem for policy makers is that the SEEA proposes three alternative valuation techniques. The techniques can produce very different cost estimates, yet each one is appropriate, depending upon the policy question under consideration. The purpose of valuation within the ENRA has been to provide policy makers with a means to add up the effects of many different kinds of degradation, providing a single bottom-line figure. But the possibility of *several* equally plausible values for this figure defeats the purpose of introducing this concept into the ENRA. The advantage of the NAMEA is that by moving valuation into the domain of policy analysis, it does not attempt to provide a unique figure; policy makers are free to tailor valuation techniques to the specific problem at hand.

A more fundamental issue is whether decisions should be made on the basis of a single-valued, summary indicator of environmental degradation and depletion, the Environmentally-Adjusted Domestic Product as it is called in the SEEA. This issue is taken up later in Section 9.3.3.

9.2.2 Implementation Issues

Even where there is agreement on methodology, implementation of ENRA can vary among countries depending on the nature of the environmental issues and the data available. Two aspects of implementation affect the use of ENRA: the nature of the data for ENRA and the modular approach to implementation that most countries take.

9.2.2.1 Data problems
The data requirements can be daunting for many countries, especially developing countries. Many of the data must be estimated, which can raise questions about credibility. This is a serious issue because, in order to be useful, data must be seen as credible by policy makers, technical experts, and the general public, especially data about controversial environmental issues.

For most of the asset accounts, reasonably sound data can be obtained from formal records, though water remains a problem in many countries. Records are also often available for the use of important resources like energy, though it may be difficult to obtain information at a detailed sectoral level. Data for some parts of the ENRA, like pollution and land degradation, are usually not directly observed and must be estimated on the basis of models. Some guidance for estimating these figures has been provided by (United Nations, 1999), but it is still a difficult process. Usually these models have been developed in industrialised countries and the detailed information required to customise the models for other countries may not be routinely collected, especially in developing countries. For example, estimation of the emission of atmospheric nitrogen from combustion of fuel depends not only on information about the quantity and type of fuel used in each sector (often available), but also on the type of combustion equipment used (often not available). The result can be data of uncertain quality. The quality problems are compounded for the monetary accounts of the SEEA by the added difficulties of valuation.

9.2.2.2 Modular approach

In response to the difficulty of constructing complete ENRA, many countries have chosen to implement ENRA in a modular fashion, similar to the way in which national economic accounts have been introduced in many countries. This flexibility is a great strength of the system because it allows countries to concentrate on aspects of the accounts that are most useful to their own situation. For example, a country in which fisheries are relatively unimportant economically may choose to construct asset accounts for other resources and delay accounts for fisheries.

There is a danger in the modular approach, however, because it requires that policy makers fully understand what information they need and what they can expect to obtain from ENRA. These conditions are not always met because many countries have relatively little expertise in environmental economics and because ENRA are fairly new so their potential uses are not well understood. It is relatively easy to construct SNA in a modular fashion because it is well established and its policy applications widely understood compared with the much newer ENRA. Statisticians may find themselves spending a lot of time on accounts for the ENRA that turn out to be of limited use.

The unique contribution of ENRA is a framework that is comprehensive and which, therefore, provides the ability to describe a system. This is especially important when it comes to the activity accounts of the ENRA, which correspond to the Supply and Use Table (SUT) in the national accounts. The modular approach succeeds when the principle of comprehensiveness is maintained within each module. A comprehensive framework may not require that every possible cell is filled, but it does require that all the major cells are filled.

Like the SUT, the activity accounts of the ENRA can be viewed both column-wise (by economic activity) and row-wise (by type of resource or pollutant). The ENRA will be of limited use if entries for pollution, for example, do not address all, or at least all the major, sources of pollution. In the Philippines, for example, the activity accounts included ten types of air pollution and fourteen industries which accounted for only 15 per cent of GDP (NSCB, 1998). However, there was no single pollutant which was estimated across all fourteen industries, even though some pollutants were significant in all industries. The pollutant with the most extensive coverage, particulate matter, was estimated for only seven of the fourteen industries; another four pollutants were estimated for three industries, and the other pollutants were each estimated for just one or two industries. If the omitted industries were not significant sources of a pollutant, this would not matter, but this was not the case. This approach in the Philippines has severely limited the ability to carry out multi-sectoral comparisons and analysis (Lange, 1999a).

9.2.3 Harmonisation of ENRA

Comparable international databases are indispensable for addressing global and regional environmental issues, and for making general international comparisons. Great progress has been made toward standardisation of environmental accounting which will eventually allow international comparisons, just as the nearly universal adoption of the SNA allows international comparisons of economic performance. Obstacles to harmonisation include different levels of coverage in each country and the use of different methods and data. The modular approach to constructing ENRA reduces international comparability.

With regard to asset accounts, many countries are close to harmonisation. The major methodological issue (which method should be used to value assets, net price or net present value), has largely been resolved in favour of the net present value (NPV). The values for certain parameters used with the NPV method (the opportunity cost of capital invested in an extractive industry and the discount rate) vary among countries. To the extent that they represent real economic differences among countries, these differences need not lead to incompatibility among the asset accounts of different countries. Some countries use moving averages of prices to value assets while others do not, though this is not a very serious problem.

A methodological issue that has not yet been resolved is the definition of mineral reserves which are considered economic assets. The SEEA proposes that only economically-proven reserves be valued. A number of countries, such as Australia, include both proven and probable reserves (or some proportion of probable reserves) in their economic assets.

Harmonisation of the ENRA activity accounts will be more problematic because these accounts are more extensive, varied, and present more complex data challenges. The fundamental controversy over valuation and appropriate valuation techniques has not yet been resolved. Eurostat is working toward a harmonised system of ENRA for Europe, but one based on the NAMEA which excludes valuation from the accounts.

9.3 CASE STUDIES

Many countries have come to recognise the alarming degradation of the environment and scarcity of natural resources, and the need to design a strategy for development that takes these constraints into account. The implementation of strategies for sustainable development relies, in part, on two key activities: 1) continuous *monitoring* of the state of the environment and economy, and progress toward meeting the goals identified in the strategic plans; and 2) *policy analysis* of specific elements of the plans. The ENRA have been used to contribute to both of these activities. However, the ENRA often play a somewhat different role in industrialised and developing countries.

Industrialised countries generally have had a longer history of environmental data collection and policy analysis, so the role of ENRA is to bring the data, often compiled by different ministries for their own purposes, into a comprehensive framework linked to economic accounts. A comprehensive framework allows standardised treatment of issues such as pollution, and cross-sectoral analysis of multiple environmental issues, for management as a single interdependent system rather than as separate parts. Many developing countries do not yet routinely carry out extensive environmental data collection and policy analysis. In these countries, ENRA can act as a powerful catalyst for a wide range of macroeconomic and sectoral analyses. In this section, the policy applications of the ENRA are discussed in terms of its two basic components: asset accounts and activity accounts. A final section discusses the use of summary indicators.

9.3.1 ENRA Asset Accounts

The asset accounts, physical and monetary, are used to monitor national wealth, the economic value of natural assets, how natural assets compare to manufactured capital, and the cost of depletion or accumulation of natural capital. In some instances, the physical accounts alone can provide a striking picture of the state of a resource that is highly informative and useful for policy. For example, the physical asset accounts of Namibia's fish stocks since the 1960s were used to provide a very clear picture to policy makers of the devastation of an important national asset resulting from uncontrolled, open-access fishing (Figure 9.1). However, a more complete assessment of sustainability requires that the economic value also be known.

Economic sustainability requires that national wealth is not decreasing over time (Pearce and Atkinson, (1993). See Gowdy and O'Hara (1997) for a critique). One of the fundamental indicators of sustainable development is the value of a country's total wealth, both manufactured and natural. (Human capital is also important, but a satisfactory way to measure it has not yet been found.)

Figure 9.1 Biomass of commercial fish species in Namibia, 1963 to 1998

million of tonnes

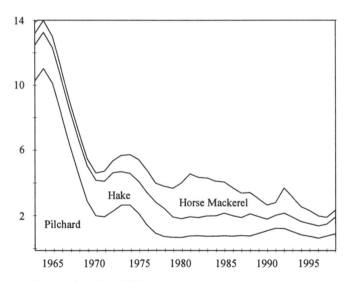

Source: Lange and Motinga (1997).

A comparison of manufactured and natural capital indicates not only *total wealth*, but also the *diversity* of wealth, and its *volatility* due to price fluctuations, an important feature for economies dependent on sensitive commodities. A number of countries now routinely report figures for natural (non-produced) assets along with produced assets, for example, Australia (Figure 9.2) and Canada.

In the case of Australia, its non-produced assets, consisting of land, subsoil assets, and forests, account for 34–40 per cent of the value of total assets. Land accounts for most of the value.

Botswana, a country highly dependent on mineral resources (averaging 30 per cent of GDP), has adopted a development goal of diversifying its economy to reduce dependence on minerals. The combined asset accounts for manufactured and natural capital are one method used to monitor progress toward diversification. While total capital has been increasing, manufactured capital has gradually substituted for natural capital: manufactured capital accounted for only one-third of total assets as recently as 1990, but has since increased to about 50 per cent (Figure 9.3).

Figure 9.2 Value of produced and non-produced capital assets in Australia, 1989 to 1998

billions of Australian dollars

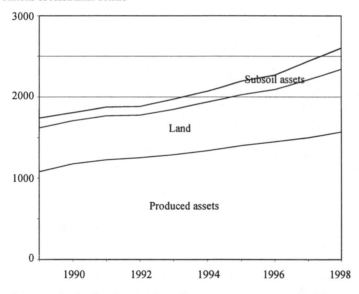

Source: Table 1, Consolidated Balance Sheet (Australian Bureau of Statistics, 1998).

The value of resources stems from the resource rent that they generate, that is, a high profit, in excess of the opportunity cost of capital, due to the scarcity of the resource. From an economic perspective, sustainable and equitable resource management requires that the resource rent be recovered by the government through appropriate taxes and used for the benefit of all citizens.

Non-renewable resources like minerals (or renewable resources like fisheries that may be harvested unsustainably) will eventually be exhausted, and the employment and income they generate will end. Economic sustainability requires that some portion of these rents be re-invested in other assets or economic activities which can replace the employment and income from the resource-based industries once the resources are exhausted.

Figure 9.3 Shares of manufactured assets and mineral assets in Botswana, 1990 to 1996

per cent of total assets

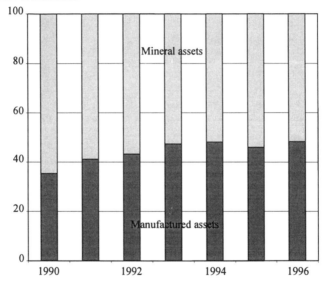

Source: Lange and Gaobotse (1999).

Renewable resources, like forests or fisheries, are capable of providing an income for all future generations if managed sustainably. Policy instruments to guarantee sustainable management include setting limits to the amount that can be harvested and levying royalties or fees to provide an economic disincentive to over-exploit a resource. Recovery of resource rent is also an issue of equity, especially in developing countries that rely heavily on extractive industries. The excess profits can be used to support development that betters the lives of all citizens, not only the minority who may own companies.

The economic rent generated by a resource, which is used to construct the monetary asset accounts, is a useful indicator in its own right, and is used to help address a number of critical policy issues:

- How much rent is being generated, and is the resource rent being recovered successfully by government?
- Is rent being used to promote a sustainable economy?
- Is the maximum rent being generated by natural resource policies?
- If not, are there other objectives that are being met, for example, equity and employment creation?
- What are the economic trade-offs between economic efficiency and equity/employment creation?

Figures 9.4 and 9.5 provide examples of rent generated by the commercial mining and fishing industries in Namibia, and of how much of that rent is being recovered through quota fees.

Figure 9.4 Resource rent and taxes from all mining activities in Namibia, 1980 to 1997

millions of current Namibian dollars

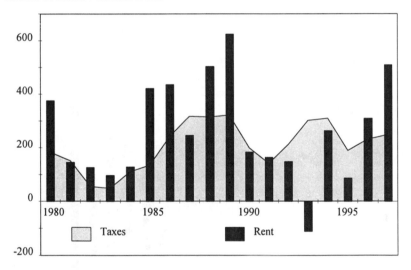

Source: Lange and Hassan (1999).

In both industries, significant amounts of resource rent are being generated. However, rent recovery is markedly different in the two sectors: most is recovered from mining, but most of the resource rent is *not* being recovered from Namibia's fishing industry. While there are a number of reasons for the failure to collect the rent, this observation has helped to spur a review of Namibia's fisheries policy.

The issue of whether extractive industries are being used to promote sustainable development is an important one for all economies. If renewable resources are not over-harvested, then the activity can continue indefinitely, meeting the criterion of sustainability. However, non-renewable resources (and renewable resources being overexploited) must meet different economic sustainability criteria, since, by definition, the activity cannot continue indefinitely. The promotion of a sustainable economy from non-renewable resources requires that the rent generated by these resources be reinvested in other activities that can eventually take the place of the exhausted resource.

Botswana has implemented two approaches to measure whether rent from non-renewable resources are used in a manner that promotes sustainable development. One approach considers sustainability from a fiscal point of view, through the Sustainable Budget Index (SBI) (Ministry of Finance and Development Planing, 1997). The other approach considers sustainability from an economic point of view, utilising the user-cost approach of (El Serafy, 1989). The two approaches have resulted in quite different policy recommendations for the management of resource rents.

Figure 9.5 Resource rent and taxes from fishing in Namibia, 1980 to 1997

millions of current Namibian dollars

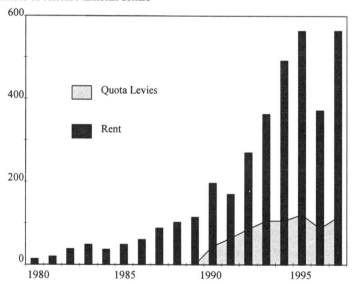

Source: Lange and Hassan (1999).

Fiscal sustainability, measured by the SBI, is based on the idea that government should not come to depend upon revenues from a non-renewable resource for its current expenditures. In other words, all rent recovered by government from non-renewable resources should be reinvested. In Botswana, fiscal sustainability is thus measured as the ratio of the recurrent budget (minus spending on education and health (human capital)) to the recurrent (non-mineral) revenues. As long as this ratio is less than 1.0, the rent is being reinvested. If it is greater than 1.0, then current expenditures are being partly financed from mineral rent. Revenues from mining in Botswana have clearly been managed sustainably according to the rule for fiscal sustainability, though there is a trend toward an increase in the ratio in recent years (Figure 9.6).

Economic sustainability is based on the idea of ensuring a permanent stream of income in the future once the minerals are exhausted. Establishing this permanent income stream may not require investment of all the rent in every year; if the entire rent is reinvested, which is the principle of fiscal sustainability, there may be an unnecessary sacrifice of consumption by the present generation for the future. The 'user-cost' method distinguishes between the portion of the resource rent that needs to be reinvested, and the residual amount that can be consumed as current income.

Figure 9.6 Sustainable budget index for Botswana, 1983 to 1998

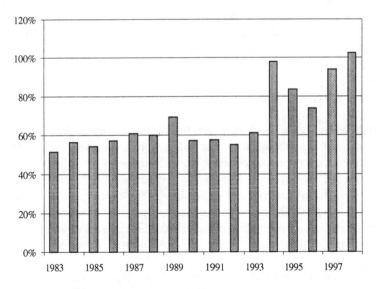

Source: Lange and Gaobotse (1999).

Under very conservative assumptions, this approach indicated that only about 50 per cent of Botswana's rent from minerals needs to be reinvested; the rest can be used to fund current consumption. It suggests that more can be done to benefit citizens in the current period, such as further alleviation of poverty.

Finally, the ENRA have been used in Namibia to explore current policies to generate the maximum economic rent from fisheries, and to estimate the cost of the trade-off between economic efficiency and equity considerations. In Namibia's fishing industry there is a great deal of over-capacity, in part due to government's policy to encourage Namibian companies to enter an industry that was previously controlled almost entirely by foreign operators, and to create employment by encouraging on-shore processing (Manning and Lange, 1998). In this case, there has been a trade-off between economic efficiency (maximising rent) and equity or broader socio-economic objectives (Namibianization and employment creation). Consequently, there is a wide range of rent per ton of fish generated by different companies; some earn almost no rent at all and some earn much more than the average.

The detailed information on fishing companies used to calculate the resource rent for the ENRA shows that the high-rent earners in the Namibian fishing industry are typically the well-established, larger companies, while the low earners are typically the inexperienced newcomers, the targets of government's policy (Lange, 1999b). The rent generated by the high earners has been used as a preliminary indication of the rent that could be generated if the industry operated in a more efficient manner. The difference between the rent from efficient operators and the actual rent is an indication of the economic cost of promoting equity. In this way the ENRA was able to address important policy issues using the same underlying data used to construct the ENRA.

9.3.2 ENRA Activity Accounts

The activity accounts are much more extensive than the asset accounts and their applications are subsequently that much more extensive. The activity accounts consist of three components: use of resources (in physical and monetary terms), the resource degradation and emission of pollutants (in physical and monetary terms), and expenditures for environmental protection. At their simplest, the activity accounts are used to monitor the trend over time of resource use, pollution emissions, the costs of environmental degradation, and environmental protection expenditures, both total and by industry.

The construction of environmental-economic profiles, or 'eco-efficiency' indicators has become a common way of monitoring sustainability. The eco-efficiency indicators report each industry's percentage contribution to the national economy in terms of value-added, employment, and environment impact such as emissions of various pollutants. These descriptive statistics provide a first approach to identifying major users of resources and sources of emissions, and provide a comparison of each sector's relative environmental burden and economic contribution. (For an example, see Figure 9.7.) These accounts have been constructed for a number of European countries (*Structural Change and Economic Dynamics*, 1999).

Figure 9.7 Shares of greenhouse gas emissions, value-added, and employment by selected industries, Germany 1993

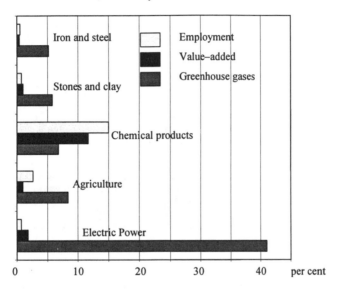

Source: Figure 6 in Tjahjadi et al. (1999).

Another way that eco-efficiency profiles can be calculated is as emissions per unit of sectoral value-added. For example, Figure 9.8 shows the comparative economic benefits of water use between South Africa and Namibia, two countries that share increasingly scarce water sources. This information, on a more detailed level, has been used both for internal policy analysis and in the ongoing negotiation between South Africa and Namibia over how to share their water in the future.

This kind of analysis is particularly useful for putting a concrete figure to ideas that may be commonly held but not quantified sufficiently for sound policy decisions, especially in developing countries. For example, most countries use a great deal of their water for crop irrigation which is known to be a low-value use of this resource. Putting a value on the water use in agriculture relative to other sectors has provided Namibian and South African policy makers with a more sound basis on which to discuss future policy for agriculture as well as other sectors.

Figure 9.8 Value-added per cubic meter of water input by sector in Namibia and South Africa in 1996

rand per cubic metre

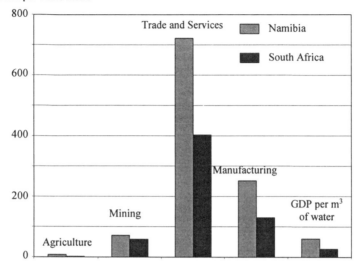

Source: Lange and Hassan (1999).

While the eco-efficiency indicators shown in Figure 9.8 report the *direct* generation of pollution associated with production, it is useful for policy makers to understand the *driving forces* that result in such levels of pollution. The driving forces for economic production are the final users. Input–output analysis has been used to measure the total impact (direct plus indirect) of a given final use. This approach is especially useful in understanding the effects of different patterns of household consumption or trade on the environment (Duchin and Lange, 1998). Figure 9.9 provides an example for Sweden. Similar statistics have been constructed for countries such as the Netherlands (Keuning et al. 1999), Germany (Tjahjadi et al. 1999), Canada (Statistics Canada, 1997), Norway (Sorensen and Hass, 1998), and the UK (Vaze, 1999).

The ENRA have also been used to address other policy issues that are important for resource management, for example the subsidy for water received by each industry in Namibia and South Africa (Figure 9.10).

The monetary accounts for water report both the cost of delivery and the market price charged for water; the difference between the two is the subsidy.

This information has been used in a review of water sector policy to address both sustainable management of resources (there is little incentive to conserve low-priced resources) as well as equity (identifying which groups in society receive the greatest subsidy).

Figure 9.9 Direct and total emissions of SO_2 by industry from the Swedish environmental accounts, 1991

kg SO_2 per million SEK industry output

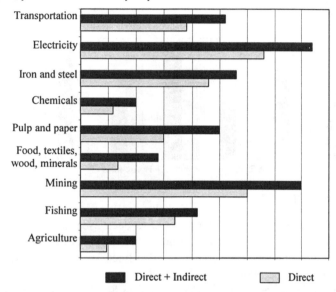

Source: Table 9 in Hellsten et al. (1999).

One of the most important applications of the ENRA activity accounts is for strategic planning. Most governments carry out some kind of indicative planning based on multi-sectoral economic models. Economy-wide modelling is used to examine policy issues which have far-reaching effects that can only be anticipated in a comprehensive modelling framework, such as what will be the effect of population growth, changes in consumption or trade patterns, or the introduction of cleaner technology? Planning for *sustainable* development requires an integration of environmental and economic modelling. In the past, it was difficult to integrate environmental and economic planning because the underlying database for such models did not exist. The contribution ENRA make is to provide the economist with a consistent, systematic, and reliable set of environmental accounts that are linked to the economic accounts.

Figure 9.10 Water subsidy by sector in Namibia and South Africa in 1996

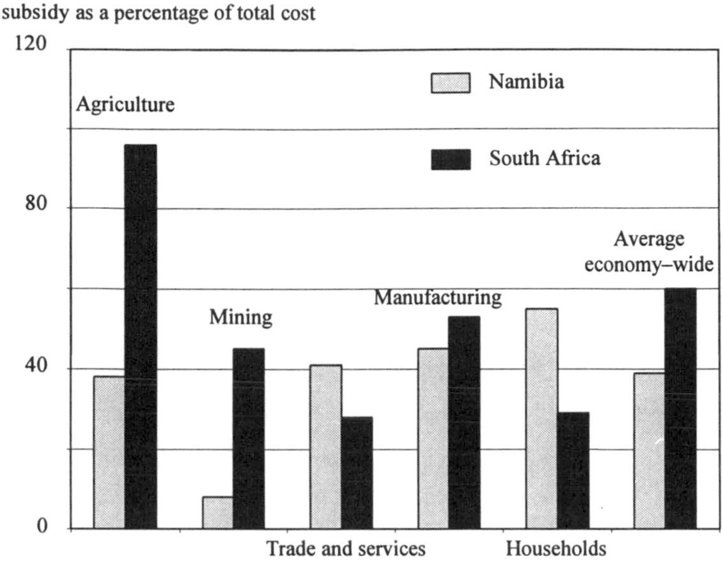

subsidy as a percentage of total cost

Source: Lange and Hassan (1999).

Integrated environmental-economic models have been used in a number of European countries to explore various policy issues, such as calculating the shadow-prices of pollutants, the economy-wide effects of a carbon tax, and the effect on economic growth of emission caps.

A similar modelling approach has been used in South Africa to explore the economy-wide effects of a new water pricing policy based on full-cost recovery (Hassan, 1998), and in the Philippines to assess the environmental impacts of trade liberalization (ENRAP, 1996). ENRA were also used in a modelling exercise for strategic analysis of Indonesia's Second Long-Term Development Plan (Lange, 1998). The analysis sought to anticipate emerging conflicts between economic development and sustainable resource management, and to identify the kinds of technological changes that might make it possible to achieve Indonesia's development objectives within the constraints posed by the natural resource base.

9.3.3 Summary Indicators: Environmentally-Adjusted Domestic Product and NAMEA Themes

Some policy makers would like a 'bottom line' for decision making, that is, a single figure that indicates where the economy is in relation to its goals for sustainability. The SEEA and the NAMEA represent two very different views on the usefulness of such an indicator. The SEEA supports this approach to decision making, providing a single-valued indicator, Environmentally-Adjusted Domestic Product (EDP) which is meant to represent the monetary value of all depletion and degradation.

The NAMEA provides summary physical indicators for each environmental theme derived by weighting emissions according to the strength of their contribution to an environmental problem such as climate change, acidification, or eutrophication. These theme indicators, being in physical units, cannot be added to the monetary indicators like GDP produced by the national accounts. On the basis of economic theory, the NAMEA rejects valuation of the physical accounts as a component of the statistical database, though the physical data can be used in a policy model to calculate an EDP. While the theoretical issues will be discussed elsewhere in the book, of interest here is the policy implication of this choice.

At issue is whether policy makers should be encouraged to adopt decision making based on a single, 'bottom-line' indicator. For certain kinds of decisions, a single indicator may be adequate. It has been argued, however, that environmental decisions are often the kind that are poorly served by a single, summary indicator (Craig and Glasser, 1998). Several countries have implemented the NAMEA system, especially since Eurostat has adopted it, but few have fully implemented the SEEA's EDP. Canada publishes its own series of physical indicators derived from their ENRA (Statistics Canada, 1997). Several developing countries have constructed EDP, such as the Philippines (National Statistical Coordination Board, 1998) and Korea (Korea Environment Institute, 1998), though EDP has not influenced policy in these countries. The United States has also accepted the principle of EDP (although differing with the SEEA on some methodological issues), but has not yet implemented it (Nordhaus and Kokkelenberg, 1999).

It is significant that Norway, the country with the longest experience of ENRA, rejects the use of a single-valued figure for decision making in favour of a more complex, multi-dimensional decision making process (Alfsen, 1996). The adoption by Eurostat of the NAMEA approach would seem to indicate that this view is shared by other European countries. Sound arguments can be made for or against the usefulness of EDP for policy; the choice reflects a national preference about how decisions concerning the environment are made in each country.

9.4 CONCLUSION: GREEN ACCOUNTING AND THE OPERATIONALISATION OF SUSTAINABILITY

The conclusion summarises the contributions that have been made so far by environmental accounts to improved environmental policy. Effective institutions, linking those who compile accounts and those who use them, are essential for effective use of the accounts. Some aspects of these institutional criteria are reviewed here and recommendations for improving the integration of environmental accounting and environmental policy are provided.

A wide range of policy applications have been made with environmental accounts, though applications vary among countries. One of the most common uses is the construction of asset accounts for a better understanding of a country's wealth. The uses of activity accounts are more varied, though many countries construct some form of eco-efficiency profiles to compare industries in terms of their relative economic contribution and environmental burden. The activity accounts are also being used increasingly in economy-wide models. Summary, monetary indicators like EDP do not seem to be widely used at this time.

Despite the creative uses to which ENRA have been put in different countries, their full potential has not yet been tapped in many countries. Partly, this is because ENRA are quite new, so that our understanding of the accounts and their uses is not as extensive as our understanding of economic accounts to which ENRA are linked. In addition, the environment has not yet been 'mainstreamed' into economic analysis in many countries, so the demand for environmental-economic analysis is still often limited to a relatively small number of professionals in a ministry responsible for environmental issues, rather than a broad range of key ministries.

A number of developing countries decided to introduce ENRA after signing Agenda 21, which calls for environmental accounting. Thus, the decision to implement ENRA was more a top-down decision about compliance with an international agreement rather than a clear assessment of a country's informational needs for sound environmental-economic policy making. For ENRA to be useful, it must be driven by policy needs; it is much less likely that policy applications will follow simply from the construction of accounts (Lange, 1996).

Two actions would contribute to more effective use of ENRA. First, information about policy applications of ENRA needs to be more widely disseminated in order to provide countries with examples of the kinds of analysis that can be done. This will also encourage international comparisons and the harmonisation of ENRA. Second, when a country is considering implementing ENRA, it should be encouraged to *begin* the process with an identification of the specific policy issues to be addressed, and how ENRA will address them *before* ENRA are constructed. While most countries begin by identifying policy concerns at a broad level, they usually do not identify, for example, the specific indicators they need, or the kind of questions they might address with an environmental-economic model. The following is an example of the process that would lead to more useful ENRA.

A Ministry of Finance or of Planning might have identified 'sustainable development' as a broad objective. Under this objective, a Ministry of Water might then identify a long-term problem of water scarcity (or water quality) and a strategy to address this of promoting more efficient use of water. The Ministry most likely would further identify specific policies to bring this about, such as pricing (water tariffs and effluent charges), building codes and performance standards for industrial and household equipment, public education, etc. It might further target production technologies in specific industries like agriculture, food processing, paper and pulp.

ENRA could be constructed to assist in monitoring progress toward sustainable development by monitoring the stocks of water, and the use of water by different industries (various forms of eco-efficiency profiles for water would be constructed.). In addition, the activity accounts could be used with an environmental-economic model to assess the impact of the different policies designed to achieve the goal of reducing water use. While the policy uses of ENRA need not be limited to these uses, it provides very concrete guidance to those who will construct the ENRA, and, by targeting well-defined policy concerns, is more likely to be useful and, therefore, used.

REFERENCES

Alfsen, K. (1996), 'A green GDP: do we need it?' *Economic Survey*, **6** (1), 33–9, Oslo: Statistics Norway.

Australian Bureau of Statistics (1998), *Australian National Accounts: National Balance Sheet*. Canberra: ABS.

Craig, P. and H. Glasser (1998), 'All of Keynes' horses', Paper presented at the Fifth Biennial Conference of the International Society for Ecological Economics. Santiago, Chile, 15–19 November.

Danielsson, A. (1999), *Draft Environmental and Economic Accounting for Fisheries*. Prepared for the UNSD/FAO Joint Workshop on Integrated Environmental and Economic Accounting for Fisheries. New York, 14–16 June, New York: United Nations.

Duchin, F. and G. Lange (1998), 'Prospects for the recycling of plastics in the United States', *Structural Change and Economic Dynamics*, **9** (3), 307–31.

El Serafy, S. (1989), 'The proper calculation of income from depletable natural resources', in Y. Ahmad, S. El Serafy, and E. Lutz, (eds), *Environmental Accounting for Sustainable Development*. Washington DC: World Bank.

ENRAP (1996), *The Philippine Environmental and Natural Resource Accounting Project Main Report, Phase III*, Quezon City, Philippines: ENRAP.

Gowdy. J. and S. O'Hara (1997), 'Weak sustainability and viable technologies', *Ecological Economics*, **22** (3), 239–48.

Hassan, R.M. (1998), 'Evaluating the economy-wide impacts of the new water policy in South Africa: a SAM approach', Presented at the First World Congress of Environmental and Resource Economists, 25–27 June, Venice, Italy.

Hellsten, E., S. Ribacke and G. Wickbom (1999), 'SWEEA: Swedish environmental and economic accounts', *Structural Change and Economic Dynamics*, **10** (1), 39–72.

Keuning, S., J. van Dalen and M. de Haan (1999), 'The Netherlands' NAMEA: presentation, usage and future extensions', *Structural Change and Economic Dynamics*, **10** (1), 15–37.

Korea Environment Institute (1998), *Pilot Compilation of Environment-Economic Accounts*, Seoul: Korea Environment Institute.

Lange, G. (1996), 'Initiating processes to reform the System of National Accounts in Africa', Paper presented at the Workshop on Using Economics as a Tool for Conservation at the IUCN World Conservation Congress sponsored by WWF (World Wide Fund for Nature) and IUCN (International Union for the Conservation of Nature), 16–20 October, Montreal, Canada.

Lange, G. (1998), 'An approach to sustainable water management in southern Africa using natural resource accounts: the experience in Namibia', *Journal of Ecological Economics*, **10** (2), 113–34.

Lange, G. (1999a), 'Policy uses of the Philippine Environmental and Natural Resource Accounts', Paper presented to the National Statistical Coordinating Board. Manila, 10 November.

Lange, G. (1999b), 'The value of natural capital, resource rent, and sustainable development in Namibia', Draft Research Discussion Paper, Directorate of Environmental Affairs, Ministry of Environment and Tourism. Windhoek, Namibia.

Lange, G. and D. Gaobotse (1999), 'The contribution of minerals to sustainable economic development in Botswana', Draft Discussion Paper No. 2. Botswana Natural Resource Accounting Programme, National Conservation Strategy Coordinating Agency and Central Statistics Office: Gaborone, Botswana.

Lange, G. and R. Hassan (1999), *Natural Resource Accounting as a Tool for Sustainable Macroeconomic Policy: Applications in Southern Africa.* Policy Brief of IUCN Regional Office for Southern Africa. IUCN-ROSA: Harare, Zimbabwe.

Lange, G. and D.J. Motinga (1997), 'The contribution of resource rents from minerals and fisheries to sustainable economic development in Namibia, 1980 to 1995', Research Discussion Paper #19, Directorate of Environmental Affairs, Ministry of Environment and Tourism: Windhoek, Namibia.

Manning, P. and G. Lange (1998), 'The contribution of resource rent from Namibian fisheries to economic development: an evaluation of policies favoring Namibian ownership of fishing companies', Paper presented at the Fifth Biennial Conference of the International Society for Ecological Economics, Santiago, Chile, 15–19 November.

Ministry of Finance and Development Planning (1997), *Mid-Term Review of NDP7*, MFDP: Gaborone, Botswana.

National Statistical Coordination Board (1998), *Environmental and Natural Resources Accounting*, vol. 1 *Philippine Asset Accounts,* vol 2. *Environmental Degradation due to Economic Activities and Environmental Protection Services*, Manila, Philippines: National Statistical Coordination Board.

Nordhaus, W. and E. Kokkelenberg (eds) (1999), *Nature's Numbers*, Washington, DC: National Academy Press.

Pearce, D. and G. Atkinson (1993), 'Capital theory and the measure of sustainable development: an indicator of weak sustainability', *Ecological Economics*, **8** (2), 103–8.

Sorensen, K. and J. Hass (1998), *Norwegian Economic and Environmental Accounts Project*, Oslo: Statistics Norway.

Statistics Canada (1997), *Eco-Connections: Linking the Environment and the Economy*. Ottawa: Ministry of Industry.

Structural Change and Economic Dynamics (1999), 'Environmental extensions of national accounts: the NAMEA framework', *Structural Change and Economic Dynamics* **10** (1), (whole issue).

Tjahjadi, B., D. Schäfer, W. Rademacher and H. Höh (1999), 'Material and energy flow accounting in Germany: database for applying the national accounting matrix including environmental accounts concept', *Structural Change and Economic Dynamics*, **10** (1), 73–97.

United Nations (1993), *Integrated Environmental and Economic Accounting*, Studies in Methods, Handbook of National Accounting, Series F, No. 61, New York: United Nations.

United Nations (1999), *Integrated Environmental and Economic Accounting – An Operational Manual*, New York: United Nations.

Vaze, P. (1999), 'A NAMEA for the UK', *Structural Change and Economic Dynamics*, **10** (1), 99–122.

10. Constructing Green Accounts

Prashant Vaze[1]

10.1 INTRODUCTION

This chapter sets out to dispel the idea that constructing environmental accounts is something you can learn from a manual. It draws on the experience of establishing the UK environmental accounts. The environmental accounts branch was established in July 1995 within the national accounts research division of the Office for National Statistics (ONS), then known as the Central Statistical Office (CSO). The UK had hosted the inaugural meeting of environmental accountants working in national statistical offices a year earlier, the group thereafter known as the London Group. Perhaps as a result of this, the topic of environmental accounting enjoyed the support of senior officials.

Bureaucratically speaking, environmental accounts units either develop from national accounts departments or from environmental statistics departments. Inevitably offspring resemble their parents, but less so in the UK compared to most other countries, since the unit never succeeded in recruiting staff that knew anything about national accounts prior to accepting their job.

The reasons for compiling environmental accounts are a mixture of political fashion, defensiveness and lack of imagination. This might seem harsh but the environmental accounts are not a 'must have' statistic that Government needs to manage the economy. Very few people lobby for their compilation. Within the UK the most vocal campaigners were an NGO, the New Economics Foundation, and a handful of academics that believed that GDP grossly misrepresented welfare by excluding all the ills that befall the environment. Our output must always have been a great disappointment to this constituency because we resolutely refused to value pollution.

The completion of the SNA93 (System of National Accounts), and more specifically the publication of System of Integrated Economic and Environmental Accounts (SEEA) (United Nations, 1993), had created a world-wide impetus to compile environmental accounts. Every self-respecting statistical office was embarking upon a programme to compile some form of environmental accounts. Within Europe extra momentum was provided by a communication from the European Commission (European Commission, 1994) to member states, requesting that they develop environmental accounts, and more specifically a generous line of budget that the European Statistical Office (Eurostat) made available to obliging member-state statistical offices.

The objectives of our branch were to:

- Create policy-relevant environmental statistics that integrated environmental and economic statistics to aid sustainable economic policy formulation.
- Become a world leader in methodological issues and an active participant in the international development of accounting methodology.
- Sustain a high media profile.

Our own motives were therefore a mixture of idealism and vanity. We saw our role as providing user-friendly environmental statistics to economists and senior policy makers in a format that could be plugged into economic models as easily as possible.

10.2 METHODOLOGICAL INFLUENCES

By 1995 there was already a wide divergence between the 'environmental economists' approach to environmental accounts whose research agenda was then inspired by John Hartwick, and the 'Social Accounts Matrix extensionists' who saw environmental accounts as the logical progression of input-output (I–O) tables. The former school of thought placed great emphasis on the valuation of pollution and resource depletion to adjust macro-economic aggregates. The most famous practical paper written from this perspective was probably that by Bob Repetto and his colleagues at the World Resources Institute (Repetto et al., 1989). The latter approach concentrated on industrially disaggregating environmental impacts between industries often using the input–output tables to define the industrial split. This approach originated with Wassily Leontief (Leontief, 1970) who had explored the integration of physical flows into the environment with I–O analysis in the 1960s and 1970s. It has been championed mainly by ecological economists and I–O analysts ever since.

As late as 1992 the World Bank issued collections of essays bringing these two approaches together (Lutz, 1993). There has been relatively little dialogue between the two schools since then. The I–O point of view has prevailed in statistical offices.

Several off-the-shelf models were available and ours most closely resembled the Canadian model. However, the German and Norwegian systems were also important influences. The European Union as a whole has settled on the Dutch NAMEA, developed by Steven Keuning as its preferred model (see Chapter 5). This integrates not just I–O tables but also takes account of the generation and allocation of income and components of the financial accounts (Keuning and Steenge, 1999). Sadly, the SEEA manual on environmental accounting proved to be of little practical use in compiling the accounts.

Environmental accounting research has been particularly fertile within the EU and Canada. Work in the EU has been co-ordinated and funded by Eurostat. Eurostat staff are themselves amongst the most experienced environmental accountants working in the field. They established small task forces of national experts (typically 3 to 5 member states each) to agree best practice and operationalise the calculation of accounts using a shared methodology. Eurostat also organised regular workshops so that other member states could learn from the experiences of the task forces. This method was successful at ensuring countries pooled their experience. The leading countries within Europe have been the Netherlands, Germany, Denmark and more recently the UK. Typically, environmental accounts units comprise between 1 and 5 staff and so they are susceptible to the departure of key members. Canada has for a long time been at the vanguard of research on environmental accounts. It has a large and dedicated environmental accounts staff, and the department itself has been active for almost a decade.

The US has been quiet at an official level since Congress directed the Bureau of Economic Analysis (BEA) to suspend research on the subject in 1994, shortly after publication of the first Integrated Environmental and Economic Satellite Accounts. The US National Research Council (NRC) has been asked to review the US BEA work and agree whether the national accounts should be broadened to encompass environmental issues. This report is now complete (National Research Council, 1999) and it is possible that the US may soon resume work on the subject. The absence of the US in the formative years of environmental accounting has almost certainly meant their present structure is different to how it would have been. The work on mineral assets the US carried out between 1992 and 1994 is bewilderingly different to that occurring elsewhere. For instance, the US treat new discoveries of minerals as capital formation (a return on spending on exploration). Other less anthropocentric statistical offices see discovery as a fortuitous gift from God.

10.3 MODE OF OPERATION

In some, ways compiling statistics is like writing a best man's speech. A good statistical series has to pander to the tastes of the audience. However, there are a variety of different audiences. If the material is too racy, you risk offending the senior members of the family. If it is too anodyne, you threaten to bore your friends. Our own potential constituency consisted of NGOs, journalists and economists and statisticians in other Government departments.

Concurrent with the development of environmental accounts, the Department of the Environment (now DETR) was creating the first batch of environmental indicators. This was more explicitly focused on the interests of journalists and politicians.

As a result of having no powerful political lobby, it was important to form alliances both within and outside Government. We established two Groups so that the work programme received advice and feedback from potential users of our data. The first, the interdepartmental group on environmental accounts, was a working-level group of economists and statisticians from other Government departments, who were simultaneously users and suppliers of data. The second group, the Advisory Group on Environmental Accounts (chaired by the journalist Frances Cairncross), included membership from NGOs, academia, industry and senior civil servants. With one exception we were unsuccessful in attracting business interest. Both groups operated successfully and ensured that the UK environmental accounts work programme did not stray too far from the needs of our users.

Like the rest of the national accounts department, environmental accounting was a secondary user of data. It never funded any survey work, nor carried out any primary data collection. Since the branch did not need to concern itself too intimately in the logistics of organising surveys, it had more time to devote to the conceptual development work. It also meant that at least in our early years we had little say in the quality or structure of the primary data that we used.

The work of actually compiling the environmental accounts, of fusing data sets and reconciling information, was carried out entirely within the branch. We made relatively little use of data from the ONS itself. Our main data suppliers were the Department of Trade and Industry, the Department of Transport, Department of the Environment, and the outside research bodies, most notably the National Environmental Technology Centre (NETCEN), which is responsible for calculating the UK National Atmospheric Emissions Inventory.

10.4 THE ENVIRONMENTAL ACCOUNTS FRAMEWORK

The main distinguishing feature between environmental accounts and environmental statistics is structure. Statistics are numbers in isolation; accounts are numbers living in a system. Perhaps the main reason why the national accounts have successfully captured the imagination of policy makers and academics has been their intellectual elegance and parsimony. Literally thousands of individual data go into the national accounts and yet they can be boiled down to a few key indicators, such as GDP, balance of payments, investment and net savings. In the UK national accounts the following surveys provide the core of the national accounts:

- Family expenditure survey – consumer spending.
- Trade data – balance of payments.
- Annual census of production – industrial output of manufacturing industry.
- Purchasers Inquiry – inter-sector purchases (used to populate the input–output tables).
- Inland Revenue data on earnings and profits – value added by industries.

As well as these principal data sources, scores of other surveys are used to compile accounts for particular sectors (e.g. agricultural incomes survey, international passenger survey). The accounting process has to reconcile sometimes wildly conflicting views of the economy from these disparate data sets. This reconciliation process uses the accounting identity, which states that:

gross domestic product = total income earned (profits + wages)
= total output of industry less sales to other firms
= total spending by final consumers (households, Government, investment and exports less imports).

The holy grail for environmental accounts is to produce a system of holding and rationalising data on the interactions between the economy and the environment so that it has the same elegance, internal consistency and authority as national accounts.

10.5 VALUATION

The environmental accountant first problem is to decide what unit to measure the environmental accounts in. These issues have already been discussed in some detail in Chapter 7. Despite the many years of work that have gone into developing techniques to place financial values on the environment, many environmental accountants still feel uneasy using techniques such as contingent valuation, hedonic pricing, travel cost method and actual damage costs to convert physical flows into monetary terms.

This discomfort arises for both practical and conceptual reasons. At a practical level many environmental *flows,* including water emissions, have not been valued. The same is true of environmental *stocks*, such as our wealth of biodiversity, the ozone layer and the radiative forcing provided by the atmosphere. Emissions of SO_2, CO_2 and PM_{10} have been subjected to numerous valuation exercises but the range of values different analysts calculate is so wide as to make the whole exercise of questionable value.

At a conceptual level, there are fundamental differences in the underlying models used by different valuation techniques. National accounts uses market prices to value goods and services. There are a small number of occasions where prices are imputed, the most important example of this (as a share of GDP) is probably the notional rent owner-occupiers pay themselves. This ensures a consistency in magnitude of GDP between countries where renting of homes is the norm and those where owner-occupation is more common. This sleight of hand imputing a transaction where none really occurs is small compared to juggling necessitated by environmental valuation.

The market price for goods bought and sold on markets is the result of a balance between the costs of producing the good, and the benefits purchasers hope to experience when they buy the good. In the economists' lexicon, it is the intersection of the supply and demand curves. Techniques of environmental valuation hardly ever seek to find this precise point of balance between supply and demand. Contingent valuation technique, the most widely researched of the methodologies, elucidates hypothetical demand curves using questionnaire-based surveys. Similarly, hedonic pricing and travel cost methods use actual expenditures on houses and travel to create a demand schedule for the environmental goods (typically scenic views) they are seeking to value. In neither case is there any attempt to balance these postulated demands with the cost of supplying the environmental good or service.

Other environmental valuation techniques, such as the replacement cost or the mitigation cost methods, attempt to value the cost of supplying the environmental good. These use engineering data to calculate the cost of providing an environmental service. The authors of the SEEA manual have taken the view that the latter is the correct basis for valuation in environmental accounting. The two methods, however, create widely different cost estimates. Many environmental services, such as the ozone layer, are almost impossible to value – though there have been valiant efforts to do so anyway

(Costanza et al., 1998).

We decided to maintain a watching brief over externality valuation techniques but not to initiate any work on the subject ourselves. On the other hand, many statistical offices had carried out work on valuing reserves of economic assets (most notably fossil fuels) and the methodology to do this is now already quite well developed. Our first environmental accounting article was on the subject of valuing sub-soil assets (Vaze, 1996). This is discussed in more detail below.

In order to produce policy-relevant data it is necessary to reduce the number of data series that are being produced. Most substances can harm human health if they are ingested in sufficient quantities, the definition of pollution depends on where and in what quantity substances are emitted. A comprehensive list of all such emissions would run to many pages, and would be unmanageably large and difficult to interpret. The ONS decided, where possible, to aggregate atmospheric emissions according to their contribution to a limited number of environmental themes, following the lead taken in the Dutch NAMEA. This was the first time that emissions had been aggregated into themes in this way in the UK. The themes used in the pilot accounts were climate change, acid rain precursors and ozone layer depletion. A compound can contribute to more than one environmental theme; for example, CFCs are both greenhouse gases and ozone depleters. The advantage of the theme-based approach is that data on economic activity are being linked to widely recognised environmental problems. The main disadvantage is a practical one. Though we might understand why a particular emission is of concern, measures of relative damage are extremely uncertain. This uncertainty reflects either limited scientific knowledge, the variability of impact due to factors such as the weather, different susceptibilities of people and ecosystems, or different persistence of emissions. The ONS has made use of the best scientific advice to weight different pollutants. In practice we were able to find weights that were acceptable for greenhouse gases, acid rain precursors and ozone depletion. On the theme of health, we were keen that WHO ambient concentration limits be used as a weighting factor.

10.6 STRUCTURE OF THE ACCOUNTS

In order to operationalise the development of environmental accounts we proposed the development of series of accounts. These consisted of the following:

- Asset accounts.
- Physical flows accounts.

- Environmental protection expenditure accounts.

Figure 10.1 Links between the environmental accounts and the national accounts

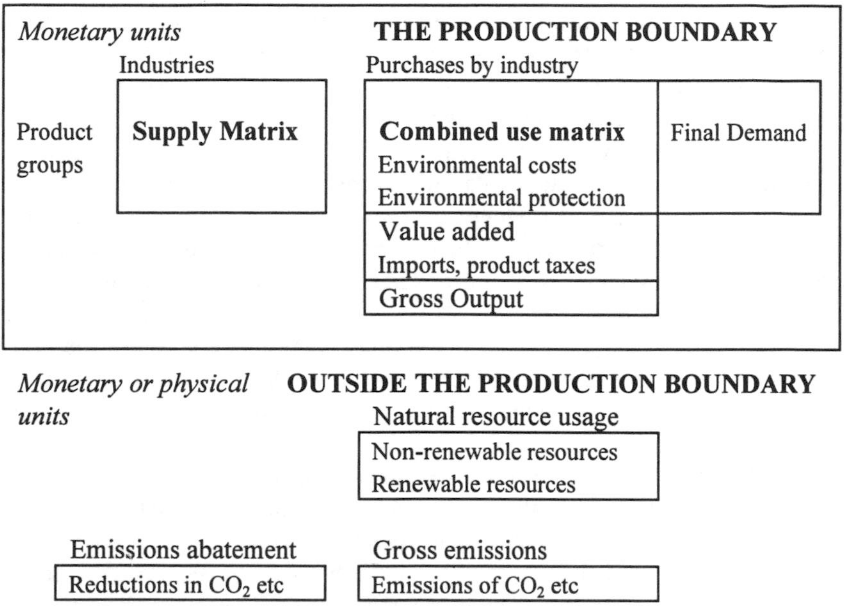

Monetary units	**THE PRODUCTION BOUNDARY**	
Industries	Purchases by industry	

Product groups	**Supply Matrix**	**Combined use matrix** Environmental costs Environmental protection	Final Demand
		Value added Imports, product taxes	
		Gross Output	

Monetary or physical units **OUTSIDE THE PRODUCTION BOUNDARY**

Natural resource usage

| Non-renewable resources |
| Renewable resources |

Emissions abatement	Gross emissions
Reductions in CO_2 etc	Emissions of CO_2 etc

Asset accounts

	Economic assets	Renewable resources	Non-renewable resources	Environmental services
Opening Stock				
Depletion/Harvesting Regrowth New discoveries Reclassifications Other volume changes				
Closing stocks				
Revaluations				
Closing stocks				

The physical flows accounts and the environmental protection expenditure accounts are linked to the supply and use tables in the economic accounts, through the use of consistent industrial and product classifications.

The *asset accounts* contain data on the stock of environmental assets at the start and the end of the accounting period, and categorise the changes that arise during the accounting period. The *physical flows accounts* are concerned with sectorally disaggregating the changes arising during the accounting period. Typically, they contain details of how the environmental assets are used by economic sectors, the flow of matter between the economy and the environment and the use of energy by the economy. (The energy account typically only covers the flows within the economy, not the full account between the economy and the environment.) The *environmental protection expenditure accounts* contain data on environmental spending in the economy arising, for example, from environmental regulation and environmental taxation. These lie within the production boundary, since these are financial flows that already appear (though are not separately identified) within the national accounts.

Figure 10.1 is loosely based on a similar figure that appears in the pilot accounts (Vaze and Balchin, 1996) shows how the different accounts fit together. They are linked to the national accounts through the supply and use tables.

In the environmental accounts, extra accounts are added beneath the economic account's 'use' table to symbolise non-market resources used by sectors, additional to the intermediate purchases and factors of production that are already 'used' by sectors. Two extra physical flows accounts can be added below the use table. These are the *Natural Resource Use* account, which contains data on biological, water, mineral and energy resources extracted from the environment. The *Gross Emissions* account contains information on the wastes released into the environment prior to any savings from environmental expenditures. Data for the latter can be aggregated into environmental themes, condensing the large number of separate contaminants into a shorter list of environmental concerns.

10.6.1 Physical Flows Accounts

The physical flows accounts show the flows of resources and wastes into and out of an industry respectively. They are measured in physical terms or monetary costs (including environmental valuations).

Conceptually, it is possible to think of an *Emissions Abatement* module below the supply table. This module contains data on emissions successfully abated as a result of environmental expenditures. It therefore presents the physical 'non-market' production arising from environmental regulations.

10.6.2 Asset Accounts

The environmental asset accounts can be thought of as extending the conventional stock accounts to include categories of assets excluded from the core accounts. Broadly, environmental assets can be split into two sorts: environmental resources and environmental services. Environmental resources are withdrawn from the environment and converted into economic goods. These can be further split into three categories:

- Fully renewable assets (e.g. water).
- Conditionally renewable assets (e.g. fish, endangered species, forests).
- Non-renewable assets (e.g. fossil fuels, high-grade metal ores).

10.6.3 Environmental Protection Expenditure

Environmental protection expenditure is defined as 'capital and operating spending which has been incurred, and can be attributed directly to, the pursuit of an environmental objective'. These items are expressed in financial terms and already appear in the core national accounts, either as intermediate spending or as investments by industry in compliance with regulatory standards. These expenditures yield *emissions abatement* rather than *marketable output*. As such they represent 'polluter pays charges'. Environmental expenditure also includes environmental taxation. These are product or emissions charges that raise the price of resources or emissions, thereby creating an incentive to reduce throughput of materials or reduce emissions.

The environmental expenditure accounts recategorise existing national accounts flows to highlight environmentally significant items. For example, the conventional use tables (and conventional sources of industrial statistics) make no distinction between purchases to manufacture marketed goods and purchases to abate emissions. These would be separated out in an environmental protection expenditure account.

10.6.4 Environmental Costs

A second type of financial item related to the environment is the actual costs incurred by firms and final demand sectors to mitigate or repair the effects of pollution. These *environmental costs* are from the perspective of victims of emissions. They are 'victim pays' estimates of remediating damage rather than 'polluter pays' costs of avoiding emissions described in the section above. Examples might be the costs of cleaning the exteriors of buildings in a smoky area, or the costs of illness brought about by pollution. Such environmental costs are often used as the basis for valuing the environment.

10.7 COMPILATION OF THE ENVIRONMENTAL ACCOUNTS

At the outset, ONS decided to use a high level of industrial disaggregation to compile the accounts. The 2-digit NACE Rev. 1 (the same as SIC92) industrial classification system formed the basis from which further disaggregation of environmentally active industries was carried out. This higher level disaggregation was used for Chemicals, Ceramics, Basic metal and Other land transport. We also tried to disaggregate the electricity industry (by fuel) and sanitary services (by separate landfill, incineration and wastewater treatment), but found the classification system unsympathetic to this. The only way of obtaining data on employment or turnover within these industries was to go back to the basic data gathered by surveys, or to the company accounts. Altogether, the environmental accounts broke the economy down into 91 sectors.

In the first meeting of the inter-departmental group we established the priorities from other Government departments and obtained a feel for the data that were available. Several other departments wrote scoping papers on data that they held and accounts that might be calculated.

Like most other countries, the UK decided to develop accounts where we knew the data to be good and where we might make rapid progress; i.e. accounts of air emissions and oil and gas depletion. The energy sector and the agriculture sector are probably the two most actively surveyed sectors of the economy.

10.7.1 Oil and Gas Asset Accounts

The Oil and gas sector is a major source of Government tax revenue, and is particularly rich in data. The same cannot be said for other sub-soil assets. Data for coal and mineral extraction (sand, gravel, clay, hard rock) is good but very little data exists on remaining reserves. There is now virtually no mining for metal in the UK.

The taxation regime on oil and gas extraction means that the Department of Trade and Industry (which sponsors the sector) collect data not just on oil and gas production, but also capital investment, operational spending and estimates of reserves, categorised according to their probability (P) of production. This latter data were used to judge the extent of remaining oil and gas reserves. These are:

Proven   ($P > 90\%$);   Probable   ($50\% < P < 90\%$);
Possible   ($0\% < P < 50\%$),   Undiscovered.

The first three categories describe fields that have been developed or at least appraised. Data on undiscovered oilfields are obviously the most contentious, since they rely on Monte Carlo simulations of how much oil might be found in new fields, depending on the geology and the pattern of former discoveries.

The difference between a narrow definition of reserves and a broad definition is very great. In the UK proven oilfields represented about six years production and had done so for the past two decades. If all known and undiscovered reserves are included, there is enough oil and gas for about 40 years. Unhappily (for the statistician but happily for everyone else) the stock on the broad definition of reserves has been growing over time.

The oil and gas reserve account was the only account where we have imputed values on environmental assets – the value of oil and gas in nature. Environmental goods, such as oil and gas, once they are processed have well-defined market prices. This is quite unlike environmental services (screening of UV radiation, global temperature regulation) which no one pays for. Our approach to valuation was to use the market price for oil and gas and subtract the full economic cost of extraction, to arrive at the value of the asset in the ground to the oil industry (its 'economic rent').

$$R = G - (O + r.K)$$

Where:

R – total rent earned by oil or gas industry in year
O – operating costs by oil or gas industry in year
G – revenue earned by oil or gas industry in year
r – rate of return expected by oil or gas industry
K – total net fixed capital

This is a fairly standard way of calculating the economic rent earned from the sector, though not all commentators agree it to be a valid basis for working out the value of sub-soil assets. In the Index of Sustainable Economic Welfare (ISEW), oil and gas is valued at its replacement cost (which is given as the cost of producing an equivalent amount of energy from a large-scale sustainable source of energy). The US Bureau of Economic Analysis favours using the cost of discovering new oil and gas reserves as one means of valuing the minerals.

Even amongst those who agree that the economic rent is the correct basis to start the valuation of sub-soil assets, there is considerable disagreement about how much of the rent should be assigned to the depletion. We took the view that the depletion should be valued as the whole of the rent. Others, most notably the OECD, believe that depletion shortens the time span of the reserve and so the depletion allowance should be the change in the net present value of the reserve (assuming that depletion occurs at a constant linear rate at the same rate as present). This latter value is much lower.

10.7.2 Physical Flows Accounts

The UK, in common with other EU countries, has to produce annual inventories of many gaseous pollutants as part of its commitments to the Montreal Protocol (ozone-depleting substances), the Framework Convention on Climate Change (greenhouse gases) and the Convention on Long Range Transboundary Pollutants (SO_X, NO_X, NH_3). Inventories are also calculated for local air pollutants such as VOCs, carbon monoxide, lead and particulates. This means that there are well-established and internationally agreed methodologies on how to calculate and report these emissions.

The main challenge was to convert emissions from processes ('small combustion', 'transport') to the standard industrial classification. This meant finding a way of assigning all of these emissions to actual industrial sectors. Data on emissions contributing to an environmental theme were calculated by the ONS in three steps. First, the ONS, assisted by the DTI, carried out a detailed breakdown of fuel use, including petrol and diesel, by households and industries. Fuel-related emissions were calculated by multiplying fuel use by emission factors. These were added to emissions that were unrelated to fuel use (for instance carbon dioxide from lime in cement production). In the case of ammonia, emissions are entirely unrelated to fuel use. Thirdly, emissions of different pollutants were aggregated to themes.

These physical accounts were accompanied by tables presenting value added (contribution to GDP), gross output, and the number of people employed for each industry. Gross output is often the best variable for modelling emissions: in general, changes in an industry's emissions will be most closely related to changes in gross output. However, gross output is subject to double counting and 'superficial' changes in the production process (e.g. whether a firm does work itself or subcontracts it to another firm). To provide a consistent measure of economic activity value added (or net output) is used, as it avoids the problems associated with gross output. The number of people employed gives each industry's contribution to employment; this information is useful for placing emissions into an economic and social context.

Physical emissions into water are much more difficult to accommodate in an environmental accounting framework. First, the data are either of poor quality or non-existent. Secondly, it often makes little sense to the policy maker to hear about emissions into the UK waters. What is required is information on emissions into a particular catchment area or even a particular stretch of river. The Department of the Environment and Office for National

Statistics carried out some research on the feasibility of calculating physical flows accounts for water. Results, published as a chapter of the environmental accounts book (Vaze, 1998), suggested useful data were available, but numerous assumptions would be needed to obtain even a crude attribution to particular industries. The majority of emissions into rivers and coastal waters originated from sewage treatment works, which themselves received pollutants from discharges by households, businesses and industry.

A third physical flows account was of international material flows between the UK and its trading partners (Vaze et al., 1998). The UK is self-sufficient in fossil fuels and has a high level of self-sufficiency in food but depends on imports for forest products and metals. There is relatively little trade in non-metallic minerals, because of their low value relative to their mass. This international trade account adopts a thematic approach to aggregating materials. The themes chosen were:

- Agricultural production (aggregated by land equivalents).
- Fossil fuels (aggregated by energy content).
- Metal and ores (aggregated by mass of pure metal).
- Forest products (aggregated by the wood raw material equivalent).
- Non-metal minerals (aggregated by mass).

The quality of trade data collected by Customs and Excise are generally good. However, the creation of the single European Market in 1992, and the removal of border controls on intra-European trade, have had a negative impact. The account used trade data on raw materials and semi-processed and finished goods where possible, converting these to their raw material equivalents. In the case of wood this meant using data on trade in timber, paper pulp, newsprint and printed paper goods.

This work has clear links with research on ecological footprints and material flows analysis, as undertaken by Mathis Wackernagel and Bio Schmidt-Bleek respectively, though it is more conservative in the way it uses the data, avoiding the reduction of materials as disparate as metals and wood to a single measure (land and mass, respectively).

10.7.3 Environmental Protection Expenditure Accounts

Environmental regulations have tended to increase the business costs faced by industry. Desulphurisation equipment installed at power stations can cost hundreds of millions sterling. In order to comply with sulphur caps, refineries pay a premium for low-sulphur crude oil. Policy makers are keen to discover exactly how much extra business is being forced to spend. Ideally, they would like to know how much pollution will be abated as a result of this spending also.

Environmental expenditure covers capital and operating expenditure which have been incurred by companies in order to meet some environmental objective, normally to comply with environmental regulations. Expenditure includes 'end-of-pipe' investments, which generally treat or control emissions or waste materials at the end of the production process, and 'integrated processes', where pollution abatement is designed into the core structure of the equipment. Operating expenditure includes spending by companies on their own account (for example, for staff working on waste treatment plants) and on payments to others for the purchase of environmental services, principally for waste management and wastewater treatment. In some instances industries might react to environmental regulations by limiting their output, or withdrawing a product from the market. This sort of cost to the industry will not be picked up by the inquiry.

Unlike all other data that make up the environmental accounts, there was no long-standing primary data available to calculate the environmental protection expenditure accounts. The DoE financed a survey for 1994 and then again for 1997. Eurostat had developed a methodology to calculate environmental spending (SERIEE). This set out which expenditures should be included and how they should be classified. To avoid double counting, spending by the environmental industry (such as wastewater treatment plants) were excluded.

10.7.4 Environmental Taxation

Environmental economists have been keen to point out the virtues of discouraging pollution by applying taxes set at the level of the externalities. Environmental taxes are taxes levied either directly on emissions or on the use or purchase of substances that give rise to pollution. The most frequently found environmental tax is that levied on road transport fuels. In the UK the list currently includes other energy taxes and landfill levy. The climate change levy is due to be introduced in 2001.

The unit created a taxation account in 1998 (Schweisguth, 1998). It drew on data collected by Customs and Excise on the yield of the environmental taxes. The definition of such taxes is determined not by the intent of the tax (for instance no one argues that Gladstone's motivation for introducing transport fuel taxes was environmental), but by its likely impact. The UK chose not to include the revenue earned from oil and gas extraction as an environmental tax, since it merely captures the rent earned by the industry and ought not to influence the rate of extraction. Also the yield of this tax is highly variable, in line with the volatility of world oil prices, and these perturbations dwarf the yields from all the other environmental taxes, except road transport fuels.

10.8 THE FUTURE

It remains a hope for many people that the value of environmental services and depletion of environmental resources should become fully integrated into the core economic accounts and therefore be recorded as a cost to set against GDP. This is not a hope I share. My own vision is that the environmental accounts remain as a satellite account and are used as an organising framework for a small number of environmental indicators. Ideally, these environmental indicators and the environmental accounts should have a status equal to that of the national accounts and the main macroeconomic indicators.

This is not as far-fetched as it sounds. More than half of the firms in the UK's FTSE100 now issue environmental audits alongside the more conventional financial accounts. The triple-bottom line – economic, environmental and social – is gradually becoming more than just a buzzword. If businesses can see the need to focus on more than just one indicator of success, it seems an overly pessimistic assessment of policy makers to conclude we must adjust GDP to capture our social and environmental problems.

The current revision of the SEEA is placing considerable store on articulating the physical flows accounts in more detail. This is in recognition of the work taking place in statistical offices in Europe and Canada, which stresses getting the underlying physical flows of emissions and resources correctly accounted for and attributed to industries.

Environmental accounts still have to demonstrate their usefulness in public policy making. To do so they have to answer the questions policy makers are asking. These questions are about the impacts of new environmental taxes on emissions, of new regulatory standards on the costs faced by firms, on the least-cost means of achieving an environmental outcome or the trade-offs between employment and environmental regulations. None of these questions is served by the valuation of externalities and the attempt to collapse the environment into an adjustment to GDP.

REFERENCES

Costanza, R., R. D'Arge, R. de Groot, S. Farber, M. Grasso, B. Hannon, K. Limburg, S. Naeem, R.V. O'Neill, J. Paruelo, R.G. Raskin, P. Sutton and M. van den Belt (1998), 'The value of the world's ecosystem services and natural capital', *Ecological Economics*, **25** (1), 3–15.

European Commission (1994), 'Directions for the EU on environmental indicators and green national accounting', COM(94) 670 final, Brussels: Commission of the European Communities.

Leontief, W. (1970), 'Environmental repercussions and the economic structure: an input-output approach', *Review of Economic Statistics*, **56**, 262–71.

Lutz, E. (1993), 'Toward improved accounting for the environment', UNSTAT-World Bank Symposium, Washington DC: The World Bank.

Keuning, S and A. Steenge (1999), 'Environmental extensions of national accounts: the NAMEA framework', *Structural Change and Economic Dynamics*, **10** (1), 1–13.

National Research Council (1999), *Nature's Numbers: Expanding the National Economic Accounts to Include the Environment*, Washington: National Academic Press.

Repetto, R., M. Magrath, C. Wells, C. Beer and F. Rossini (1989), *Wasting Assets: Natural Resources in the National Income Accounts*, Washington DC: World Resources Institute.

Schweisguth, D. (1998), 'Environmental taxation in the UK', *Economic Trends*, October, London: The Stationery Office.

United Nations (1993), 'Integrated Environmental and Economic Accounting', Sales No. E.93.XVII, Statistical Division, New York: United Nations.

Vaze, P. (1996), 'Valuing the depletion of oil and gas reserves', *Economic Trends*, April, London: The Stationery Office.

Vaze, P. (1998), 'An illustrative water account for England and Wales', *UK Environmental Accounts 1998*, London: Office for National Statistics.

Vaze, P. and S. Balchin (1996), 'The Pilot United Kingdom Environmental Accounts', *Economic Trends*, August, London: The Stationery Office.

Vaze, P., D. Schweisguth and J. Barron (1998), 'Analysis of the flow of material resources between the UK and other countries', *UK Environmental Accounts 1998*, London: Office for National Statistics.

NOTES

1	Between 1995 and 1998, Prashant Vaze was Head of Environmental Accounts at the UK Office for National Statistics. He is a member of the London Group and co-ordinated the writing of Chapter 1 of the revised SEEA manual between 1998 and 1999.

11. Corporate Environmental Accounting: Accounting for Environmentally Sustainable Profits

Rupert Howes

11.1 INTRODUCTION

It is abundantly clear that current patterns of industrial production and consumption are unsustainable. The evidence is all too pervasive. While companies 'add value' through their activities, they also extract value for which they do not pay. Their activities and operations give rise to external environmental impacts such as the contamination of ground water, traffic congestion, poor urban air quality, global climate change and so on. The costs of these external impacts are paid by the rest of society. Prices do not reflect costs and as such companies (and individuals) are not paying the full/true costs of their production and consumption decisions. Instead, sub-optimal and inefficient decisions are continually being made in response to imperfect and distorted price signals.

So what does all these mean at the level of an individual company? Quite simply, profits as reported may not be environmentally sustainable. The degree to which an individual company is genuinely 'adding value' through its activities is also uncertain and if the company is making dividends, they could be being paid out of *natural* capital rather than income, a situation which is clearly unsustainable over the long term. The 'going concern' assumption upon which the company's annual accounts are drawn up may also no longer be valid.

For a company committed to moving towards environmental sustainability, the challenge is to determine what its 'true' profits' (i.e., its environmentally sustainable ones) may be, and hence to gauge to what extent it is really adding value. To do this it needs to begin to account for the environment. It should take account of its most significant external environmental impacts and, in effect, to determine what profit level would be left (if any) if it attempted to leave the planet in the same state at the end of the accounting period as it was in the beginning.

Why should companies be interested in doing this? Because their own sustainability and long-term future are inextricably linked to their ability to reduce their environmental impacts and to continuously improve their overall environmental performance. Legislation is increasingly forcing companies to internalise some of their external costs. Consumer and local community expectations as to what constitutes good corporate environmental governance are increasing, and financial institutions are also starting to take an interest in corporate environmental performance. Without the right systems in place, companies will be unable to meet the future expectations of their customers, shareholders, regulators, as well as a more environmentally aware financial sector. 'First movers' will clearly have an advantage and this is a challenge to which some leading UK companies, such as Interface Europe, Anglian Water and Wessex Water, are already beginning to respond.

This chapter provides an introduction and detailed account of some of this innovative and experimental work. The remainder of the chapter is divided into four sections. Section 11.2 offers a brief rationale of why 'nature' needs to be taken into account if we hope to be able to transform our economic systems and get them onto a more sustainable trajectory. Section 11.3 outlines two components of corporate environmental accounting. The first is accounting for environmentally related expenditure already incurred and captured within the company's nominal ledger/accounting system, but perhaps lost in general overheads. The second is the identification, valuation and internalisation of environmental externalities into the company's accounting and reporting system. This aspect of corporate environmental accounting forms the focus of the case study presented in Section 11.4, which summarises the results of one company's, Interface Europe's, attempts to account for their external environmental footprint. Working with Forum for the Future, a UK-based Sustainable Development organisation, the company has been investigating how it can develop more integrated and complete management and financial accounting and reporting systems that specifically take into account the most significant environmental impacts resulting from their activities. The key innovation in the project has been the linking of monetarised corporate environmental data to the company's financial accounts, in order to arrive at a figure for the company's environmentally sustainable profits. Interface Europe's environmental accounts for the period to December 1997 are presented in this Section.

Section 11.5, considers possible ways forward to encourage other companies to take greater account of the environment. Detail is also provided, in appendices 11.2.1 and 11.2.2, on other examples of corporate environmental accounting in practice.

11.2 NATURE AND CORPORATE ACCOUNTS

For those working in the more forward-looking corporations, industry may appear to be tackling its environmental impacts far more strategically and positively than it was 10 years ago. Most leading companies produce environmental policy statements, have certified environmental management systems, specialised environment teams reporting directly to the board and so on. Many are also reporting their performance publicly, detailing performance targets and quantitative indicators (Bennett and James, 1998). While this does represent progress, are those responsible justified in believing that they are now beginning adequately to address the environmental challenges we still face? The answer depends, of course, on one's starting point. Sitting outside the company and looking in from a public policy perspective, the picture is less attractive. On a range of issues, from local air and water pollution, through to acid rain and climate change, industry is seen by outsiders to be contributing to environmental damage and resisting policy measures which would lead to environmental improvements. Such opposition has most recently been demonstrated by UK industry's fierce and concerted attack against the Government's proposed climate change levy. There appears to be a conflict between the internal perspective, which emphasises business processes and for which profits remain central, and the external perspective, which focuses more on environmental outcomes (Howes et al., 1997).

11.2.1 The Maintenance of Natural Capital: Something is Missing from Corporate Accounts

Can wealth creation and environmental sustainability ever be reconciled or is there an inherent conflict between profits and the environment? Much of the business school rhetoric, from the late 1980s to the present day, would suggest there is no conflict. The talk is all of 'win-win' or 'double dividend' opportunities, measures that bring reduced environmental impact and enhanced profitability. Clean and efficient industries, it is said, will produce new products and technologies without environmental destruction. But despite their obvious appeal, the adoption of clean technology, waste minimisation and the pursuit of energy and eco-efficiency in isolation will never be enough. While these activities need to be encouraged and actively promoted, given the magnitude of the environmental challenges we face, it would be naïve to rely on what industry deems to be 'win-win' to deliver necessary environmental improvements. Producing more from less is not the same as sustainable industrial production.

11.2.2 The Role of Natural Capital

The problem, in part, stems from the failure of accounting systems – at the national level (as discussed elsewhere in this publication) and at the corporate level – to account fully for 'natural' capital. While companies account for the depreciation of manufactured capital, to ensure that productive capacity and hence the ability to generate future returns and income is maintained, no account is made for the degradation of natural capital when calculating corporate profits. Natural capital can be thought of as the exploitable re-sources of the earth's ecosystem, its oceans, forests, mountains and plains, that provide the raw material inputs, resources and flows of energy into our production processes. It also consists of a range of 'ecosystem services'. These services include the provision of an atmosphere and a stable climate, a protective ozone layer, and the absorptive capacities to disperse, neutralise and recycle the material outputs and pollution generated in ever increasing quantities from our global economic activities. While some account is taken of the depletion of resources, no account is taken of the degradation of what has been described as 'critical natural capital', the essential ecosystem services without which no life, let alone economic activity, would exist.

Evidence of this incomplete accounting is abundant. For example, while companies may account for the timber (i.e. the actual resource) which they extract from a forest, they do not account for the ecosystem services provided by that forest. These include water storage, soil stability, habitat and the regulation of the atmosphere and climate. Unfortunately, the cost of these essential ecosystem services becomes all too apparent when they start to break down. In China's Yangtze basin in 1998, for example, deforestation triggered flooding that killed 3,700 people, dislocated 223 million and inundated 60 million acres of farmland. This $30 billion disaster forced a logging moratorium and a $12 billion emergency reforestation programme (Lovins et al., 1999). Similarly, external costs of global climate change are beginning to become more obvious. Storm and extreme weather-event-related damage (global climate change is expected to increase the frequency and severity of such events) caused upwards of $90 billion of damage in 1998 alone. This represents more weather-related damage destruction than reported in the entire decade of the 1980s (Lovins et al., 1999).

The key to resolving the conflict between profits and the environment, as many have pointed out, lies in getting the prices right. Businesses (and consumers) should pay for the external costs of their activities. Farmers should pay for the contamination of ground water (and not be subsidised to pollute the water in the first place); timber companies should pay for the destruction of water catchments and industry should pay for its myriad external environmental impacts. These include industry's contribution to global climate change, its impact on poor and declining urban air quality, loss of agricultural production and productivity as a result of aqueous and gaseous emissions and direct impacts, and disposal of waste to land. Until this happens, the conflict will remain. Only when these costs have been internalised will profits, as reported in financial accounts, approximate to what can be regarded as environmentally *sustainable* profits.

One way of getting the prices right is through the process of ecological tax reform (ETR); i.e. moving taxes from the goods, such as employment and profits, to the bads of resource use and pollution. The UK's landfill tax and the climate change levy are examples of ETR. The revenues raised from these taxes are redistributed back into the economy by reducing employers' National Insurance (NI) contributions. However, neither of these taxes fully reflects the extent of the external impacts resulting from the disposal of waste or the business use of fossil fuel-derived energy.

In the absence of the political will to establish a comprehensive and radical ETR programme, companies committed to improving their environmental performance need to move beyond simple corporate environmental reporting, to begin to account more completely and transparently for both their internal environmental costs and their external impacts. In effect, they need to begin to account for the depreciation of 'natural capital' in the same way that accounting rules and standards require them to account for the depreciation of manufactured capital. Once these costs are internalised, everything changes: prices, costs and what is or is not profitable.

11.3 CORPORATE ENVIRONMENTAL ACCOUNTING: WHAT IS IT?

Corporate accounting for environmental sustainability is a new area, with no hard and fast rules or standards, and it is one in which very few companies are actively engaged. If a company is seriously committed to the idea of decreasing its environmental footprint, it needs to manage and control both its internal environmental costs (such as the costs relating to waste management, energy consumption, etc.). It also needs to begin to reduce the external environmental costs resulting from its activities. These costs are currently borne by the rest of society and represent 'value extracted' by the company, but not paid for.

For a company embarking on environmental accounting, the identification of internal environmental costs provides a useful starting point. These costs can include the following:

- Costs of monitoring emissions.
- License, permits and authorisation costs.

- Special insurance fees to cover the use of hazardous chemicals.
- Payment of fines and charges.
- Costs of operating an environmental department.
- Capital spending with an environmental component.

There is no one definition of what constitutes environmentally related expenditure and the importance of various categories will clearly vary depending upon the nature of the company and its principal activities. A more rigorous allocation of these costs can bring many benefits in itself. Often, environmental costs are hidden in overheads or allocated somewhat arbitrarily across departments/cost centres. Leaving aside the difficulties in determining and defining what exactly constitutes an environmental cost, studies such as the World Resource Institute's (WRI) Green Ledgers (Ditz et al., 1995) have shown that these costs can be substantial. The six case studies presented in the WRI study show that for certain products and facilities, environmental costs can account for 20 per cent of total costs.

When environmental costs are this significant, tighter and more transparent accounting can more than pay for itself. Traditional cost allocation methods (on the basis of machine hours, output or perhaps headcount) can lead to a situation where products with relatively low environmental costs subsidise those with higher costs. This results in poor product-pricing decisions, as managers respond to distorted internal 'price signals'. The case of Spectrum Glass, one of the companies reviewed in the WRI study, illustrates this point. Their principal environmental concern was the use of the colourant cadmium oxide, a chemical used for only one product: 'ruby red' glass. This product is responsible for the bulk of the hazardous waste produced by the company. At the time of the study, with environmental costs being allocated across all products, 'ruby red' glass appeared profitable. However, if pending legislation on the release of cadmium takes effect, the firm will discontinue the production of 'ruby red' glass.

Spectrum Glass may not be typical of the ease with which environmental costs are directly attributable to particular products. But it is indicative of how internal subsidies, created through a misallocation of costs, can lead to inappropriate pricing and product-mix decisions. With more transparent and complete accounting, firms are more likely to be able to identify cost-saving opportunities, make better decisions with regard to product mix and pricing, and also be able to avoid future costs through inappropriate investment decisions. At the very least, making the link between environmental and financial performance more apparent can make it easier to take and win support for further environmental initiatives.

Internal costs, however, are just one part of the equation. The next essential step for companies committed to moving towards sustainability is to begin to account for their external environmental impacts, and the next section offers a case study of this process.

11.4 INTERFACE EUROPE: A CASE STUDY EXAMPLE

This section details the outcome of a collaborative project between Forum for the Future, a UK-based sustainable development organisation, and Interface Europe, a multinational manufacturer of carpet tiles and floor coverings. The overarching aim of this ongoing initiative is the investigation of how companies can develop more integrated and complete management and financial accounting and reporting systems, that specifically take into account the most significant environmental impacts resulting from their activities.[1] One of the core aims has been to calculate the 'sustainability cost' of a company; i.e. the notional cost the company would need to spend to restore or avoid the environmental damage caused by its activities.[2] The key innovation has been the linking of corporate environmental data to the company's financial accounts, in order to arrive at a figure for the company's environmentally sustainable profits.

The remainder of this section reviews the approach taken to defining and identifying the company's environmental impacts; the approach adopted in relation to the monetary valuation of those impacts; a review/insight into the methodology developed; and a discussion of why such experimental and innovative projects are needed. The environmental accounts produced for Interface during the first phase of work are also presented. An overview of the company and a brief description of its main manufacturing processes is provided in Appendix 11.2.

11.4.1 Approach to the Study

Both aspects of corporate environmental accounting are being investigated in this ongoing initiative. This case study focuses on the externality costing and integration component of the project; the identification and valuation of external costs is the first step in assisting Interface's management to begin to address how these costs can be managed and ultimately reduced. Consideration is in progress on how the company can more effectively identify and manage its internal environmentally related costs; i.e. those costs actually incurred by the company and already captured in the accounting system.

The three key stages in the externality project are listed below.

• The identification of the most significant/major environmental impacts resulting from Interface's activities and operations.

- The valuation of those impacts.
- The development of a set of environmental accounts incorporating these values and subsequent estimation of the company's sustainability cost and environmentally sustainable profits.

This last step, the linking of monetarised corporate environmental data to the company's financial accounts (in order to arrive at a figure for the company's environmentally sustainable profits), represents the main innovation of the project. The following sub-sections detail the approach taken and methodology developed for each of these stages.

11.4.2 Identification of Impacts

Working closely with Interface, the principal and most significant external environmental impacts resulting from the company's operations were identified, through detailed discussions and interviews with company employees, site visits and a review of relevant company documents.

Methodologically difficult areas in this first stage of the study included the issue of where to draw the system boundaries; i.e. to what degree the life cycle impacts of Interface's activities and operations should be taken into account in determining the company's sustainability cost. Depending on the nature of the company, these cut-off considerations could significantly affect the magnitude of the estimated *sustainability cost* of the company's operations. For example, the estimated sustainability cost for Interface would probably increase substantially if the upstream impacts associated with the production of energy-intensive raw-material inputs, such as nylon and PVC, were taken into account. Similarly, the inclusion of downstream impacts, resulting from the final disposal of end-of-life carpets to landfill or incineration, could also be significant. For non-manufacturing/service based companies, these considerations are probably less significant.

Given that the objective of the study was to estimate Interface's sustainability cost (i.e. the notional sum that Interface would need to spend in order to restore or avoid the environmental damage caused by its activities), it seemed reasonable to apply fairly narrow system boundaries. Consequently, only direct or first level impacts (i.e. those environmental impacts the company was directly responsible for and had greatest ability to control), plus the second-level impacts resulting from Interface's high use of electricity, were accounted for. In effect, the study attempted to apply the polluter pays principle to Interface, i.e. to an individual company. If this principle were applied equitably and consistently, all other producers (and consumers) would also be responsible for the direct environmental impacts resulting from their own production and consumption decisions. If they all calculated their own sustainability cost based on the same tight/narrow definition of system boundaries it would ensure that all significant external impacts are accounted for once and only once; i.e. there would be no danger of double counting.

Consequently, for a company committed to moving towards greater environmental sustainability the key information flows will be those that relate to their own direct emissions and impacts – the ones which they have the greatest ability to control and influence.

11.4.3 The Environmental Impacts Accounted for in the Study

Not surprisingly, on this basis, the most significant environmental impacts resulting from Interface's operations were determined to be those relating to: the company's high use of electricity and natural gas, direct production emissions resulting from the various manufacturing processes; and transport-related emissions from the use of company cars, freight distribution and air travel. This is reflected in the headings of the environmental accounts. Emissions to water were not found to be significant/material for any of the production sites. Costs relating to the disposal of solid waste to landfill and incineration, generated in the manufacturing process and through normal day-to-day operations are, to a large extent, already captured within the accounting system. While these internal and hence realised costs may not represent the 'full' or 'total' cost of disposal, it was beyond the scope of the study to attempt to estimate and quantify any difference.

On the basis of the rationale outlined above, the environmental accounts produced for the study have focused exclusively on emissions to air. These include carbon dioxide (CO_2), nitrogen oxides (NOx) and sulphur dioxide (SO_2) emissions resulting from the use of natural gas and electricity; emissions of volatile organic compounds (VOCs), carbon monoxide (CO), NOx and SO_2 emissions resulting from the various manufacturing processes (direct production emissions); and transport-related emissions of CO_2, NOx, VOCs, CO and particulate matter (PM). The accounts may be developed further to include emissions to other media if further investigation suggests they could be material.

Once the gaseous emissions had been quantified, the next step of the study involved estimating what Interface would need to spend in order to rectify or avoid the environmental damage caused by its activities. In effect, this calculated a notional sum that it would need to spend in order to restore the biosphere to the state it was in at the beginning of the accounting period. The following sub-section details the approach taken.

11.4.4 The Valuation of Environmental Impacts

There are a number of ways of valuing environmental costs (and benefits). Those that attempt to value actual damage costs, 'to place a value' on external environmental impacts, such as the loss of visual amenity following forest dieback (due to acid deposition), or the human health costs resulting from pollution (such as advanced deaths attributable to transport-related emissions of particulates), are steeped in controversy. Even if a value for actual damage costs could be obtained (which is possible in certain circumstances), there is then the immense problem of determining, and subsequently allocating, the proportionate responsibility for those costs between a potentially vast but unknown number of contributors. Many of these valuation techniques, such as contingent valuation, hedonic pricing and the 'travel cost' method, are imprecise and extremely subjective. Contingent valuation, for example, attempts to determine a value for a particular environmental cost (damage cost or benefit) on the basis of assessing what people would be 'willing to accept,' by way of compensation, to tolerate a particular cost, or their 'willingness to pay' to keep or receive a particular benefit. The aim of the technique is to elicit valuations, or bids, which are close to those that would be revealed if an actual market existed.

The approach to environmental valuation taken in this study avoids these shortcomings. No attempt has been made to estimate the actual damage costs/environmental impacts resulting from Interface's activities and operations. Instead, the impacts resulting from the company's activities have been valued, as far as possible, on the basis of what the company would need to spend in order either to restore the environmental damage caused, or to avoid the impacts in the first place.[3] 'Real' or market-based prices have been used as much as possible. This approach is straightforward and uncontroversial. However, establishing appropriate avoidance or restoration costs for all impacts, as discussed below, is not always straightforward and can be difficult. The use of avoidance or restoration costs is in line with United Nations recommendations for environmental adjustments to the national accounts (United Nations, 1993).

Valuation of environmental impacts on this basis offers a mechanism to link corporate environmental performance data to the mainstream financial and management accounting systems. Valuation of environmental impacts (by any means) also enables a positive value to be placed on environmental quality and hence underlines that environmental goods and services are not free. Consequently, experimental projects of this kind are needed to determine to what degree the monetarisation of impacts can assist in developing more integrated accounting systems, systems that are capable of assisting management in their day-to-day operations, strategic planning and in meeting the expectations of their various stakeholders for higher standards of corporate environmental governance.

The following subsections detail how the various avoidance and restoration costs disclosed in the accounts, in Table 11.1, were determined.

11.4.4.1 The valuation of carbon dioxide emissions

Given the current dependence of our production and consumption systems on fossil fuel-derived energy, it is not surprising that carbon dioxide emissions result from virtually all of Interface's activities. Significant emissions result from the direct use of gas and electricity in the production processes, from the distribution of finished goods and work in progress, and from the substantial amount of road and air travel incurred by company personnel. The use of propane-fuelled forklift trucks in the distribution and manufacturing centres also contributes to the company's total level of emissions.

There are currently no cost-effective methods to 'capture' carbon dioxide emissions at source (in a similar way that sulphur emissions can be captured in flue gas desulphurisation equipment). Emissions can either be reduced by reducing overall consumption levels (e.g. driving fewer miles, using less electricity and burning less gas), or avoided by switching to non-fossil-fuel energy sources. Reductions in emissions can also be achieved through improvements in energy efficiency. However, for an expanding company absolute reductions in energy consumption, other than those achievable through efficiency measures, are not an available short-term option.

Emissions from Interface's use of electricity could also be avoided, or at least reduced, by switching, where possible, to electricity generated from renewable energy sources such as wind, hydro, biomass or solar. The opportunity to buy electricity generated from renewable energy sources has increased following the liberalisation of the UK electricity market. Several suppliers, such as SWEB, have been attempting to differentiate themselves in an increasingly competitive market by offering a number of *new* products/services such as 'green electricity'; i.e. electricity generated from renewable energy sources and hence carbon-neutral (well nearly). Consequently, this option represents an increasingly available (and viable) strategy for any company committed to reducing its emissions of carbon dioxide. It is on this basis, using a premium of 1p/kWh over typical tariffs of 4p/kWh, that Interface's emissions of carbon dioxide from electricity consumption have been valued. This represents the cheapest way of avoiding these emissions (compared to the costs of carbon sequestration; see below) and hence is the most appropriate valuation to use in the accounts.

At present, emissions of carbon dioxide from transport are also difficult to avoid, other than by reducing the overall level of company road and air miles.

Table 11.1 Interface Europe, 1997: consolidated environmental accounts

Atmospheric Emissions	Emissions (Tonnes)	Unit Cost £ (where relevant)	UK Pounds £	
Natural Gas Consumption				
26 million kWh				
CO_2	4761	6	29,000	
NOx	4	14,000	56,000	
SO_2	4	2,400	9,600	
Total				95,000
Electricity Consumption				
17 million kWh				
CO_2	7537	N/A		
NOx	20	N/A		
SO_2	43	N/A		
Total (avoidance)				170,000
Direct Production				
Emissions				
NOx	3	N/A		
SO_2	0.3	N/A		
VOC	17	N/A		
CO	4	N/A		
Total (avoidance)				350,000
Transport (Distribution)				
4.645 million kms				
CO_2	3,079	6	19,000	
NOx	34	14,000	476,000	
VOC	1	7,200	7,000	
CO	9	40	-	
PM	2	2,800	6,000	
Total Haulage/Distribution				508,000
Transport (Company Cars)				
8.875 million kms				
CO_2	2,026	6	12,000	
NOx	(50%) 2	14,000	28,000	
VOC	low	7,200	-	
PM	low	2,800	-	
LPG Net Conversion Costs		265,000		
LPG Annual Fuel Savings		(283,000)		
			(18,000)	
Total Company Cars				22,000
Air Travel				
6.397 milliom kms				
CO_2	1,215	6	8,000	
NOx	4	14,000	56,000	
Total Air Travel				64,000
Rounding				*41,000*
Total Sustainability Cost				**1,250,000**
Operating income per the Financial Accounts				**17,000,000**
Environmentally Sustainable Profit				**15,750,000**

Note: All figures apart from unit valuation costs have been rounded to the nearest £100 or £1000.

To some extent, Interface is attempting to do this by investing in, and encouraging, video conferencing. The company is also relocating its main European transport depot from Amersfoort in the Netherlands, to the manufacturing site at Scherpenzeel, also in the Netherlands, to reduce container lorry journeys between the two centres and hence total overall mileage. However, for the foreseeable future, and in the absence of the development and widespread availability of alternative renewable transport fuels, emissions from road transport in particular will remain substantial.

Given that it is currently not possible to switch to carbon neutral and renewable sources of energy to replace Interface's high demand for natural gas or to meet transport needs, Interface is unable to avoid (or to substantially reduce) their energy-related emissions of carbon dioxide, other than the emissions associated with electricity use (as discussed above). However, it is possible to mitigate the effects of these emissions through carbon sequestration (the process of effectively 'locking up' or fixing carbon in growing trees). About 50 per cent of a mature tree's bulk is made up of carbon, fixed by the tree (or any green plant) through the process of photosynthesis. While there is considerable controversy over the validity of sequestration projects as a response to the challenge of global climate change, particularly with regard to large-scale forestry projects in the Southern hemisphere, individuals and companies are now able to purchase *carbon-friendly warranties* (or their equivalents) that guarantee that an agreed number of tonnes of carbon will be fixed in this way; i.e. a market price is available. It is on this basis, the cost of mitigating the effects of Interface's emissions of carbon dioxide, that the company's gas and transport-related emissions have been valued in the accounts. The current price used, as shown, is £5.45 per tonne. This represents the market price being charged by Climate Care (formerly the Carbon Storage Trust, a UK-based organisation) to sequester one tonne of carbon dioxide (this equates to £20 per tonne of carbon).

11.4.4.2 The valuation of direct production emissions: VOCs, NOx and SO$_2$

The emissions of VOCs, NOx and SO$_2$ shown in the accounts (Table 11.1) are the total emissions of these gases from all three production sites: Scherpenzeel, Shelf and Providence Mills, and Craigavon. Emission levels are calculated on the basis of periodic monitoring checks, undertaken as part of Interface's compliance requirements under the UK's Integrated Pollution Control (IPC) legislation and equivalent Dutch legislation, and total recorded operating times of the relevant production lines.

The nature of the pollution impacts associated with the emission of these gases makes the estimation of what it would cost to restore any damage caused extremely difficult (the estimation of the damage cost itself would be even harder). Much would depend upon the nature of the receiving environment and the local atmospheric/weather conditions at the time. Because of this, the approach taken in this study has been to estimate what it would cost to avoid the emissions in the first place, or more precisely, what it would cost to prevent the emissions produced from being released into the atmosphere.

Most air pollutants can be either destroyed, through thermal incineration, or at least removed by some sort of scrubbing or electrostatic precipitation process. While the ideal would be to avoid the emissions in the first place, through the development of new production processes and perhaps also through materials substitution, 'end of pipe' treatment can offer an immediate and interim solution. The valuation of Interface's direct production emissions have been made on this basis. The values shown in the accounts are estimates from environmental technology/air pollution abatement equipment suppliers and represent the cost of fitting scrubbing units, ducting, prefilters, coolers and additional precipitators as required to the numerous point sources of these emissions. As shown, the total estimated cost of avoiding these emissions is in the region of £350,000.

11.4.4.3 Valuation of transport-related emissions of NOx, VOCs and PM

As noted in Section 11.4.4.1, as a global pollutant, most of Interface's emissions of carbon dioxide have been valued at the current per tonne market price to sequester carbon dioxide. Production-related emissions of NOx and VOCs have been valued on the basis of the capital cost of appropriate end-of-pipe pollution abatement equipment, equipment capable of capturing and hence avoiding virtually all of the production-related emissions disclosed in the accounts. Unfortunately, there are no such easy (and justifiable) complete avoidance cost valuations available for Interface's transport-related emissions of these gases. Instead, as discussed below, emissions of NOx and VOCs from transport have been valued by a composite of valuation techniques.

Interface's entire fleet of company cars is under three-years old. Most have petrol engines and all are fitted with three-way catalysts. They conform to the highest emission standards (ECE Stage 1 vehicles) and there are currently no readily available technical means to capture the remaining emissions of NOx, VOCs and particulates from petrol vehicles. Had they been older vehicles, it would have been possible to value a substantial proportion of the emission of these gases on the basis of what it would have cost to upgrade them to meet these higher standards. This would have involved retro-fitting three-way catalysts and other modifications. For example, based on motorway driving conditions, ECE Stage 1 vehicles emit 0.371 grammes of NOx per km. In contrast, petrol cars (without catalysts) sold between July 1983 and July 1992 (which make up 68 per cent of the total car fleet in the UK) emit in the region of 3.8 g/km; i.e. some ten times as much.

Hydrogen fuel cells, which have the potential to emit only warm-water vapour, offer the prospect of avoiding harmful vehicle emissions almost entirely (during the use phase of a vehicle's lifetime at least). However, the widespread commercial availability of such vehicles still remains some time off, despite the development of a number of prototypes. An interim partial solution is offered by the use of alternative 'clean' fuels; these include Liquid Petroleum Gas (LPG) and Compressed Natural Gas (CNG). While emissions of carbon dioxide remain similar to those of conventional petrol and diesel vehicles, emissions of PM, VOCs, and NOx are substantially reduced. Compared to petrol engines, for example, oxides of nitrogen are reduced by some 40 per cent and hydrocarbons by between 40 and 95 per cent with LPG vehicles. Emission levels are reduced even further with CNG vehicles; however, given the current limited CNG refueling infrastructure within the UK, this option has not been considered in this study.

Consequently, a significant proportion of transport-related emissions (excluding carbon dioxide) can be avoided by either purchasing or leasing LPG vehicles. There is now a very strong business case to switch to LPG. Government grants through the Powershift Programme, administered by the Energy Savings Trust (EST), are available for both converting existing vehicles to run off LPG or to contribute to the purchase of factory-produced LPG vehicles. Typical conversion costs are in the order of £1500 per vehicle. Grants of up to 75 per cent of these costs are available depending upon the type of vehicle. In addition, despite a 15–20 per cent reduction in fuel efficiency, overall fleet fuel bills are likely to be substantially reduced given the current price differentials between LPG, petrol and diesel. Per litre, LPG costs about 25p, petrol 75p and diesel 78p (as at January 2000). Consequently, for a company with a predominantly petrol fleet, such as Interface, total fuel bills could be reduced by nearly two-thirds. For an individual car traveling about 30,000 miles per year, this equates to a reduction in the fuel bill of around £1500 which is approximately the conversion costs and, as noted, these could largely be covered by a Powershift grant.

It is on this basis, the net capital cost of converting their company car fleet to run off LPG, that 50 per cent of Interface's non-carbon dioxide transport-related emissions (company cars only at this stage) have been valued. Assuming the full conversion grant of 75 per cent for the company's UK fleet (167 cars) and full conversion costs for the remainder of the fleet (135 cars), conversion costs total £265,000. Annual fuel savings are estimated at £283,000 and hence the avoidance of these emissions is shown as a credit of £18,000. It should be noted that these are approximate figures and are included in the accounts principally to illustrate that a viable option, both technically and economically, is now available to avoid a significant proportion of non-carbon dioxide transport-related emissions.

Problems still remain with LPG. Although both Shell and BP Amoco, for example, have plans to install several hundred LPG filling stations by 2001, the widespread availability of refuelling infrastructure is still limited in some parts of the country. However, given that the fuel saving of £283,000 is an annual saving, (no account of this is made in the environmental accounts) Interface could consider investing in their own refuelling facilities. British Gas estimates that this would cost in the region of £250,000 to upgrade a commercial filling station to be able to supply LPG; this is more than covered by the annual saving on total fuel costs. Some suppliers will install on site refuelling points for considerably less than this.

Carbon dioxide emissions have been valued, both for distribution vehicles and company cars, at £5.45/tonne (i.e. their sequestration costs). The valuation of NOx, PM and VOCs from commercial/distribution vehicles, and 50 per cent of these emissions from company cars, are based on valuations determined by BSO Origin, one of only three companies in the world which have made attempts to account for their wider environmental impacts (see Appendix 11.2). [4] The figures of £14,000 per tonne of NOx, £7,200 per tonne of VOCs and £2,800 per tonne of particulate matter, have been used on the basis that they have been obtained from an extensive literature survey and official Dutch Government reports and action plans (the Dutch National Environmental Protection Action Plan (NEPP)). [5] As these figures relate to a European-based organisation, and as Interface Europe has a major manufacturing site in the Netherlands, it seems reasonable to use these unit cost figures until such time as more appropriate and Interface-relevant figures can be estimated/calculated.

Sulphur dioxide emissions from Interface's consumption of natural gas have been valued at £2,400. This equates to the Swedish sulphur tax, which is based on estimates of the external costs associated with such emissions. Nitrogen oxide emissions from gas consumption are valued at £14,000; i.e. at the same rate as non-company car transport-related emissions of these gases.

11.4.5 The Environmental Accounts and Sustainability Cost of Interface's Activities and Operations (for the year ended December 1997)

This section presents the 1997 consolidated environmental accounts produced for Interface Europe during the study. As shown in the accounts, the sustainability cost of the company's activities in 1997 was estimated to be £1.25 million (i.e. about 7.5 per cent of operating income). This cost is simply the summation of all of the various quantified and valued (on the basis of their avoidance or restoration costs) environmental impacts detailed in the accounts. It represents the calculated cost to Interface to reduce their environmental impacts to a socially acceptable and sustainable level. No distinction has been made between capital and revenue items; i.e. all costs, including provisions for/investments in end of pipe pollution abatement equipment to avoid production emissions, are charged to the current year's profit and loss account.

This figure is clearly sensitive to the underlying assumptions used in the valuation of the various environmental impacts, and to the degree to which life-cycle impacts are accounted for. Given these limitations, it is important not to place too great an emphasis on the 'precise' sustainability cost obtained. In isolation, the figure has limited value to both the company and to external audiences. Much of the value obtained by a company from producing environmental accounts, as noted below, derives from the process itself and from the wider potential benefits associated with public reporting and disclosure. However, for Interface, the significance of the estimate of their sustainability cost is that it is not beyond the realms of possibility for the company to begin to provide/set up a provision in their accounts to pay for the cost of avoiding the environmental impacts disclosed in the accounts, or where this is not possible, to provide for the cost of the restoration of the damage caused as a result of their activities. It is within their reach to make this transition. Had the sustainability cost been, say, 70, 80 or 120 per cent of operating income, it would be harder to see how Interface could have embarked on (and justified to their shareholders) such a transition (in isolation), without a fundamental rethink about the nature of company's core business activities.

11.4.6 The Value/Use of Calculating a Company's Sustainability Cost

The value for a company that embarks on producing such accounts derives from the process itself and from the subsequent management and control of the environmental costs identified. The insights gained from preparing environmental accounts can help to focus management's attention on the most pressing and potentially costly environmental issues facing the company. External costs can quickly become internalised through legislation or, indeed, as demonstrated by Shell's experience over the disposal of the Brent Spar oil storage platform, by the expression of wider societal demands over what does (and does not) constitute good/responsible corporate environmental governance. Being aware of these costs (i.e. the company's exposure to potential environmental problems, before they become issues), can assist the company's management in their forward/strategic planning and consequently help to reduce the company's exposure to future environmental risks and liabilities.

As the value of corporate environmental reputation becomes an increasingly important issue, the publication of environmental accounts could also provide a signal to external stakeholders that the company is committed to becoming a more sustainable enterprise. Even if the accounts are not published in full, the disclosure of the company's sustainability cost over successive accounting periods (assuming it is calculated in a consistent manner) could provide an indicator of the company's overall progress towards environmental sustainability. A downward trend in the sustainability cost would indicate that the company's external environmental impacts were being reduced, while a rising trend would indicate that they were increasing and hence that the company was moving in the wrong direction.[6]

If other companies were to make similar disclosures, either on a voluntary basis or as a result of some form of mandatory reporting requirements, the publication of an individual company's sustainability costs could also enable a distinction to be made between companies with good and positive approaches to the environment from those with poor or less proactive approaches. In an increasingly global and competitive world, this could eventually offer a mechanism for companies to differentiate themselves from their competitors and thereby attract new markets/customers or, at the very least, maintain their existing customer base.

11.5. CORPORATE ENVIRONMENTAL ACCOUNTING: CONCLUSIONS AND NEXT STEPS

This chapter has briefly outlined the inadequacy of current accounting practices to take 'nature' into account. As a consequence of market failures, prices do not reflect costs. This leads to a sub-optimal allocation of resources and the perpetuation of an inherently unsustainable system of economic activity. The planet's essential or critical 'ecosystems services' upon which all life, and economic activity depend, are being routinely and increasingly degraded. Continued and unabated degradation threatens our ability to create wealth and, ultimately, our very survival.

Some companies are already beginning to respond and have made significant progress in improving their environmental performance and overall governance, aided, in part, by the use of environmental accounting techniques and methodologies. Greater attention to the treatment of internal environmentally related expenditure can bring many 'win-win' benefits in itself. This has been demonstrated by the work conducted by the World Resource Institute (WRI) outlined in Section 11.3. However, given the scale of the challenges we face, the realisation of these win-win opportunities, in isolation, will never be enough to make the transition towards a sustainable economy. Making more from less does not equate to a sustainable system of industrial production.

Until natural capital is accounted for in corporate accounts, in a similar fashion to the treatment of manufactured capital, reported profit and income figures will inevitably overstate the degree to which an individual company is genuinely adding value. The declared profit levels are unlikely to be sustainable over the long term and the going concern assumption, upon which the company's accounts are drawn up, may also no longer be valid.

Government clearly has a vital role to play in setting the right enabling macro economic and policy framework, to enable companies, on the basis of a level playing field, to begin to account more fully for their external environmental footprint. The most effective way to achieve this would be through an ambitious and comprehensive programme of ecological tax reform (Ekins and Simon, 1998) as part of a balanced policy response. However, in the absence of the political will to implement such a reform, individual companies committed to transforming themselves into more sustainable enterprises can begin to take 'nature into account' through the internalisation of monetarised impacts into their accounting systems. Section 11.4 outlined how one major UK manufacturing company has attempted to do this. While there are clearly limits to what an individual company can do in isolation (one cannot have a sustainable company in an unsustainable economy), there are many benefits to be derived for identifying and recognising what are the most pressing and significant environmental challenges facing an organisation. External costs can quickly become internalised through environmental taxes, legislation and through consumer expectations over what constitutes good corporate environmental governance. Those companies that develop appropriate systems to assess and enable them to begin to address their most significant impacts in advance of legislation are likely to gain a comparative advantage over their competitors, in terms of reputation and ability to respond more quickly to changing circumstances. They are also more likely to be able to meet the expectations of their customers, shareholders and an increasingly inquisitive and environmentally aware financial community.

While the methodology developed for Interface is experimental and under development, several more leading companies are embarking on similar externality costing and integration initiatives. These include two of the UK's leading water companies, Anglian Water and Wessex Water, which are both working with Forum for the Future to determine their own sustainability cost and estimate of their environmentally sustainable profits.

More companies are likely to follow. The UNEP (1997) Benchmark Survey of 100 Corporate Environmental Reports (CERs) also suggests that the monitarisation/valuation of environmental impacts, and their integration into corporate accounting, will become an increasingly important issue. The need to account and report on environmental performance, to integrate their reporting streams and to focus reporting on financial market users are among

12 key recommendations to those responsible for preparing CERs. The report also suggests that new sources of data and information will be required from the companies that financial markets insure, lend to or invest in. They predict that this will be a priority area for chief financial officers in the early years of the 21st century (The United Nations Environment Programme (UNEP), 1997). Greater levels of monetarisation in CERs will also be necessary to assist in benchmarking between companies.

Appendix 11.1 Interface Europe: The Case Study Company

Interface Europe is part of Interface Inc., the world's largest manufacturer of carpet tiles and floor coverings for commercial, institutional and residential use. Interface Europe accounts for about 25% of the company's consolidated turnover of $1.2 billion (in 1997) and employs about 1200 people across Europe. In the year ended December 1997, the company operated four manufacturing sites across Europe: at Scherpenzeel in the Netherlands, Shelf and Providence Mills in West Yorkshire and at Craigavon in Northern Ireland. Additional manufacturing facilities in the UK were acquired after the year-end. The company also maintains several sales centres across Europe and Scandinavia. Interface Europe's head offices are located at Ashlyns Hall in Berkhamstead. Corporate headquarters are located in Atlanta, Georgia, in the USA.

In brief, the production of carpet tiles involves weaving (or tufting) carpet yarn (mainly nylon threads) into some form of backing substrate material. The underside of the tufted cloth is then coated in a liquid latex or polyvinyl chloride (PVC) plastisol coating, prior to the application and subsequent fixing of further backing materials, either more PVC plastisol or a bitumen/limestone mix. The backing materials are necessary to bulk up the product and add weight to ensure that the carpet tiles remain fixed/secure once fitted. While the precise processes vary depending upon the type and nature of the product being produced, they are all extremely energy and materials intensive. In the year ended 31 December 1997, European production facilities consumed over 6000 tonnes of nylon, 17,000 tonnes of bitumen, 28,000 tonnes of limestone, 12,000 tonnes of latex and 2,000 tonnes of PVC. Direct energy consumption (gas and electricity) amounted to some 43 million kWhs. Interface recognise that their activities are damaging the environment and are therefore 'extracting value' for which they do not pay. Ray Anderson, Chairman and founder of the company, has publicly stated that Interface is now seeking to become the world's first sustainable corporation, and then ultimately, to become a restorative company, one that actually puts back more than it takes. This would be no mean feat, given their starting position, but one to which the company is devoting considerable resources and energy.

Appendix 11.2 Accounting for the Environment: The Experience of BSO Origin and Landcare Research (New Zealand) Ltd

A11.2.1 BSO Origin

In 1990, BSO Origin, a Dutch management consultancy company, produced an innovative set of environmental accounts. The accounts attempted to quantify, in financial terms, the value extracted by the company but not paid for. BSO Origin continued to produce environmental accounts for several years until the company was eventually sold to a large Anglo-Dutch multinational. In the 1990 accounts, the net value lost (or 'cost of environmental effects') is deducted from the conventional economic value added by the company to produce a net value added. This project has drawn on the pioneering work undertaken by BSO Origin. However, there are several differences in the approaches adopted by the two studies. The most important concerns the approach to environmental valuation. In their 1995 report, BSO state that their preferred approach to valuing environmental impacts is to make use of actual damage cost estimates. This is in sharp contrast to the approach taken in this study (see Section 11.3). BSO also make use of prevention and restoration costs. Consequently, the numbers are not comparable. As Gray et al. (1993) note, BSO 'add possible apples to approximate pears and subtract the result from hypothetical oranges'. By focusing on avoidance and restoration costs based on actual market prices, this study hopes to avoid this problem. In addition, this study has attempted to determine an estimate for Interface's environmentally sustainable profits. The sustainability standard adopted is effectively zero. In arriving at the environmentally sustainable profit estimate, avoidance or restoration costs have been determined on the basis of reducing emissions to zero or nearly zero. Internalising external damage costs could still result in a level of activity that was unsustainable.

A11.2.2 Landcare Research (New Zealand) Ltd – (Manaaki Whenua)

Landcare Research is a Crown Research Institute that conducts research into the sustainable management of land ecosystems, including their productive uses and conservation of natural resources. The Landcare project also drew on the pioneering work undertaken by BSO Origin. However, in common with the Interface project, it attempted to apply the idea of the sustainability cost calculation to an individual organisation. It was the first such practical experiment of this kind. The method used involved modelling a series of incremental cost steps the organisation would have to go through in order to move towards sustainability. The financial quantification of an organisation's impacts was separated into two parts. The first related to the incremental costs associated with purchasing from more sustainable sources. The second related to the cost of remedying the environmental effects arising from the organisation's activities. However, no options for purchasing goods and services from more sustainable sources were found and the financial quantification of impacts was limited to some cost estimates relating to carbon emissions only. The authors concluded that that the clean-up costs associated with emissions, except for carbon, could not be estimated (Bebbington and Tan, 1996, 1997). This was due to the uncertainty that surrounded the way the emissions interact and on how to remedy their effect. Unlike the Interface project, no attempt was made to link the organisation's environmental performance data to the company's financial accounting information; i.e. to estimate Landcare's sustainable profits.

Apart from the different approaches adopted to environmental valuation, one notable factor that distinguishes the above studies from the Interface project relates to the nature of the organisations themselves. Both BSO Origin and Landcare Research are service-based organisations. Interface, in contrast, is a large, international manufacturing company. Consequently, the scale and magnitude of the environmental impacts that need to be addressed tend to be greater. In addition, manufacturing organisations tend to have a greater diversity of impacts, the most obvious of which are those resulting directly from the production processes. These differences create particular methodological challenges. As far as we are aware, the Interface project is the only initiative currently underway that is attempting to estimate the environmentally sustainable profits of an organisation of this type.

REFERENCES

Bennett, M. and P. James (1998), *The Green Bottom Line: Environmental Accounting for Management Current Practice and Future Trends*, Sheffield: Greenleaf Publishing.

Bebbington, J. and J. Tan (1996), 'Accounting for sustainability', *Chartered Accountants Journal of New Zealand*, **75** (6), 75–6.

Bebbington, J. and J. Tan (1997), 'Landcare research and accounting for sustainability', *Chartered Accountants Journal of New Zealand*, **76** (1), 37–40.

Ditz, D., J. Ranganathan and R.D. Banks (eds) (1995), *Green Ledgers: Case Studies in Corporate Environmental Accounting*. Washington DC: World Resource Institute.

Ekins, P. and S. Simon (1998), 'Determining the sustainability gap: national accounting for environmental sustainability', in *UK Environmental Accounts 1998*, P. Vaze and J.B. Barron (eds), London: The Stationery Office.

Gray, R., J. Bebbington and D. Walters (1993), *Accounting for the Environment*, London: Paul Chapman.

Howes, R., J. Skea and B. Whelan (1997), *Clean and Competitive: Motivating Environmental Performance in Industry*, London: Earthscan.

Lovins, A.B., L.H. Lovins and P. Hawkins (1999), *Natural Capitalism: Creating the Next Industrial Revolution*, London: Earthscan.

The United Nations Environment Programme [UNEP] (1997), *The 1997 Benchmark Survey*, The third international progress report on company environmental reporting (Engaging Stakeholders), London: UNEP.

United Nations (1993), *Handbook on Integrated Environmental and Economic Accounting*, Studies in methods. Series F, No. 61, New York: United Nations Statistical Division.

NOTES

1   Funders for this project included the Chartered Institute of Management Accountants (CIMA), with in-kind support from Interface.

2   The sustainability cost approach is one of three ways identified by Rob Gray to enable organisations to begin to account for sustainability (Gray et al., 1999). This project draws on

this concept in developing a methodology that could be employed by companies to account for the external environmental impacts resulting from their activities

3   There is no necessary relationship between damage, restoration and avoidance costs. However, where that damage has been inflicted on an economic asset (i.e. the damage is clearly visible) restoration and damage costs can be equal. Where the damage is done to an ecosystem, this connection is lost.

4   The other organisations are Landcare Research, a Crown Research Institution in New Zealand, and Ontario Hydro, a Canadian power company.

5   The BSO valuations are based on an exchange rate of about 3 Dutch Guilders to the UK Pound and have been rounded to the nearest £100.

6   The sustainability cost can be reduced over time by improvements in technology, for example, through producing the same (or different) carpets with less materials and energy. It can also be reduced by physically closing the 'gap,' by driving fewer miles, producing less carpet and hence using less materials and energy in absolute terms.

12. Setting the Agenda for Green Accounting in the 21st Century

Sandrine Simon and John Proops

11.1 GREEN ACCOUNTING FOR THE 21st CENTURY

In this conclusion, our objective is to recapitulate the main outcomes of each part of the book and to pay special attention to a set of fundamental questions that research in green accounting should help to answer. From this, a synthesis of the main characteristics of research in green accounting for the 21st century is finally presented.

The general focus of this conclusion needs to be on the paradigm of ecological economics and on the concept of sustainability, both in the context of research in green accounting. This is because we have examined these issues from:

- an epistemological, social, historical and political angle in Part One,
- a methodological and theoretical viewpoint in Part Two, and
- practical and implementation points of views in Part Three.

This is also because we wish to conclude whether research on green accounting fits within the paradigm of ecological economics, and relates to the concept of sustainability, as was originally mentioned in our introduction.

The evolution of this area of research shows that the choice of methodologies used to construct this new type of national accounts has animated much controversy. Some of the approaches have not been in agreement with the new concepts put forward in ecological economics. One could even stress that, for a while, research in green accounting was not related to the concept of sustainability in any way. However, here we wish to convince the sceptics that most current developments in green accounting have changed direction, and that most future directions in this area of research will benefit from the insights of a new conceptual and methodological framework. This framework, that of ecological economics, might thus prove to be very useful in helping operationalise sustainability in the future.

Examining the controversy concerning green accounting and sustainability has highlighted two important points.

The first is that the reform of the SNA is not a 'mere technical' problem. It is politically loaded, relates to fundamental social issues and its rationale is extremely closely related to the principles of those who advocate a reform of the standard economics paradigm. The correction of the shortcomings of the SNA, although approached from many technical angles, is very much related to our conceptions of how the economy and the environment relate. Reforming the accounting policy tool implies questioning our economic paradigm. Although it makes reference to them, this book has not been exclusively focused on the description of the various existing methodologies in green accounting. Rather, it has tried to show that this area of research is being progressively understood in the context of ecological economics.

The second point relates to the most recent directions of research on green accounting. If one accepts that efforts are being more and more turned towards the attempt to represent and implement the concept of sustainability, in the context of ecological economics, a new technical concern appears. How well equipped is the ecological economics paradigm to provide us with descriptions of complex dynamic systems that characterise sustainable processes, and what type of policy tools, related to the accounting framework, can it offer?

While the first point refers, mostly, to the evolution of past research in green accounting, the second critically investigates new advances in such research, and attempts to examine the position of research in green accounting in the context of future interests and needs in ecological economics. Let us now examine how each part has contributed to this discussion.

11.2 PART ONE: THE HISTORY OF NATIONAL ACCOUNTS

In Part One, Christine Cooper and Ian Thomson first focused on the social, political and epistemological dimensions of the national accounting tool and, by extension, of green accounting. Anthony Friend added an historical dimension to this discussion and explained what green accounting was derived from, both from a methodological and a policy perspective. Sandrine Simon finished this part by focusing on two fundamental links; that between green accounting and sustainability, and that between green accounting and ecological economics.

The implications of the outcomes delivered by Part One are important for future research in green accounting. National accounts have orientated economic policies and shaped the economic reality with which we are familiar. Their reform is therefore crucial, if they are to represent and implement sustainability. The correction of their shortcomings is not only a technical and methodological matter. It is profoundly social and political and is closely related to the reform of our economic paradigm itself. Despite its apparently radical dimension, this reform is only following the natural course of historical developments in accounting. New policy and societal needs have thus encouraged the construction of better adapted policy tools and new political and societal aspirations have, in turn, favoured the adoption of certain paradigms in which to carry out research focused on this reform.

In our case, the paradigm of ecological economics is presented as the most appropriate one to help construct a system of green national accounting that is conceptually and practically related to the concept of sustainability.

11.3 PART TWO: GREEN ACCOUNTING AS A POLICY INSTRUMENT

The selection of various technical methods for greening the accounts through time, and the reasons for this selection, were presented in Part Two. Examining this technical dimension is necessary to understand better why certain types of research in green accounting can contribute to a change in the policy-making process, and to the operationalisation of sustainability, while some others cannot.

Steven Keuning showed that research in green accounting is closely related to the issue of 'indicators of sustainability'. Such indicators are perceived as the first step in the direction of the operationalisation of sustainability and green accounting. Research in green accounting also provides new insights concerning the construction of 'indicators of sustainability' as an 'integrated framework of indicators', such as the Dutch NAMEA. The modelling foundations of green accounting were presented by Kirk Hamilton, who discusses how simulation models and green accounting can actually complement each other, and hence considerably improve the policy process in the direction of sustainability. Similarly, the revival of input–output analysis, discussed by Carsten Stahmer, brings fundamental insights to the green policy process in relation to green accounting research. For instance, it shows the importance of indirect effects (so often hidden and ignored in analysis) and also the importance of the benefit of structural disaggregation and transparent illustration of the interdependencies in the green accounts. Fulai Sheng and Sandrine Simon argued that certain policy motivations have orientated the choice of various green accounting methodologies through time. They reviewed the issues of satellite accounts versus aggregate indicators, that of valuation in green accounting and physical versus monetary accounts, that of indicators versus frameworks of indicators of sustainability, and finally, the issue of complementarity between green accounting and other research exercises (such as modelling).

11.4 PART THREE: USES OF GREEN ACCOUNTING

In Part Three, the emphasis was on the practical dimension of green accounting. Thus, Glenn-Marie Lange explained the policy implications of green accounting in the case of various developing and industrialised countries. She also stressed that the full potential of green accounting has not yet been tapped. Prashant Vaze showed how institutes, such as the UK Office for National Statistics, select a methodology and construct green accounts. He also showed the link which exists between the green accounting initiative and the UK commitments to international environmental protocols, such as the Framework Convention on Climate Change and the Convention on Long Range Transboundary Pollutants, thus emphasising the bridge between national policy tools, their methodological developments, and large-scale political agreements. Finally, Rupert Howes also explored the links between green accounting initiatives at various geographical scales, by focusing on corporate green accounting as a specific and practical exercise which is part of a broader methodological and policy initiative.

These practical considerations remind us that conceptual and methodological developments for future research need to motivated by practical policy needs, if green accounting is to become a useful and recognised tool to operationalise sustainability.

11.5 SUGGESTIONS FOR FUTURE RESEARCH

A certain number of conclusions can be drawn from this book concerning the future of research in green accounting.

First, research in green accounting is still active and in evolution. Although the motivation behind such research seemed, for a while, to be centered on technical issues, and generated by a competition between not always compatible green accounting methodologies, the research climate seems to be now more positive and promising. The pros and cons of the numerous approaches have been discussed at length in numerous publications. The common approach now seems to be policy-oriented and related to the contribution of green accounts to the operationalisation of sustainability.

The original rationale of green national accounting has thus been revisited and the 'correction of the SNA's shortcomings' has acquired more meaning.

This correction is now envisaged in the context of research on indicators of sustainability. Thus, correcting the shortcomings of the SNA is not understood any more as synonymous with constructing an accounting indicator (or framework of indicators) of sustainability. Also, the correction of the shortcomings has to be done in such a way that it responds to policy requirements. In order to operationalise sustainability, policy makers need a certain type of information and some clear understanding of the interrelations between the environment and economic activities, and also of the impact of our economic activities on the environment. Green accounting must provide this information and attempt to answer policy-related questions. From a reactive attitude (the correction of a problem, ex-post), research in green accounting is thus now becoming proactive (the construction of a useful policy tool).

The representation of sustainability, and of the economy-environment interactions within the accounts, remains a difficult issue. As we are now coming better to understand the complex and systemic concept of sustainability, we are also making progress in representing it. It has often been concluded that a single aggregate indicator was not a good representation of sustainability, nor did it help us to understand the practical implications of sustainability. However, the translation of this better understanding into policy applications still needs to be improved, and is related to the structure of the accounts and how policy makers use this information. It is also, clearly, related to the issue of valuation.

The issue of valuation remains central to research in green accounting. As alternative valuation methods provide the opportunity to envisage monetary valuation from a different perspective, and to communicate integrated information to policy makers in a different form, the questions of who values the environment, and of who is the policy maker are addressed. Is it corporate businesses (through their corporate accounts)? Is it the variety of stakeholders involved in different environmental debates and practical issues (through the deliberative evaluation processes they are involved in)? This area of research is still in need of further effort. New alternative valuation methods need to be more related to research in green accounting. Also, research in corporate accounts, and how they relate to national green accounts, needs to be pursued.

This set of issues clearly shows that research in green accounting has not been merely a technical matter, but has also involved a rethinking concerning our economic paradigm. The epistemological study of the role of national accounting in society has also revealed that reforming the SNA encompasses a fundamental political and social dimension that we need to investigate more in the future.

It is from this perspective that research in green accounting seems to generate most promising and useful outputs. However, acknowledging the importance of these new dimensions in research in green accounting also means that we are including in our research some factors that are not easy to deal with, such as the recognition of remaining uncertainty in our understanding of our relations with the environment, or the complexity and systemic dimension of the sustainability of ecosystem functioning. Future research in green accounting will have to acknowledge that our knowledge and ignorance are evolving, and that they have progressively to be reflected in the construction of green accounts. This means that the structure of environmental accounts would benefit from being engaged with 'time', rather than being presented in a definite and universal way.

To some extent, developing a variety of 'creative' green accounts that would respond to different institutional settings, environmental resource constraints, and policy needs, does not present a huge methodological problem and has widely been observed so far. A forum (such as the London Group, created under the initiative of EUROSTAT) where advances in research in green accounting can be exchanged is, however, very useful. Although the SEEA has been created and is constantly improved, it should be interpreted as a point of reference and a source of research insights rather than as the absolute and unique way of constructing environmental accounts.

Finally, research in green accounting needs to be open to related areas of research. As well as that of environmental valuation, institutional ecological economics, research on ecosystem functioning, research in modelling and simulation, are promising complements to research in green accounting. This is because, while accounts illustrate, ex-post, the results of a policy and the way in which the economy has been organised during a period of time, simulation models and input-output analysis can greatly contribute to the analysis of various policy scenarios and to their selection. The complementarity between modelling exercises and green accounting would considerably help in initiating the transition towards sustainability.

11.6 CONCLUSION

Is research in green accounting in line with the principles and objectives of ecological economics? Can green accounts become a useful policy tool, with the ability to help put sustainability into practice?

We hope that this volume has been successful in persuading the reader of the necessity of carrying out research in green accounting in the context of ecological economics.

A further challenging conclusion can be derived. If it is genuinely possible to develop methodologies and policy outcomes in the context of ecological economics, this implies that the paradigm of ecological economics, which is often viewed as conceptually very strong but lacking in theoretical instruments, does provide us with a range of useful technical insights regarding current and future improvements of green accounts. Thus we could argue that ecological economics contributes to the reform of the discipline of economics not only conceptually but also from a theoretical and methodological perspective. This suggests that, through economic instruments such as green accounting, ecological economics has the potential to have a direct policy impact at local, national and international levels.

Index